PENGUIN BOOKS

Skin to skin

Carol Archie is a broadcasting journalist who, for most of her career, has worked in television news, current affairs and documentaries. She was a journalist and producer for Mana Maori Media, supplying Maori perspective programmes to Radio New Zealand. She published her first book, *Maori Sovereignty – The Pakeha Perspective*, in 1995.

skin to skin

Carol Archie

PENGUIN BOOKS

PENGUIN BOOKS
Published by the Penguin Group
Penguin Group (NZ), cnr Airborne and Rosedale Roads, Albany,
Auckland 1310, New Zealand (a division of Pearson New Zealand Ltd)
Penguin Group (USA) Inc., 375 Hudson Street,
New York, New York 10014, USA
Penguin Group (Canada), 10 Alcorn Avenue, Toronto,
Ontario, Canada M4V 3B2 (a division of Pearson Penguin Canada Inc.)
Penguin Books Ltd, 80 Strand, London, WC2R 0RL, England
Penguin Ireland, 25 St Stephen's Green,
Dublin 2, Ireland (a division of Penguin Books Ltd)
Penguin Group (Australia), 250 Camberwell Road, Camberwell,
Victoria 3124, Australia (a division of Pearson Australia Group Pty Ltd)
Penguin Books India Pvt Ltd, 11, Community Centre,
Panchsheel Park, New Delhi - 110 017, India
Penguin Books (South Africa) (Pty) Ltd, 24 Sturdee Avenue,
Rosebank, Johannesburg 2196, South Africa

Penguin Books Ltd, Registered Offices: 80 Strand, London, WC2R 0RL, England

First published by Penguin Group (NZ), 2005
1 3 5 7 9 10 8 6 4 2

Designed by Mary Egan
Typeset by Egan-Reid Ltd, Auckand
Printed in Australia by McPherson's Printing Group

ISBN 0 14 301962 7
A catalogue record for this book is available
from the National Library of New Zealand.

www.penguin.co.nz

Contents

Kia ora

For nearly 30 of the years I've been in journalism, my work has often focused on Maori/Pakeha issues.

That was particularly true of the time I spent with Mana Maori Media which, since 1990, has been explaining and reflecting the Maori world back to Maori and other New Zealanders.

Often I would interview people – all the way up to the prime minister – who were concerned about the divisions between Maori and Pakeha. But, of course, the relationship isn't just about debate and conflict.

Two Treaty workers, Moea Armstrong and Mitzi Nairn, set me thinking about that – and prompted me to start planning this book.

They have helped other New Zealanders understand what the Treaty of Waitangi means and are well aware of the political tensions coming from the Maori sense of betrayal over Article Two of the Treaty.

But they are also aware of the tens of thousands of Kiwi families who are embracing both Maori and Pakeha cultures. Such families, at a personal level, are in a cultural partnership that works.

A comment from Professor Ranginui Walker also pointed to the prospect of a book like this. He once said race relations might be solved in the bedrooms of New Zealand. And perhaps that is what is happening.

There was also another aspect I wanted to explore – the situation of the children from Maori/Pakeha marriages. They seldom get the chance to talk about their experience of belonging to both camps, or how they feel about being called 'half-caste' or 'part-Maori' and so on.

Then there is the question of what some see as the 'browning' of New Zealanders, not just in skin tone, but in our thinking. In contrast, some worry that Maori culture is being diluted.

Whatever processes are at work, it is clear that big numbers of Kiwis are caught up in them. Recent research from Dr Paul Calister, at Victoria University, shows that half of all Maori living as a couple have a non-Maori partner. Nearly 70,000 New Zealand couples are in Maori/non-Maori relationships. When you consider the numbers of people in their wider families, that's a lot of interaction going on.

There was a time when those marriages tended to be Pakeha men marrying Maori women. But nowadays Maori men are just as likely to have a non-Maori wife. And, the figures suggest, a Maori who is well educated is more likely to have a non-Maori spouse.

This book includes the stories of more than 30 people from 10 New Zealand families of mixed ethnicity. As you will see, their experiences throw some light on how people in such families cross the cultural divide.

There is something to be learned from their lives and their responses. Even the participants were surprised, on occasions, to find how other family members were reacting to the cultural differences. And, so I'm told, there were lively debates within some whanau as these concerns were aired. I trust, though, that their generosity and courage in sharing their stories will lead to more than just a few sparks within the family, and that their observations will help a number of readers in similar situations.

The emphasis in this book is on Maori and Pakeha, because they are the two peoples whose relationship has largely shaped New Zealand's colonial history and development. But I have included a Maori marriage to a Thai/Chinese, and another union between a Maori and a Fijian, to acknowledge that our Kiwi melting pot is becoming more and more complex these days.

This book is not an academic work. Nor is it trying to prove any particular point of view. I am leaving it to you, the reader, to reach your own conclusions.

There are, however, themes that keep surfacing. Like the different experiences of racism from generation to generation. Or the differing attitudes (between Maori and Pakeha) to food, hospitality and concepts of family. Or the sheer diversity within the Maori world.

The stories remind us, too, how differently our two peoples deal with death – and how powerfully a tangi can affect Pakeha unused to that process. Then there is the pattern of the Maori partner being the most likely one to be making the compromises in a mixed marriage.

I thank everyone who helped or encouraged me in this project. It has been a privilege to work with you all. Thanks to Finlay Macdonald, Alison Brook, Gary Wilson, Siobhan Wilson, George Andrews, Jennie Rowe, Janet and Rennie Barrett and Paul Diamond for their support. Special thanks to Trina Maniapoto and Marie Williams who helped with transcriptions and to Anahera Vercoe and Numia Ponika-Rangi who are always generous with Maori translations. My husband, Bill, as always, was hugely supportive, made hundreds of cuppas and was willing to critique draft after draft.

I hope you enjoy these stories – and that they will help us as New Zealanders to understand ourselves a little better.

DEIRDRE *Walker, a Pakeha, has done her bit to assist the 'browning'*
of New Zealand with three children, nine grandchildren and
one great-grandchild. Her prominent Maori husband, Professor
Ranginui Walker, is often quoted as saying New Zealand's race
relations may be solved in the country's bedrooms. Deirdre agrees.
She has supported Ranginui's endeavours to increase Pakeha
understanding of Maori and their culture. The couple married in

---

PHOTOGRAPH:

Back (l to r) Rangi and Deirdre Walker with first child, Michael; Molly Dodson
Front (l to r) Isaac and Wairata Walker; Andrea Walker; Francis Dodson

the 1950s when cross-cultural marriages were less common and less

acceptable in many circles.

Deirdre Dodson was born in Matamata in the early 1930s and raised in
Tirau, Palmerston North and Auckland. Her English-born mother and
father, Molly and Francis Dodson, had to scrimp to survive but Deirdre
says she, her sister, Anne, and twin brothers, Maurice and Guy, had
a happy life. Their father had trouble finding work because he had
an upper-class education in an English public school and most New
Zealand employers had little use for Ancient Greek and Latin. After a
string of jobs during the depression, he eventually found a niche as an
apiary instructor.

Deirdre remembers a family story about a time when the Tainui
leader, Te Puea Herangi, brought a concert party to Tirau to fundraise.
'The local church asked my parents if they would billet one of these
people. My mother was horrified because she was influenced by the
posters which showed a warrior doing the haka and poking his tongue
out. In the end she agreed, as a good Christian, to have one of these
"savages" in the house. When he came he had a suit on and was well
educated, beautifully spoken, and she said he was as good as my father,
as far as manners and charm go. She was stunned. It altered her
perception of what Maori could be like.

'When we moved up to Auckland and I went to Takapuna Grammar,
Maori just didn't exist as people in my mind. I was at teachers' college
in my second year when I met this young man called Rangi. And he
didn't seem any different to other boys. Just like a Pakeha fella. We
went out a few times and went to the Easter show and when we came to
that thing where you swing the hammer and ring the bell, well, he hit
the bell! And I thought, "He's clever, strong and good-looking – what
more do I want?"

My mother thought Rangi was Christmas, but my father was very English and there were two sorts of people he was not comfortable with: one was coloured people and the other was Catholics. And Rangi was both!

'Dad behaved like a real English gentleman, very polite, never said anything, and he tried so hard to cover up his feelings that it seemed false. I could always sense an awkwardness between Rangi and my father.

She felt impatient with her father for his prejudices while respecting him for trying so hard not to show it. Underlying racist attitudes in the Dodson family were well illustrated by one of Deirdre's uncles in England who cut her out of the family Bible when he heard she was 'marrying a black man'. 'There is a hole in the family Bible where my name was. And yet later when we went to England and visited him, you couldn't have wished for a better host. I don't know if he changed his mind over the years or was just being polite. He never told us he had cut my name out. It was his friend who told us. I thought it was hilarious and was not offended.

'My mother went to England in 1952 to visit her mother, and she was talking with her brother's wife about New Zealand and Maoris. Mother must have said Maori are just ordinary people like us, and her sister-in-law said, "But what would you think if your daughter wanted to marry one?" and my mother just said, "Well, I think one of them is likely to." It was a different scene over there in England. However, back here in New Zealand my twin brothers were okay about our relationship and so was my sister.

'When I announced to the principal, at the school where I was teaching, that I was getting married to "Rangi Walker", I didn't say he was Maori, but he guessed by the name. So the principal advised me not to let him "go back to the mat" or allow his family to move in with us. "Go back to the mat" was a saying in those days which meant living like stereotypical Maori.

'The funny thing was that it was my brothers who moved in with us later on. They and Rangi all started uni together, so my brothers spent a lot of their time at our place – talking, eating and studying. They even came on our honeymoon with us! We were going to the beach so they came too.'

Deirdre found Rangi's parents easy to get on with. 'Before we were married, his father told Rangi I looked like a film star and he didn't think film stars made really good wives. One day his mother was talking to her sister about a niece marrying a Pakeha and she said, "Oh well, never mind, at least he's a Catholic." But they never said anything to make *me* feel uncomfortable.

'Rangi's parents had a dairy farm at Kukumoa near Opotiki. They had the same kind of Christian values I was used to. They went to church. They didn't drink, smoke, gamble or party. Depending on the topic, they sometimes spoke Maori. I never felt they were speaking about me or to cut me out. They were lovely people, so there was no hassle. I noticed a vast difference because we were city people and they were country. That difference was much greater than that of Pakeha and Maori. And they had a large family! Rangi's mother took in social welfare kids and adopted about four other children. Another contrast was that between immigrants and non-immigrants. My parents talked about Britain as "home" and their identity was rooted in England. My father never identified as a New Zealander, even in his eighties, although my mother became a real Kiwi.'

Outside the family, people made many comments that Deirdre found 'interesting'. Some people thought it wasn't good to marry a Maori, others thought it wasn't good to marry a Catholic. But, she says, most people accepted their marriage because Rangi was educated and doing well. 'They thought he was French or Italian.'

My neighbour said to me one day, 'He's very dark, isn't he? Is he Italian or Egyptian?' and I said, 'No, he's Maori.' And she said, 'Oh, he's lucky. He doesn't look like one.'

Deirdre gave up teaching when she and Rangi married and they moved to Oakura near Russell. He taught at Punaruku School and Deirdre soon became pregnant with their first son, Michael. She had morning sickness for months but neither she nor Rangi twigged that she might be pregnant until another teacher suggested that might be the cause of the sickness. 'Rangi's attitude was, "My aunties would go down and weed the row of kumaras, and go inside and have their babies and come out and finish the row." And he couldn't understand why I went to bed for days, weeks or months.

'When we had our babies I liked their light brown skin. I thought other babies looked sickly and white. Ours weren't that brown, but they looked healthy.

'We were offered a house here in Auckland so Rangi could go to uni. He began with Maori studies part-time. Rangi spoke Maori when he was a little boy but he didn't speak Maori to me or the children. He was busy working and studying and we did very little socialising, so he had few opportunites to mix with other Maori in those early years. Our life was focused mainly on our family.'

Rangi studied for seven years to get his BA, three to get his Masters and another three for his PhD. Meanwhile Deirdre began relieving work in kindergartens when her last child, Wendy, was small. She remembers a kindergarten teacher saying to Wendy one day, 'Eat that orange somewhere else. You smell like a Maori.' It was another little story of prejudice to add to Deirdre's repertoire. She resumed teaching in 1964 at Beresford Street School in Ponsonby. 'Once, one of the staff said disparagingly, "Oh, Maori time" when someone was late. And I said, "My husband is Maori and he is never late." Those comments are irritating. People said them in front of me because they didn't know my connection.'

Rangi emerged as a public person with a strong Maori identity after completing his doctorate in 1969 and joining the Auckland District Maori Council. 'People saw him as being Maori and he relearnt the language and became involved in Maori issues, and then it all changed. From then on we mixed with lots of Maori.

'To me the Maori side was like the jam on the bread. It provided new interest in my life. There were hui to go to. I enjoyed it – the company, different people, wonderful people. I was always the one keen to go. Rangi's not social. He does things only for work or politics, never just for fun – unless it's fishing. Rangi goes to tangi only when he feels he has to.

'The first tangi I went to was his father's. That was a cultural shock. He died in 1960 at our home after being very sick for a long time.

At the tangi I could hear the people in the kitchen laughing and I was horrified. 'How dare they laugh when this much-loved man has died!'

'I couldn't believe it. Of course, I realise now the laughing is all part of the tangi.

'After the tangi they tramped the house, in a ceremony called takahi, which I thought was strange at the time. A priest went to each room scattering holy water and praying to lift the tapu because Rangi's father died in our home. Rangi was no longer a Catholic by that time and he would have preferred a Maori priest. But it was what his mother wanted.

'Rangi was a whangai so it was actually his adopted father who died. His birth mother was his mother's sister. His adopted mother was always worried that the birth mother would want him back, so she kept her immediate family separate from those whanau members. It created tension until after Rangi's adoptive parents died. Now we're all the best of friends. Because of the lack of contact, Rangi's birth family thought he was whakahihi, or stuck up, and wouldn't have anything to do with them. He, on the other hand, thought they had disowned and rejected him. It was a shocking waste of years!'

Deirde didn't know about the Maori custom of sharing babies around the whanau. As a Pakeha mother, she was not prepared to entertain the idea. 'When Michael was three months old, Rangi's parents asked if they could take him back to Opotiki for three months. I nearly died! I'd never heard of such a thing! I was upset because Rangi wanted them to have the baby. I think he thought it would repay his adoptive parents for what they'd done for him. I cried and cried and they said, "Oh well, we won't take him." I think men are different. Rangi would've been happy to let the baby go, even if he missed him, because he felt his mother and father would have loved so much to have him. As a grandmother myself I now understand that.'

As chairman of the Auckland District Maori Council, Ranginui was exposed to considerable public hostility. He was speaking out on controversial issues like immigration, police discrimination against Maori, the insensitivity of coroners, the importance of Maori language, the effects of colonisation and many other topics. Angry letters to the newspapers and scathing editorials criticised his 'radical' views. Some people wrote him nasty personal letters too. Deirdre was annoyed by it but she says it didn't concern Rangi.

I used to worry about him being put down in public. I was frightened he would get into some sort of trouble and I hated the way it made him seem like a troublemaker.

'He had a lot of courage. He was totally committed to Maori issues and never gave away anything to placate Pakeha. I always thought he was right and supported him.

'One day I took a document with a Maori pattern around it to the chemist for framing and he said, "What name?" I said, "Walker", and he said, with some disgust, "Not Dr Rangi Walker?" So I said, "Yes. Lucky, aren't I?" And he said, "I don't think so. He's bitter and twisted and he's got a chip on his shoulder." And I said, "He's not like that in real life. You are just going by what you have read in the papers and seen on TV." And this man said, "He hates Pakehas." So I said, "Well, he thinks I'm all right!"' Deirdre is very amused by this story.

'I remember going to a tangi in a real *Maori*, Maori community. I was the only Pakeha there. And this woman, who was what I call a real "flax root person", was sitting opposite me. Someone passed her the salt, and nothing came out when she shook it. And she said, "Just like a Pakeha, absolutely useless." I was amused. I thought fair enough, because, to her, they probably are. I just laughed.

'Someone said to me. "Oh, I feel so sorry for you. You go to these Maori meetings and listen to what they say about Pakeha." And I would say, "Don't worry about it. I think the same." Most of the time I would agree with the issues, but I wasn't anti-Pakeha – just pro-Maori. I could see reasons for their criticism of Pakeha.

'You can be a very liberal Pakeha, but unless you've lived with people's pain and anger, then you can't really understand what they're on about. Once you live with it, like I did, then you understand. Just hearing about the beatings of Maori by police, the loss of land, the injustices and unfairnesses. I'm talking about the issues that came up at Maori Council meetings: racism in getting accommodation and jobs, discrimination, not being able to get into a taxi, not being served when it was your turn at the shop. All these little things that mount up.'

For the 21 years that Rangi was on the Maori Council, Deirdre went with him to meetings. She sat near the back and listened. She says Maori made her welcome, were accepting, friendly and respectful. Lately, Rangi has been hearing Wairarapa claims as a member of the

(l to r) Wendy, Stuart and Michael. Circa 1965

Waitangi Tribunal so Deirdre travels down to the Wairarapa with him and can be found sitting down the back as usual, taking it all in. She says none of the other Tribunal members have their spouses with them but she goes to keep Rangi company 'so he won't be lonely and nor will I'.

'The kids had very little experience of Maori things when they were little. We used to take them to Opotiki for Christmas. I don't think they would have heard much Maori being spoken – certainly not to them. Their grandfather died when the kids were very young, but their grandmother taught them a lot about their Maori side. They didn't get much from Rangi. When they got older they went to her for holidays. They learned a bit of language and the boys helped their grandmother rebuild the marae. They were very fond of her. She was a good teacher and good person.

I remember at school Michael and Stuart were labelled 'Maori boys' from a young age. They weren't that dark, and it always

interested me how people could pick they were 'brown'. 'Maori'
was not merely descriptive – it was a put-down.

'I didn't ever make any attempt to tell them they were Maori. It was not part of our lifestyle then. We didn't go to tangi or hui. I don't know how people found out, but the boys certainly got labelled very early on.

'At school each year the Maori kids were counted for statistical purposes. When Stuart was in the fourth form the teacher said, "Hands up all the Maori kids," and he put his hand half up. "Is your hand up or down, Stuart?" He replied, "I can't remember what I was last year."

'When he was little, Stuart, our middle boy, always said he was English. I have no idea why. One time my father who *was* English had his shorts on at the beach. And Stuart said, "Ew, you've got white legs! Is that what Englishmen look like?" And he didn't want to be an Englishman any more.

'When they were in their teens, Rangi was in the Maori Council and that's when they started thinking consciously about who they were. I don't think it bothered them one way or the other, though. In 1972 Rangi and I went to England for six months. Michael was at university and Stuart was in his last year at school. The two boys joined Nga Tamatoa and became very involved in Maori issues. Before we went, they didn't openly embrace that thinking, although they were always interested in what Rangi was doing. The boys joined protests and demonstrations as members of Nga Tamatoa. They were free agents and learnt quite a lot of Maori language in that six months too.

'I always felt society treated kids from cross-cultural marriages unfairly. Society labelled them "Maori" and then blamed them for not knowing what that meant, and in the same breath, challenged them, "What's *Maori* about you?" There are a lot of brown-skinned people who don't know anything about their history or culture. They don't know anything – except that society labels them. There may be nothing

Maori about them other than their brown skin. With our boys I didn't
know myself what it was they were supposed to be. It didn't seem
important to me at that stage. I left it to them and when they thought
it was important then they chose. Now, however, I am assertive in
reinforcing the value of their Maori heritage to my mokopuna.

'Our children all identify as Maori. All of them are on the Maori
electoral roll. Michael is also involved in Maori issues through
his work.'

Although she sees her own relationship as very successful, Deirdre
is wary about encouraging others into Maori/Pakeha marriages. 'We
have seen so many break up where each is a good person, but the
Maori partner sometimes gets involved in Maori issues as they get
older and the Pakeha partner can't understand what it's about. As a
result, they drift apart. The Pakeha partner needs to understand and
become involved too.

'When our whanau get together, fishing, Maori politics and rugby
are the main topics of conversation. I look at the young Pakeha partners
of our grandchildren and imagine their reaction. "Oh no, not that topic
again!" It could be hard for them if our grandchildren get more and
more into Maori things as they get older.

*I was amazed at the instant reaction in our extended family
to the government's stance on the foreshore and seabed. All of
them are so angry about it, and regard it as the last rip-off.*

'And yet they're city people. They don't really live on the coast. It
interests me that these people for whom it means nothing, in a way
– they are not going to own a beach – are so angry.'

Deirdre is proud of what Rangi has achieved. 'In the 1970s and '80s
Rangi was seen as a permanent thorn in the side of many Pakeha. It's
not like that now. He hasn't changed but he's a respected elder because
the rest of the world has caught up.

'No couple goes into marriage as identical people with identical backgrounds. But a cross-cultural marriage may mean just a bit more learning. Fortunately, Rangi hasn't had to convince me about any of his perspectives on Maori issues. I have agreed with them. I always see the Maori viewpoint. I don't think we disagree on anything much.

'In our marriage sometimes the male chauvinist thing is strong, so gender issues have created more issues between us than race. Rangi was talking about dividing his mother's property for the boys, not including our daughter. I had to talk to him about that! Sometimes when there has been a gender issue that he hasn't understood, such as equal sharing of property between men and women, I say, "Just picture it like Maori and Pakeha. It's the same thing. Equality."

'Rangi is my darling, my best friend and the centre of my existence. We started so young at 21. We didn't see much of our relatives on either side so it was just the two of us most of the time. We had to depend on each other and we grew up together.'

RANGINUI *Walker is a member of the Waitangi Tribunal and Emeritus Professor of Maori Studies at Auckland University. He has written widely as a columnist and author about Maori history, politics and education and has been a favourite of the media as a forthright commentator on Maori issues, even though this made him unpopular in many circles in the 1970s and '80s. He says the most powerful weapon Maori have in achieving their aspirations may be intermarriage, because mixed-heritage children will identify as*

Maori and be rooted in the land.

The first six years of Ranginui's life were spent nestled in a traditional extended family in the tiny settlement of Rahui in the Bay of Plenty. His tribal roots are in Whakatohea and Maori was his first language. He thought Pakeha were 'aliens'. He lived in a safe, nurturing community with doting grandparents, nannies and great-uncles. Hunting, fishing, gathering and subsistence farming were supplemented by his father milking 40 cows.

Ranginui began to see what Pakeha were about when, as a child, he went to town in Opotiki and saw the busy little port, streets of commercial buildings and shops full of merchandise. 'I was blown away. From an early age it was quite clear to me that Pakeha had all the power and all the goodies. Compared with my nice nurturing world, it was more assertive, competitive and domineering.'

Rangi's parents moved to a farm on the other side of Opotiki, and he was sent to live with an aunt and go to a convent school in town. 'The first day I was dragged before the nuns for speaking Maori. And that's scary. All the kids ganged up on me as though I had done something heinous. It was a terrible blow to my psyche, as a kid. So I naturally learnt to suppress the language in order to survive socially. You are dominated by this foreign environment. So you act like a Pakeha, think like a Pakeha,

Rangi and Deidre at their weddding, 1953.

become like a Pakeha – but with this duality to your persona which is suppressed. That was me.

'I don't think of myself as any different from a Pakeha as a consequence. That's part of my success as an academic – being able to foot it in the other camp. I was determined to succeed in the Pakeha world, so I became competitive, the top of the class. I was socialised like a Pakeha but lived in an all-Maori family and knew the Maori world as well.'

At teachers' college in Auckland in the 1950s, Ranginui was among Maori students who flocked together like brothers and sisters because they were a minority. But with so few Maori students it's not surprising that Ranginui chose a Pakeha wife. He first met Deirdre at a dance at Ardmore after an Easter sports tournament. 'And she was a good fun person to be with. She had a good sense of humour, was good-looking, a good dancer. And so we started dating.'

Ranginui was so conscious at that time of racist Pakeha attitudes that he always dressed well to 'beat them at their own game'. But his new girlfriend showed no sign of prejudice.

He believes it was because she had never had occasion for the racist attitudes to come out and he was the first to shape her opinions about Maori.

It was a different story when Deirdre took him home. 'Her mother thought I was pretty neat but not Francis. Francis, being a typical English gentleman, had those English attitudes of superiority.' Ranginui was not impressed by the pretensions of Deirdre's father. 'I knew I was well-born in my family and cherished and came from a good life, confident with my own identity as a Maori. He didn't bug me at all. I knew I was capable, both practically, because I could tackle all the work on my parents' farm, and academically, because I was dux at St Peter's Maori College.

'I didn't like his public school old boy pretence. He was what I would call a two-bob millionaire. When I was growing up our neighbours were Scots and were always talking about "home" and how they were only here temporarily to make their pile and go home. Of course a lot of them never did. I think Francis was in that category. He never really fitted in the New Zealand scene. He was always dressed elegantly, whatever the time of day, never casual, never a Kiwi. Molly, my mother-in-law, fitted in nicely.'

Ranginui chuckles now at his naivety when he was trying to court Deirdre. The couple would go to the Crystal Palace for dances and at supper time he would brave the bunfight at the counter to bring her back a bite to eat and a cup of tea. 'I always took sugar. She didn't. But I always put sugar in her tea and she never said anything. And the other thing was, I would take her to a milk bar . . . that was the height of naughtiness in those days . . . and I would buy my favourite, which was strawberry milkshake, and I just assumed, as a dumb male, she would like that too. But she liked chocolate!'

Once they were married Ranginui noticed a few Pakeha habits of Deirdre's he didn't like – such as hairbrushes or hats on tables. He says Deirdre, in turn, had to learn to cope with Maori food. 'Like how to cook a pigeon instead of roasting it. [In Maori cuisine, pigeons should be boiled.] It didn't take her long to learn and enjoy eating them. I'd go out diving for mussels around Auckland, collect scallops in the Manukau Harbour, toheroa at Muriwai, and go out on a boat and give her some kina. For her, it broadened her experience and tastes.

She adapted to some of my cultural ways. I don't think I made any cultural compromises myself. To me the Pakeha world is the world of reality, I had to get on and deal with it. It's a pragmatic thing to do.

Ranginui says if there was any disappointment in his family that he had married a Pakeha no one said so. 'She was a hit with my grandfather. My grandfather, Wiki Walker, was half-Scottish, and when this beautiful young thing was taken down there for a holiday – she looked like the actress Claudette Colbert in those days – and my grandfather looked her up and down, and said, "Ka pai hoki tenei wahine, tupu tena – it will only take one yard of material to make a dress for her. She will be cheap to clothe." She was so slight and small. And she wasn't like a painted hussy. She was very natural and my family liked that. We were a very conservative family. My parents voted National.'

Ranginui remembers encountering racism as a student during the summer months when the teachers' college hostel was closed. 'I had to work in the freezing works to get some extra cash.

I would look up the ads in the paper for accommodation. 'Oh yes, you can have this,' they would say. And when I went to meet the person holding the keys: 'Oh, sorry, we don't give the keys to coloured people.'

Ranginui is visibly upset telling this story. 'That was one in the guts! I couldn't believe it! I said, "But we are responsible people. I am training to be a teacher." But it cut no ice. They would say, "It's not me, you understand. It's the owners." That's how they rationalised their racism.

'You feel powerless. You realise that it's a reality and you just have to deal with it. And when you find another Pakeha person who does let the room to you, then okay, that negates it. That balances the book and you get on with it. You think, "Oh, he's a nice Pakeha. Not like that other one."'

Once into teaching, Ranginui realised that what they were teaching Maori children was too far removed from their own lives and culture. A major influence on him was the late Ian Mitchell, a teacher at Hillary College in Otara. 'Ian was a remarkable man. He contacted me because, as secretary for the Auckland District Maori Council, I was at the interface between Maori and Pakeha. He was complaining about the school certificate English exam paper. I couldn't see what Ian was complaining about because I could do the paper myself. The questions involved subjects like H.G. Wells' *The Time Machine*, *The Ascent of Everest*, June Opie's *Over My Dead Body*. And the essay topics were things like "How to clean a typewriter" or "How to make a floral arrangement" – nice middle-class Pakeha things. Ian pointed this out to me. And that was when the penny dropped. So my real "politicisation" was done by a Pakeha.'

Ranginui says Deirdre understood the issues too because she was a schoolteacher at Beresford Street School in Ponsonby where there were many Maori and Pacific Island children. 'We were both conservative to start with but we went through a gradual growing process.

'To me being a radical was a good thing because it meant that you got into the root cause of issues. My thesis was about urbanisation of the Maori at Otara and in 1970 I ran a conference on urbanisation of Maori and out of that emerged Nga Tamatoa (the young warriors) – an organisation of young Maori activists. At that conference we saw the alienated urban Maori youth – angry at the loss of language, loss of culture, detribalisation, frustrated over Pakeha domination and power.

'Michael and Stuart were young teenagers then. They eventually became part of Nga Tamatoa but they weren't angry themselves because they had a privileged life. They were insulated from it because of our lifestyle. We lived in Mt Eden. We weren't in Mangere or Te Atatu or places like that, and their one focus was schooling and me as the role model. To them studying was quite ordinary and natural. Whenever Deirdre and I were going to a hui, they would say they had homework or study to do. But that didn't mean to say they denied their identity as Maori.

'I didn't talk to my kids in Maori at home. I was so busy and it was my habit to speak English. But when Nga Tamatoa came along the two boys picked up their language.

One day they got up at a huí and spoke Maorí and I nearly fell off my chair because I didn't know they could do ít. That's the ínteresting thing about identity.

'Here are these middle-class children leading a relatively privileged life and suddenly here they are pitchforked into this dynamic of cultural politics. They learnt about it at marae live-ins organised by Nga Tamatoa. They would go to a rural marae and stay over a long weekend and get the elders to talk to them and help them learn their language. Later they stayed occasionally with my mother, and she would indoctrinate them a bit more. That's how they learnt their language in a six-month period while Deirdre and I were in England.' Ranginui admits to being very proud of them.

The New Zealand Maori Council is a statutory body that is supposed to advise government on Maori policy and uplift the Maori people but Ranginui says its resources were pitiful. 'We dipped into our own pockets to pay for almost everything. I used to write my minutes up in longhand or else get Deirdre to type them on an old typewriter and I'd take them into the Department of Maori Affairs to print and circulate.'

Ranginui worked hard for the Maori Council. The meetings extended from 9.30 a.m. until 5 p.m. or even later. 'Deirdre attended them all because we are a partnership and she believes in togetherness and shared values. If you don't have shared values in a marriage, how can it endure? She helped with putting agendas in envelopes, licking stamps and addressing and so on. She's special. She's my back-up and her role has grown over the years. So she's been my research officer, and now that I am even busier in my retirement as a Waitangi Tribunal member she also manages my diary and answers important emails, setting up appointments and travel arrangements when I am out of town. She's my PA, she's my house director, my friend.'

Ranginui says Deirdre was not one to give him advice. 'She was just totally supportive. She sat and absorbed what the Maori people were saying. She just listened. She was in the background and the Maori people accepted her, as my wife and as one of them, as a loving person. They all treated her with the greatest respect and honour, because she is not pushy in the Maori domain. She just sits there quietly and will not express an opinion in the public arena. So she listens and learns.'

For some, Ranginui's activism was 'evil'. He laughs about an incident that happened to his son, Stuart, an anaesthetist. 'He wanted to find the effects of a new drug and the time to ask his questions was when the person was semi-comatose coming out of an operation. So as the anaesthetic wore off he bent over to talk to a male patient, "Excuse me. My name is Dr Walker, and I want to ask you some questions." Suddenly he watched this guy stiffen up and say, "Not Dr *Rangi* Walker! I'm not answering *your* questions!" He thought the devil incarnate had come to get him!'

Although Ranginui is depicted as a hater of Pakeha, he insists that he has never, throughout his part of the struggle, disliked Pakeha as such. 'I have never met anyone who has expressed dislike for Pakeha in my circles. My understanding is that we have a power structure, a system, that is often hostile to the needs and welfare of people. And so you deal to the system. And this is what Pakeha don't understand.

When Maori are protesting, they are protesting against the Crown. They are protesting against the government and the way that it has used its power. They are not protesting against Pakeha per se.

Ranginui believes race relations in New Zealand are getting better. 'I used to say, "Pessimism of the intellect but optimism of the heart."

When you look at the nasty nature of our history it makes you pessimistic, but you have got to be optimistic, otherwise you give up.'

Although Ranginui often says it will be sorted out in the bedrooms of New Zealand, he's not strongly advocating cross-cultural marriages. 'I have known relationships that have broken up because of the cultural differences. There has to be negotiation and give and take on both sides over the cultural differences. But actually Maori and Pakeha are much more alike than they admit. We are much more like each other than we are like our English forebears.'

He has a story which demonstrates his affinity with his fellow Kiwis – whatever their whakapapa. It was 1972 and he and Deirdre were coming home from England. Until then he had been in the habit of making scathing comments about what he saw as the 'untutored Kiwi twang'. But after six months of following English rules of polite behaviour, he boarded an Air New Zealand flight in LA and heard a Pakeha air hostess welcome them with her Kiwi accent. 'I felt like embracing her as a sister!'

It's very plain that he adores his Pakeha mate too. 'Deirdre has just gone along and listened and absorbed and blended in. She is loved by Maori wherever we go, including me of course . . . but she has also had her life enriched in the process.'

※

RATANA *Walker is a Thai of Chinese extraction married to Michael,*

the eldest of the Walker children. Appropriately, she met Michael

through the East–West Center scholarship programme in Hawaii,

designed to bring East and West together and they moved to

New Zealand 15 years ago. She works mainly for Waitemata District Health Board in Auckland and also as a health planning consultant. Michael and Ratana have two children, Leilani, 15, and Punahamoa, 12, whose mixed heritage is sometimes a puzzle for those who don't know them.

Ratana's name means 'precious stone' in the Thai language. Little did she know, growing up in Thailand, that her name in Maori culture was also precious to those who follow the Ratana faith and that one day she would link her name to a well-known Maori family.

Her mother is a Chinese/Thai and her father a Chinese from China

(*l to r*) Leilani, Ratana and Michael Walker
(*front*) Punahamoa, 2005

who worked as an accountant. Ratana had close contact with her extended families on both sides. Her mother, Suchinda, was one of 10 children. 'And each Sunday everyone in the family had to meet at our Nana's house. We had meals together and sometimes 30 to 40 people were there.'

Her upbringing was more Chinese than Thai. 'The male is dominant in Chinese culture. We lived in a compound. My father had one floor, my grandfather had one floor and whatever he said came first. So I grew up in a strong disciplined atmosphere. Education was paramount. People there believe that if you have education you will have high status in society.'

It was through her educational aspirations that Ratana met Michael. In 1982 she left Thailand to take up the East–West Center scholarship that he had won also, from New Zealand. She was there to do her Masters in Demography and a PhD in Sociology, and Michael was finishing his doctorate. She says there were so many different races of people at university in Hawaii that she was not really conscious of any differences in the beginning. The couple lived together for a while and then decided spontaneously one day to marry when they learnt that Rangi and Deirdre were coming to visit them.

'The wedding was short notice, really cheap but very good. My friend and I went to get some material at Woolworths around midnight, for about $2 per metre, and she made me a dress. Then we had a potluck party, people made me leis and the ring is my ring.

Michael and I are not materialistic, which is quite different from my background. Most people from my culture might want a rock or something, but in our marriage it's not important.

Living in Hawaii made it easier for Ratana to understand what being Maori might mean. She and Michael both belonged to the Pan Pacific Club, where they learnt traditional hula and some Hawaiian language.

'Michael learnt Thai as well, because he used to hang around with all my Thai friends.'

Now settled in Auckland, Ratana enjoys the shared ideas she and Michael have about whanau support. Her mother, Suchinda, has moved to New Zealand and now lives in a self-contained area below their house. 'It is far enough away but it's also close. And we have a strong family life with Rangi and Deirdre.' The senior Walkers live only a few blocks away.

Some marked cultural differences in the way her Thai/Chinese family sees things and the way the Walkers look at life have caused problems for Ratana. She was raised with a strong focus on value for money. 'In Asian culture we are taught to be careful and to rationalise everything because resources are so stretched, people struggle to live and therefore you value tangible things. That's why people say Chinese are always after money. And having a father who is an accountant makes it more so for me!

'When you go shopping, you bargain to get a good deal. Because when you get a good deal it is like you have won. It makes you so proud that you are so clever. The cleverness comes from outsmarting other people. And we grew up like that.'

When she met Ranginui she found his thinking on material things completely foreign and sometimes even painful to accept. When Ranginui bought a four-wheel drive vehicle he rang Ratana to ask her to come round for a drive. 'In Thailand we ask how much it costs, in New Zealand you don't ask. But I asked, "How much did you buy this car for?" And he said, "$29,600." And I said, "How much did they ask for?" And he said that was what they were asking. I said, "What?"

I couldn't believe it. He had bought the car without asking for even one dollar off!

'Then he looked at me and said, "Ratana, you know people in this country are different, they don't screw each other like that. If we can afford it at that price, we buy it at that price. They have to make a living."

'That night I just kept thinking, "Gosh! Couldn't he have knocked the price down even by $500? At least he could save $100!" I had no sleep for a couple of days. He had paid too much.'

She was even more astounded by another vehicle transaction Rangi and Deirdre made with their old car that had become a classic model. 'A boy at the garage said, "That's a nice car," and he offered them $1,000 for it. He was so excited he went to the bank to get the cash. My in-laws went home and felt guilty, thinking the car is not worth that. The next day they gave him back $500! That's them.'

Ratana says in the 15 years she has been in New Zealand she has been gradually looking at the world differently. The Walkers have taught her a lot.

In the past I used to bargain like anything and when I came home I felt so good, you know. But then they taught me to look on the other side of the coin. When you buy things it is a two-way street.

'If I screw someone, if I feel so good, then the other person probably feels equally bad. It's part of a relationship thing. Michael is the same as his father. He doesn't bargain either. It's a huge cultural difference.'

She gives another example of how Chinese approach life from her Hawaiian days. The students were living in a dormitory with a shared kitchen. 'A student from Hong Kong said while we were cooking, "I don't understand Hawaii people. You know they go out and catch fish. And they just catch one or two and then they come back. And they go out again!" He could not understand it because if Chinese people were to go out fishing they would take the whole lot.'

Ratana's viewpoint has changed so much that she's the one who moans when she sees Asian people taking more kaimoana than they need from New Zealand's coast. She's more critical of those who disrespect the environment than Michael is. 'I can see it now. It's not about individuals. It's a cultural thing, how you grew up.'

Ratana says, coming from Thailand, it's been very easy for her to fit into Maori family life and culture. For her doctoral thesis Ratana focused on conflict resolution and this has helped her to understand the Maori view of the world. 'In my thesis, I argued that law is not universal. In order to resolve conflict in non-Western societies, you need to understand and solve it within the context of that culture.'

As an example, Ratana says, in traditional Thai culture it is regarded as pointless to take an offender away to jail. It doesn't resolve the conflict for the victims. But if both the offender and his family offer to take part in a shared ceremony, that's more important than locking the offender up. This has made it easy for Ratana to understand marae justice and Maori concepts of utu, or reciprocity, and conflict resolution.

An area of conflict in the marriage is education because the importance of discipline to gain a good education is so ingrained in Ratana. 'I am much more strict with the children than Michael, although looking back into Asian society and analysing it, I realise this is a mistake, so I am trying to soften my approach. But the kids see me as more disciplined in my attitudes to their homework. In Asia, we really value education but in New Zealand I criticise the government for not valuing it enough.

Throughout Asia if you have a good education you can have social mobility. You can be poor one day and tomorrow you can be prime minister. However, I now believe Asians concentrate on education a bit too much.

'It is not very balanced. You get brilliant people without a social life.'

Over the years Ratana's father-in-law has made many controversial statements about Asian immigration to New Zealand. Ranginui says the preamble to the Treaty of Waitangi speaks of emigration from Europe and Australia, and Maori were not consulted about the change to a more multicultural society, which he sees as a threat to biculturalism. He challenges the view that immigration benefits the economy, and a major concern for him is that Maori will become more of a minority in their own country. In the future he believes Maori and Pakeha may both regret the current levels of Asian immigration.

Ratana's opinions on immigration are surprisingly aligned to his views. 'My study in Hawaii was on demographics and the impact of immigration. The New Zealand government did not do its homework well. I can cite all the books they can read. Asian migration is called "chain migration" because of extended families. For example, if you get an English couple to come here, you really get a couple. But with Asians, they come with the whole family. Mum and Dad come in; they bring their brothers and sisters too. This is a worldwide phenomenon. If the government, for instance, wants a carpenter to come here they might, instead, end up with another 10 people, through the family reunion category, who are not carpenters or immigrants with the skills New Zealand needs. If that is what the government was planning that's fine, but it's not.'

In her previous job as Resource Manager for Maori Health at the Ministry of Health, Ratana learnt some Maori language and waiata so that she could mihi when she visits marae. 'Now when I go to a Maori function, I can understand a little bit. Sometimes we get on so well you forget about your colour. Most of my good friends are now Maori and when you go places you will know so-and-so and so-and-so will know you. It is a really small world.

'I think it's a family thing as well because this Walker whanau, all our cuzzies and nieces and nephews, we are really close. I don't feel left out.

It makes the whole thing very easy because my family is the same.

'It is very important to me that my children identify as Maori. For me, working with Maori statistics, I like to have a more positive view of what Maori statistics will show in the next generation. I like to balance it out a little bit so the figures don't look so negative, so I always define them as Maori and they like it that way.

'Leilani decided to learn Maori and join kapahaka. She did it herself without us saying anything. Punahamoa looks more Chinese than Maori and probably behaves that way too. In terms of his Maori side, he doesn't show as much interest as Leilani. He doesn't do things just because others are doing them. He picks up Maori words and will hongi his grandparents but doesn't say much in Maori.

'Earlier in our marriage Michael left all the child-rearing to me but, since we talked this over a few years ago, he has taken on an equal role as a father and is very good with the children. It's not always easy being in a cross-cultural marriage but we rarely argue nowadays. Even on education matters we have both agreed to come halfway and compromise. Michael is a caring, honest and trustworthy person. I think our marriage has worked well.'

MICHAEL *Walker, the eldest son of Deirdre and Ranginui Walker,*

is an Associate Professor in the School of Biological Sciences at the

University of Auckland. He studied for his PhD in Zoology at the

University of Hawaii where he met his Chinese/Thai wife, Ratana.

Michael was an active member of Nga Tamatoa in his early years at the University of Auckland. He believes his mixed heritage has

given him an edge as a scientist in his field.

Michael Walker has been influenced by the sea since his birth when his parents lived in a bach at the beach at Oakura near Russell. While his younger brother and sister both became medical doctors, Michael was drawn to study kina for his Masters at Auckland University and, later, tuna and stingrays.

Ranginui and Deirdre expected high standards of honesty and hard work from their children. Michael describes how his father demonstrated that work ethic himself, managing three jobs – as a teacher at the local primary school, teaching English at Queen Victoria School for Maori girls, teaching Maori at night school – while going to university part time as an undergraduate.

'Having a Maori father and Pakeha mother wasn't something we noticed as children. We essentially lived a mainstream nuclear family life. It was our parents' aspiration to give us the best of that. So the Maori element was very much lived in parallel. I didn't know that the lives of Pakeha kids were any different, and I certainly would not have been able to specify what those differences were. Yet I suppose we knew the other kids were unfamiliar with Maori words like "ihu", "puku" or "hongi" – things that we understood quite naturally.'

Michael tells a story about his brother who, aged about four, told his friends that his nana had a 'lovely tan'. The little boy needed an explanation when one saw his grandmother and said, 'But she's a Maori!'

'When we went down to Opotiki to see our grandparents it was total immersion in the Maori world. They spoke Maori but only English was spoken to us. There was one uncle down there I had never heard speak Maori until I was 40. And I said to him, "I didn't know you spoke Maori. How come you never spoke it in the past?" He said he would have been afraid to, just because of the attitudes towards Maori language at that time.

'When my brother was born, and I was a year old, I stayed in Opotiki for about a month. I imagine only Maori was spoken, although I have no memory of that time. I often wonder if early exposure from my grandparents as a very small child helped write the programme in my mind and gave me a bit of an advantage picking it up as an adult compared with my brother and sister. My sister was able to study Maori at school but you almost never hear her speaking it. Whereas I am called on to speak it more and more in formal situations. I was self-taught. Languages were always my best subjects at school. I was much better at them than sciences in fact.'

Michael says his being Maori became obvious as soon as he was aware that there were two cultures in New Zealand society.

He recognised that his Maori whanau were different from what he experienced on a day-to-day basis in Auckland. 'And in the early years they were quite a significant part of our life. Not only did they come up to Auckland so my grandfather could get medical treatment, but also we went down there a lot, for the holidays and so my father could help with the farm. It was lives lived in parallel and that has been true for me professionally as well. The two don't meet very much. That is the culture of New Zealand.'

Michael believes differing cultures can potentially be a complicating factor in marriage. He says it's fortunate that his own marriage did not meet the degree of disapproval that was rife in his parents' time. 'There is nothing in my experience like my grandfather, who was racist, trying to send my mother off to England to try to prevent her marrying my father. She didn't go, because my father said, "Don't expect me to be here when you get back." They realised what was going on and fortunately my grandmother was very supportive.

'Like Dad, I never got along well with our English grandfather, because of the ways he tried to disguise what he really thought, but when I visited him just before he died, for the first time in my life I was able to respect him because he faced death with courage and without being self-serving. That respect relieved me of any guilt about my old feelings towards him.'

Michael says he wasn't affected when Ranginui started to appear in the media and attracted public criticism. 'He always shielded us very well from the vicious things. He didn't allow us to become targets. I wasn't aware of other kids giving me a hard time. It wasn't only the mainstream media attacking him, it was Maori as well. People fight hardest when they are fighting over scraps. And when the message isn't to their liking, they're not always too fussed about who they lash out at.'

Michael had no doubts that what his father was saying about Maori issues was true. 'We trusted him and we could see plenty of evidence to support the case he was making.

And, of course, we saw this contradiction in what was represented in the media about Maori and what we knew to be true from our large extended family of very hardworking and very good people. We knew the stereotypes were wrong.

The Walker children also learnt about Maori struggles at the dinner table. There were many meetings in their house over Maori issues. 'In one book by my father, *Struggle Without End*, I almost felt undressed when he published it because it was like 20 years of our dinner table conversations!'

Michael was in the seventh form when he first became involved in anti-racist, anti-apartheid and environmental movements. He says

joining Nga Tamatoa helped him to work out the identity issues that
had emerged for him. He'd lived in a white suburb in a highly charged
political environment at home and was aware that he was different.

His education, observing his father at home, proved useful for
Nga Tamatoa. As secretary for a year he brought organisational skills
to the group. 'I ran things effectively from the background and it
helped me to find myself.' Many of the 'young warriors' of that time
are now, like Michael, making significant contributions in education
and other fields. Those 'radicals' are in their fifties, but he says there's
still a need in New Zealand today for that sort of questioning. 'The
hikoi and the foreshore and seabed issue demonstrate that. Power and
money always congregate – and must be challenged.'

*Having completed his doctorate in Hawaii, Michael tried for
jobs back in New Zealand but he found out later that, in at least
one case, he was not considered because of who his father was.*

Eventually Michael took a post-doctoral position in the Zoology
Department at Auckland University. It was not until he was offered
a job at Waikato University that Auckland University finally offered
him a position. 'I used to get comments like, "You only got this job
because you are Maori." And another guy in the staffroom would say,
about some pamphlets someone had left on the table, "What's this
shit? Oh, look it's about Maoris!" and then look at me to see if I would
bite. However, the leadership and people I worked with on a day-to-day
basis gave me so much support, that stuff was all trivial. Looking back,
because of the challenges I had getting into the academic environment
here, I was able to create my own job and I've grown much more than
I might have done.'

While he has chosen to identify as Maori, Michael says this does not
mean that he is *only* Maori. 'It's like one of those assumed things. It's
not that I am *not Pakeha*. It's just that I am more than *simply Pakeha*.

However, there isn't a huge need for another Pakeha academic out in the mainstream, but there is a need for a Maori academic in sciences, given that our academic community is relatively small and our academic science community has very few Maori in it.'

This is why he puts his energies into encouraging Maori and Pacific students into the science field and promoting research for Maori development and advancement through Nga Pae o te Maramatanga, a Centre of Research Excellence. 'I'm from a privileged background. I've been given advantages I have not earned. In my life, I've seen that our society has wasted a lot of human potential, particularly that of Maori people. I could quite easily perpetuate that history by staying in the safety of the mainstream now that I'm inside the system. However, that's not good enough if I want society to be better as a result of my having existed. The logical consequence is that I should seek to make the single biggest contribution to society that I can – for me that is through education and participation of Maori in the sciences.'

Michael says being 'moderately' bicultural has been an advantage for him in the science world. His knowledge of both Maori and European styles of navigation and experience at sea in the Pacific, for example, gives him an edge over his northern hemisphere colleagues. He built the first 20 years of his career on the magnetic sense in animals and now is looking also at biological rhythms.

'My paternal grandmother used to plant kumara by the moon, so I have vivid memories of planting well into the night. There must have been some reason for doing that. And the Maori fishing calendar has given me fresh ideas about the impact of lunar rhythms – particularly on the appetite of the fish.

'Professor Mason Durie from Massey University talks about two knowledge systems. Before the Tohunga Suppression Act of 1907, Maori society had its own formal advanced education and then there is the Western-style university system. (Unfortunately the Maori form of advanced learning has been knocked around.) Mason says you can't use the methods of one to understand the other. However, there are important opportunities for those with the competencies to access both. I'm one of the few people in New Zealand in that situation.'

Michael points out how scientific thinking is beginning to converge with Maori concepts of creation, whakapapa and kaitiakitanga. In the Maori world, humans are not singled out as a special creation and they are related to all other organisms and environments by descent. The web of interrelatedness means that if humans are to prosper, then everything in the environment also has to do well. 'Now Western scientists have discovered that we share 60 per cent of our genes with a banana etc etc. If we have high sequence identity with a single-celled organism like yeast, then in fact we are highly related. Science has just caught up with the Maori view.

'We can point to clear examples where matauranga Maori has important things to say. Having these two different perspectives provides the means and opportunity to rethink and question our own assumptions. It's like marrying a person from a different culture. Your assumptions get questioned. And when your assumptions are questioned you examine yourself and you learn.'

Michael acknowledges that Ratana had to make a lot of adjustments to settle in New Zealand initially. However, he believes she now sees the advantages of this country. When the children came along, it was another challenging adjustment for both of them.

we had very different ideas about the children. The assumptions are more deeply rooted. we can make jokes about it now but it wasn't easy.

'I had been reared in a "standard" nuclear family in Auckland. But Ratana wanted to do things like having the baby in bed with us. That may be a Maori custom but my Pakeha mother did not do that. So that was one of my assumptions that went out the window and I had to get used to it. In the end, I slept in a separate room because it was easier. The world didn't come to an end. It meant that I could work late and get up early to process emails before the others woke up. I got over it.

'I don't speak Thai well and I struggle with the tones but Ratana can understand me. I know enough to order at a restaurant or get what I need in Bangkok if I'm on my own. I learnt because I was curious and wishing to impress. I was also keen to stop them gossiping about me without my knowing what was being said.

'Our kids are used to us talking to them in Thai. But they will answer in English – except with my mother-in-law who doesn't speak English. If we want them to give her a message we tell them the words to say and they can handle that. Leilani's progress learning Maori at school is slow. I thought she would be learning more there than she is. I guess I'm also a little jealous that I didn't have that opportunity and have unrealistic expectations as a consequence. On holidays now, my father is speaking more and more to them, which helps reinforce my efforts, telling them, in Maori, to shut the door, close the curtains and other minor things around the house. They know what those instructions mean. Getting them to answer or to handle more complex language is hard, though.'

Looking at his marriage Michael says the cultural issues have made for interesting times. But both he and Ratana have been prepared to change what they *do* – even if they can't change who they *are*. 'The basic underlying happiness is there, we enjoy each other's company so we make the changes. As for my children, they are even more privileged than I was and they don't see their mixed heritage as an issue. I don't think they have any idea what it was like in New Zealand 20 or 30 years ago.'

The Hirschfeld Family

CHARL *Hirschfeld (senior) is an Australian who came to New Zealand in 1955 and soon afterwards fell in love with Ngawiki, a young woman from Rangitukia on the East Coast. They had three children, Charl, Linda and Carol. Ngawiki died of a brain haemorrhage when Charl (junior), the eldest, was 15 and Carol only 10. For this, and other reasons, the family's cultural focus was largely Pakeha.*

PHOTOGRAPH:

Back (l to r) Charl Jnr, Ngawiki, Charl Snr
Front (l to r) Carol, Linda. Circa 1968

Charl Hirschfeld was born in 1931 in Western Australia. His surname is probably Jewish and his paternal grandparents were Lutherans who emigrated originally from Polsen in Prussia in 1863. However, Charl didn't know much about his paternal side because his father died in a road accident just before he was born. His mother (of Scottish and English extraction) had little money and to manage she opened a little grocery business in Perth with her brother.

Charl sees his childhood as deprived. His mother was under strain and became 'obsessed with religion'. During the war, mother, brother and young Charl moved to Melbourne where the two adults worked in a munitions factory.

'Mum became involved in a sect called Bethany. She used to take me to these tent missions – evangelical things – where people my age would go up and say, "Oh, I've seen him" and "Thank God, I've found Christ" and I'd think to myself, "Gee, I haven't had time to see him yet!" I was about 12. And the preacher prayed to bring me in and I wondered what it was about. For years I was agnostic and then I decided I didn't believe it.'

Leaving school at 15, Charl became an apprentice electrician, beginning a 50-year career working on power lines, first around Australia, then in New Zealand and Indonesia. He was recognised as an REA, or registered engineering associate, by the 1980s. For the most part, what he has learnt has been self-taught.

A tall strong man himself, Charl had already formed some impressions of Maori before he arrived in New Zealand. 'I saw Maori as quite a physically . . . I wouldn't say superior . . . but in the top physical attributes. I arrived at that conclusion by reading some accounts by early settlers in a museum display.'

Shortly after he arrived in New Zealand, Charl joined the State Hydro-electric Department and took up a job in Kaikohe building the first big power line up north. 'Apart from the foreman, I was the only

Pakeha there. I would booze with the Maori every weekend. They were very happy and carefree, it would appear in those days anyway.'

He was transferred to Otahuhu in Auckland where he was building large steel towers and living in barracks. It was about this time that he met Ngawiki at a party. 'It sort of kindled a feeling between us. She reciprocated. I think there was an empathy there because we were both very insecure people and possibly recognised that in each other.'

They started to go out together. She was a psychiatric nurse at Carrington Hospital at Point Chevalier and Charl applied to work at the Auckland Power Board. 'One of the engineers there mentioned to me, many years later, that he was not thinking of giving me a job because of my wild hair and being an Australian. It was probably unkempt. I used to like partying and drinking and things like that. I was rudderless in a way. Ngawiki and I had a courtship and after a period of time we formed a relationship.

In those days, ads in the papers for accommodation said 'No Maoris'. It was hard to find accommodation. But I fronted up to the landlords so they wouldn't know that Ngawiki was Maori.

The couple decided to get permission from Ngawiki's family to marry. Ngawiki bought herself a new dress for the journey. Arriving by train in Gisborne late at night they took a taxi to Ngawiki's home at Tolaga Bay. It was an eye-opener for Charl, although he had no insight then into the effect such an upbringing might have had on his wife-to-be. They walked across a paddock in the dark to a one-room tin shack. Inside were Ngawiki's mother, her stepfather, Doc, and three children.

'Doc was sleeping in an upturned water tank on a bed of fern fronds. The younger girl was in a cot and they had extended the cot by attaching a banana case to the end of it. The fireplace was just an open fire. I don't know if there was even a chimney. Everything had to be cooked in a blackened pot.

'I had a row with the stepfather. God knows what it was about. It got to a bit of a punch-up. Her mum didn't seem to have any idea of time. We were going to have Christmas dinner at night. During that period the husband went berserk and smashed a few pots. I had spent some years in construction camps where fights and boozing and all sorts of funny things went on so it didn't have a strong impact on me. I probably take people as I find them. The husband, Doc, was an ex-soldier and an alcoholic.

'I realised Ngawiki had had a tough upbringing, but at that time I tended to feel more sorry for myself and my own upbringing. I would be more sympathetic to her background now.

'One day, years later, when her mother was here, she [Ngawiki] said, "I've got something to tell you, Mum. Basically you sacrificed my life for the younger kids. I was always late for school. I went with holes in my trousers and always missing the bus." So she had obviously had an unhappy childhood. She ran away from her mother.

Back: Linda, Carol
Front: Ngawiki on the statue of Pania of the Reef.
Ngawiki was one of the models for the statue.
Circa 1970

'Ngawiki very rarely spoke Maori, except maybe to her sister. The only close friend she had was her sister. Her old granny came to visit one time and she didn't speak much English. Some say Ngawiki didn't speak Maori particularly well but she spent her early childhood with Maori speakers.

'We rowed continuously. I would go along with things for the most part but then a week would go by and I would be pressed and something would snap and then I would lash out. This was not a cultural thing. She was a bit obsessive about me and didn't like me speaking to anybody – especially women. However, being an only child and not having a very happy childhood, the tie to my children was very important to me. And the woman who produced the children, although we differed and fought all the time, was important too.

'We didn't really communicate much with each other about what we felt. We were too busy fighting with each other. I couldn't even tell you what we fought over. I was generally happy because I had a wife and children. At that time of my life I felt complete having a woman around the place, even if she nagged, as long as she wasn't unfaithful to me.

'She was my love. In fact, when they are the apple of your eye, you build a picture up of what you want to see. And people may tell you all sorts of things but you don't believe it. You see them in a certain light, because they are important to you.

'To be quite honest, I had to do a lot of work around the place. I used to do the washing. She hung it out. One day I hung it up and she went out and took it all down and hung it out again herself. That probably tells a story. I don't think there was much about race in this.

Our common thing was that we were both uneducated and from unhappy families.

'The children say they were terrorised by Ngawiki. To my way of thinking she was protective. You have to balance what is important. The jealousy thing made me think I was important to her. I probably went along with it. I was a lot shyer then. I always went out of my way to shield what was happening at home from the world outside. We lived in Epsom. When the girls went out to their little parties – and there was a lot of preparation, always dresses to be bought and hair to do – she went out of her way. If she looked at them they would do what she said. She was a very powerful person. I go along with certain things. But I've got certain limits. She never beat them up in front of me.

'My son, more recently, said I was a party to the whole thing. I didn't see it that way at all. I said, "Try to get it in context." She took him to rugby when I was working. As far as I could see, those kids were well looked after. It was never noticeable in marks or anything.

'We lived pretty isolated. Very few people came into our home. Apart from my family and two or three friends, I am not a very sociable beast. It is obvious to me now that Ngawiki was lonely. There are probably a lot of things I maybe could have done to help. I was at work and there she was stuck with the kids all the time. That's how I see it now.

'When we started to get a few things together, the first thing I bought – in our beaten-up old flat – was a fridge for the baby's bottles and a washing machine. And when we got to Epsom I bought a set of *Encyclopaedia Britannica* for the kids and a brand new piano, and Ngawiki, who had always played by ear before, learned music. She used to play her guitar and sing "And you'll never get another wahine like me." She was very musical. Charl, my son, also went to music lessons. All the kids put their best into their work. I am like that myself. Ngawiki had a good command of English. She wrote well. She was quite intelligent but it was all locked up in a way.

'Actually, there is a little telling thing there. And I really notice it.

It has become apparent to me and it's made me think that maybe I tend to pakeha-fy them. Why did I rename her Vicky?

'Why did I rename my late Indonesian wife Evelyn instead of Evi? I suppose I Pakeha-fied my children too, because in those days the first child was registered as a Pakeha. All the children have Pakeha names. So maybe that tells you something.

'We lived in Epsom for 11 years but we wanted a change of lifestyle and we came here to Ellerslie. I thought she wanted to not concentrate on the children so much but to get out. I tried to get her to get a job. And eventually she took one driving a cab during the day. I knew central Auckland well as part of my job. I went along with Vicky and got her through the test as a taxi driver. She only worked for six weeks before she died.

'Ngawiki is buried at Mangere. She died in the night of a brain haemorrhage. Only a few members of her Maori family came to the funeral. I didn't know any protocol or anything like that. It was all very sudden. She had a Pakeha funeral. I knew she was Anglican so I got the local Anglican minister to do it. Quite a lot of Maoris came along because I worked with a lot of Maoris. I didn't bring her back to the house because of the children and she had had to have an autopsy. I did think of bringing her back to the house but the children were in a state of trauma. To my way of thinking it was not important. Ngawiki was buried. At least I knew not to cremate her. At least I knew that much.

'Funny, I had a couple of dreams after that. One was as if there was a sort of a pillar, which had to do with her. And one night I woke up and the room was bathed in light. I told myself I had to face it. There was no supernatural. It's all to do with various factors on your mind. So I got on with things. I had some depression as a delayed reaction some time afterwards.

I didn't know the kids had any difficulty in life because they were Maori. They are Maori kids and I'm a Pakeha, but it has nothing to do with the situation.

'It's the relationship that's important. I worked with Maori guys. My prejudice is not stereotypical. I wouldn't say I like all Maoris. I don't like all Pakehas. I tend to make judgements on whatever relationship I start off with. Sometimes I start off with a bad relationship and it changes to a positive one.

'It is interesting the way kids aspire to middle-class values. Vicky and I both came from a deprived background, and, with the baggage we had between us, race was secondary. My kids are really brown Pakehas with aspirations to the middle class. I probably played a part in it because I never considered myself middle class but in fact my values may be middle class. Maybe that's because of the religious background I come from. Those things do print into you. I certainly don't reject Christian values.

'Charl, my son, is involved in Maori things. He knows his whakapapa. Even when he was not applying himself at school and became a bit of a delinquent, he always showed a keen interest in history. Maybe the encyclopaedias had something to do with that. I don't know. Against all advice I bought those encyclopaedias but it was a good thing in 1963 to buy that set. Because I didn't know much about the world around me and at least the kids had that. You can see the index is absolutely worn out.

'I don't think they have any problem with identity or knowing who they are. They are content.

They're not happy about discrimination on the basis that they are brown. And they can quote instances by the score on that, of course.

'But my advice would be, "Well, the fact that you are here and you are healthy, genetically you all seem pretty good to me, so you can all stand on your own two feet." I have always said, "It doesn't matter if you are a rubbish man or whatever, as long as you are a happy rubbish man and you've got a balanced outlook on life. What more do you want?" That's just saying words. But my actions during their lifetime have shown that. Although I might have punished them sometimes, hit them around the legs (because that's how Mum used to tell me off), they say, "You never took your frustrations out on us." And they thought that was fair.

'In 1977, an engineer I worked with asked me if I was interested to go and work in Indonesia. So I resigned after 21 years and took the girls over there. In my holidays I came back to see Charl. Then the girls went to stay with relatives in Australia and went to high school there. Linda said, in no time, Carol was the centre of attention. She got something published in a trade magazine which started her in journalism.

'I brought the kids back to New Zealand and was approached again about going back to Indonesia. I set Linda up with a car as the oldest girl, got them started again at Selwyn College and left them.'

Charl met and married his Indonesian wife, Evi, during this time. By some tragic quirk of fate she died of a brain haemorrhage too in 2003. Charl believes it's interesting that he married two brown-skinned women but he doesn't read much into that because, once again, he says race didn't come into it.

'I haven't got much to say about the race side of my relationship with Vicky. It's almost as if I've avoided it, isn't it? As I'm talking about it now I realise that I skirted every race question. I may have done that all my life. Even in Indonesia I empathised more with the indigenous people than with ex-pats. And I learned to speak the language.

'Maori and Indonesians can be racist too, of course. It is alive and well in all cultures. Even among the Maoris the different tribes fight each other. Maori don't see themselves as an entity. They're still tribal.'

Culturally, Charl doesn't know where he fits. 'Because I have observed cultural things, through my contact with Maori things, for instance, and because I travelled extensively in Indonesia over nine years, spent a couple of years in Papua New Guinea and observed them there, I think, "What is my culture?" Like, I don't feel any religious ties. I am not skilled in any performing arts from whatever culture I belong to. So in many ways I see people in cultures as trapped, by a programming sort of a situation. And yet I know that if we didn't have religion and we didn't have glue that ties groups together, we probably wouldn't be civilised. My identity is "human being". I always call myself a Pakeha. Even when I talk to my Indonesian friends I call myself Pakeha.

'Ngawiki and I never went to a marae together. I have been to tangi for people I worked with but never went with her to her marae.

I went to the East Coast a few months ago for her sister's death. When we were at the gates of the marae I started to cry.

'I sat there with the body and I cried. And then at the grave too I cried all the time. I wanted to say something. And someone said to me, "Pakehas don't have tangi like this." And I wanted to say, "Wait, wait a minute, Pakehas do care, you know." And, you know, I couldn't. I got all mixed up and just cried and cried.

'I don't know what it was that upset me about it. Maybe it was thinking that maybe Ngawiki should have been accorded that sort of thing. But that's water under the bridge and you can't keep looking back. I'm not sure if it's a guilty conscience. I'm sure one of Ngawiki's female relatives would want her dug up and taken back to her own. But I don't think like she does. Because, when I die, I want to be cremated and buried with Ngawiki. I feel that is my place, beside Ngawiki – even though I had a second wife. That is the mother of my children buried at Mangere there. I wouldn't shift her. She has become urbanised now. She's not tribal any more. And I can't provide the link. I am the link to urbanisation and I think the children see it in that way too.'

❋

CAROL *Hirschfeld is well known to all New Zealanders as a former*

TV3 news presenter. She's the youngest child of Charl and Ngawiki

Hirschfeld. She and her husband, Finlay Macdonald, have two

young children, Will and Rosa.

One of Carol Hirschfeld's early memories is how she was called a 'half-caste' at school. 'Being a child in the '70s, we were on the tail end of generations of mainstream New Zealanders who did not perceive the need to be sensitive about things Maori. So being a "half-caste" was definitely pejorative. And I was conscious that we came from a

household where one partner was brown and one partner was white and that most people didn't come from households like that.'

This perception of difference meant that Ngawiki, Charl, Linda and Carol were always striving to prove that they could fit in. Carol describes it as working harder to prove they were 'decent folk' and not the 'dirty Maoris' she heard people talk about. 'My mother tried to ensure there was no criticism by really dressing us up to the nines. When we went out we would have to be absolutely pristinely presented to the world.'

Carol Hirshfeld

Ironically their home was not kept in the same way as their clothes so Carol felt they were presenting a façade to the outside world. She says the house was chaotic at times. 'Mum would swing from being extremely fastidious and then just sort of lost. She probably suffered some form of suburban neurosis. That's what Dad thinks now, looking back.'

Even Charl senior didn't fit the norm in New Zealand society because he was Australian and Carol was conscious that he was different because he had a strong Australian accent – and does to this day.

'A highly unusual thing about Dad is his blindness to racial difference. He grew up in Western Australia and Victoria and can't remember ever seeing or hearing about anyone of a different colour until he was about seven. So by the time it came into Dad's consciousness, his attitudes were formed without ideas about people's race. And so he never saw us as being any different really. And yet clearly we are, and Mum was, and Dad's second wife, who was Indonesian, clearly was too. Yet he never characterised people according to their race.'

Until Carol was five the family lived in Epsom in a house rented from the Power Board. At school she can remember only two Maori families and lots of Pakeha children of doctors and lawyers. Charl senior thought it was an advantage to be in the area because when the school needed anything like books, mountains of books materialised. However, Carol wonders how her mother coped with life in Epsom because, at that particular school, they were 'at the other end of the socioeconomic scale'.

She is aware that race and class issues are closely aligned and that the race barrier is easier to cross if you have money and education behind you. 'Both my parents were very working class. Dad's huge drive was to educate his children so they would have choices. And he ended up with three incredibly middle-class children as a result of it. I went to university and I've got a BA, my brother has a Masters in Law, and my sister's just finishing her BA in teaching.'

Carol believes her mother, had she lived longer, might have been just as encouraging about education. Having left her home on the East Coast for good at 15, Ngawiki was seeking a very different life for herself and her children. 'Mum had a really troubled relationship with her mother. Her mother was remarried to an alcoholic, and had another family.

I'm not very close to my coast side, partly because Mum died when she did, and partly because, for a long time, I felt that her greater whanau had not cared for her or looked after her.

'The more I found out about her personal history, the more I understood why she was estranged from her whanau, except for her sister. She was very close to her sister.

'Mum's upbringing was really tough, really poor. We know the story about when Dad went back down to the coast in 1956 to ask for Mum's hand in marriage. The house that Grandma was living in with her second husband still had rushes on the floor. They used to change the rushes. One of the beds was made of crates and had newspaper underneath as a lining.

'Mum was kept back from school, from the time that she was about 10, to care for the younger children. I met my grandmother less than a dozen times in my life, before she died when I was 18. She was a tiny, tough woman, quite violent . . . very violent towards my mother. And it upsets me when I've gone back to the coast and heard people talk about how violent my grandmother had been to my mother – beating her, for example, till she fell off a horse at the age of 10, and just terrible things.

'Mum wanted to get away from that. And that's why, I think, she passed on to her children that they were middle-class and must never go back to the kind of circumstances that she experienced.'

Carol had her 'worst' experience of racism in the third form at school when 'another part-Maori boy' called her 'black'. It occurred at a time when body image was a key issue. 'My best friend at that time couldn't have been more blonde and blue-eyed. She almost won a competition for looking like Farrah Fawcett. And this boy was obsessed with her, and I was her best friend. I don't know why he turned on me one day. He was just unbelievably cruel. He ridiculed everything about me. I wore glasses and I was the tallest girl in the class, and then he called me "black" on top of it. I cried about it in the toilets all day. At home, I talked to Charl about it. And he said, "You are never ever to let anyone make you feel less than you are because you're brown." And he said, "If anyone ever does that to you again, laugh in their faces and turn it back on them." I remember it clearly. It gave me a strategy to cope in such situations.'

Carol believes Ngawiki was lost for a while in the years of bringing up her children but this was changing just before she died. Her mother was happy about becoming a taxi driver. 'She enjoyed the financial independence that brought and the contact with other people. Because she would have been in a big whanau-type community when she was younger. She would have missed that. I think she definitely felt disconnected and when we moved out into the suburbs I think that was even worse. My parents had the only house in that new Ellerslie subdivision for ages.

'They had no phone. I think Mum became so reliant on Dad. She was a savagely jealous woman, and all these factors made it worse. She had young kids, wasn't working. She had no real friends. It was actually not a great recipe. And Dad realises it now, but his great dream was to plonk us in the suburbs and get the kids into a good school.'

carol cannot remember any other Maori families in their subdivision and she realises now that her mother probably felt like a fish out of water.

'She was taken much more into Dad's world – but wanting to be there, because she was an insular person. My parents were insular people. We rarely had people come around.'

She wonders if the family was isolated partly because of their mixed cultural background. 'When they were courting, Dad said they moved into a house in Grafton and were told to move out. And, though he could never prove it, he was sure that it was because the woman who ran the house didn't want a Maori living there.

'He also talks about the fact that there were some pubs they couldn't go to. I don't know if it was because people explicitly asked them to leave or just that they felt so incredibly uncomfortable that they chose not to do those things. It staggers me that it happened, and so recently in our history.'

Carol's experience of racial issues was different during her secondary schooling in Bendigo, Australia, where, she says, everybody thought she and Linda were Greek or Italian. There was a song popular at the time called 'Black Betty Bam-ba-lam'. The other school kids would sing it when she climbed on the bus in Bendigo. But, for some reason, it didn't matter to her so much. In fact, she still rather likes the song.

'I remember working on a little community newspaper in Australia, because I was interested in journalism even then, and this guy walked in. I looked at him and thought, "Man, that's the first Maori face I've seen for two years." He was so obviously Maori, and I found him fascinating. There was a great sense of recognition. It was a really good feeling. He was somebody like me.

'That's what my sister and I constantly looked for – a situation where there were other people like us. At university we ended up being quite good friends with a number of Fijian students. They were really racially mixed – Fijian/Chinese, Indian – and one night we were invited to a party. We walked in and absolutely everybody was brown, and I thought to myself, "This is the first time I've been to a party where everybody's mixed."

I still notice when I'm the only brown person somewhere and it happens quite frequently.

When Carol talks about the racial discrimination experienced in her family, people often express surprise. She says they perceive her as having status in the community and cannot imagine such incidents could be connected to her. She remembers her mother being sensitive to situations such as service in restaurants, shops and banks.

'All those things were passed on to us. Linda, my sister, and I have talked about being highly attuned to any kind of change in people's attitudes because we're Maori. It becomes so second nature. And I realise you start practising it when you're a child. You think "Do they like me?" or "Do they have issues with me because I'm a different colour?" It just becomes part and parcel of how you cope in certain situations – that you kind of withdraw from a group of people if you think, "They see me as being different, and therefore it's probably not worth my while to stay."'

She says it's more difficult now to assess those situations because of her position as a newsreader. Many viewers don't recognise her as being a Maori. She and Finlay laugh at this because there is a tendency for people to see her as something more exotic – rather than 'just Maori'.

'I don't speak any Maori; I speak Indonesian. I studied it at university, and I can speak enough to get by on. People just assumed we were Dutch Indonesian when we were living in Indonesia.

'Linda and I, partly because there was that truncation through our lives with Mum's death, have found it hard to go home to the East Coast. This applies less to my brother, because Charl has made a real effort to go back and understand our family tree. He's helped to set up a trust, the Kaa Family Trust, to stop our land constantly being dissipated through the years.

But Linda and I find it hard in Maori situations. Sometimes I don't know what to do. I need somebody to take me through it. And I feel it really strongly when we do go to whanau occasions and Fin is looking to me to tell him what to do and I'm thinking, "I don't know. I need a guide myself."

'And I have reached this point of life, now that I'm in my forties, where I'm very conscious of needing to be the guide to take my children through.

'Charl, my brother, made a decision to find out about his roots. He wanted to understand his identity and he needed to reconcile Mum's death. When she died he was 15 and that was a very hard stage of his life to lose her. And with Charl being the first-born they had a problematic relationship. She was quite violent to him.'

Carol has not felt the same need as Charl to look for her Maori roots. 'I remember talking to my brother when I was a teenager because I became very troubled, thinking, "I've got to choose. I've got to say who I am. I know I'm Maori, but it's really hard, I don't speak any Maori and I haven't got the cultural reference points I need."'

She and her brother talked about it at length and in time he calmed her down and told her, 'You are what you are. Nobody can ever take your Maori-ness away from you. It is there; it's part and parcel of who you are; it's written into your DNA; and you'll write it into your children's DNA too.'

Carol says it made her feel more relaxed about it. Their discussions coincided with the period when Charl had just started going back to the East Coast to re-establish connections with their whanau. Carol found it reassuring to hear his perspective on their identity in view of the journey he was making.

'Also, I have thought about it very hard over the years – that I'm very much a product of the history of this country and I'm proud of that and nobody can *make* me be something. I *am* something.' She takes pride in the fact that she is truly indigenous. 'So I *do* feel strong in my identity about who I am. And that's a New Zealander – a Maori New Zealander.'

Left: Finlay Macdonald, Will (aged 5 years), Carol Hirshfeld. *Right:* Rosa (aged 2 years)

Carol's two children often ask her, 'What are you?' and 'What are we?' 'Particularly Will, because he's nine and I say, "Well, we're Maori." He says, "Dad's not Maori."' Carol laughs. '"No, no. Dad's not Maori. But that's okay."'

A journalism student asked Carol recently, in an interview, if she saw herself as a 'Maori broadcaster'. Carol says she sighed because it's a hard question to answer simply. For instance, she doesn't talk about Maori issues as part of her broadcasting career. However, she is a journalist who is Maori. 'And I do see myself as Maori.'

'It's a curious thing. I've been really heartened over the years I've been newsreading that various people have come up to me, and I can think of a bank teller, a young guy, he said to me one day, "It's really good to see a brown person doing what you're doing – in the mainstream." And that made me feel absolutely great.

'I try not to let it eat me away, but I have a huge amount of guilt about not speaking Maori. In fact I was speaking at Massey University and this young woman who'd just finished her Masters in Maori took me to task for my pronunciation in front of everyone. She said, "John, you do pretty well. But Carol, you know . . ." And there was nothing I could say. I mean, she was right. But having said that, I have made various efforts over the years to get on top of it. What can I do but try?'

As a newsreader, she's had to come to terms with the expectations that many other people place on her – about what she should do and how she should do it. They expect her to be a role model or representative for Maori in the media.

People put their perceptions on you and it bears little relation quite often to who you are. You just have to grow a thick skin about it.

Finlay reached a new understanding about race issues not long after he met Carol and was thinking of marriage. 'And my Dad, who was English (although he was actually born in New Zealand, but that's a long story), wasn't a racist but he had racial stereotypes in his mind. He would glibly stereotype or put on a Maori accent. You know, that "Eh, boy" thing. And when I said, "She's Maori", he did a bit of that. He said some little thing that he wouldn't have thought was offensive at all, and I remember bridling and realising I'll never be able to stomach that kind of shit ever again from family, from friends, from strangers. Whereas once I might have just ignored it, or glossed over it, or even (God forbid!) participated in it, that was suddenly over for me. That whole everyday, low-grade racism that New Zealand gets really used to was not for me anymore.'

Finlay describes his mother as still astonished that she came from 'white' northern England and emigrated to New Zealand in the first place. 'So to find that half of her grandchildren have Maori in them is surprising and rewarding and rich for her. I think Mum and Dad were conscious of it, and, without making it too deep, it feels like it's one of those things that connects Mum here now – that she belongs here because there's such an integration. She's never gone back to England. She has no desire to. She says her father, who died before I was born, would never in a million years have dreamt that his descendants, quite soon, would be Pacific people, that there would be Maori genes in the family. It would have never occurred to him and it happened so quickly, and there you go.'

Finlay says he doesn't remember any awareness that Carol was Maori when they met. It wasn't the first thing he asked her. 'I knew I was attracted to her, and I knew she obviously had something in her blood but it took me a while to actually bother to ask, to work it out, and someone else might've told me. And then I became interested in her family background and the whakapapa and so on. As you get older you get more interested in that anyway. And I'm interested in mine.

When you look at our family trees together you get this extraordinary Scottish clan thing mingling with the Maori tribal/iwi thing. They look so similar.

'The way lineage is recorded and cared about is really similar. My dad was really into that on the Scottish side. And Carol's brother has done quite a lot of it on the Maori side. That's nice, I like that. Makes for one hell of a complex family tree.'

Finlay found himself influenced by Maori culture when his father died. 'Without making too big a deal of it . . . we took his body home, just to my parents' house, and had him there for a few days. It just struck me that we wouldn't have done that, probably, if we weren't in New Zealand, that this was a tangible kind of tangi-like experience. I think more people are doing that sort of thing. And it wasn't particularly a self-conscious act. I was definitely aware that this is what goes on in this country and it's a bloody good way of dealing with things like that. It was very helpful for everybody. My mum was very aware of that, she was glad to have him at home.'

Carol says she has discussed with her brother and sister what they might do with their dad (Charl senior) when he dies. 'We have to give Dad a full form of tangi for our sake. We couldn't possibly not be with his body for a while. We would have so much to say, we would absolutely need to have time with him. Yeah, our Australian father!

'Dad always maintains the fact that he has had two wives of different skin tone to himself is irrelevant. He says it was totally a man/woman thing between them; it really didn't matter; it was just coincidental. I don't know if that's true. He always refers to us, his three children, as his "New Zealand souvenirs".'

Carol and Finlay say they never argue about racial issues. Finlay says he's a Maori sympathiser. 'I tend to side with them on most issues. Once I realised that Carol was Maori (like when we turned the light on!), then I thought it was really great, I got off on it, I thought it was fantastic. I was born in England so I was four when my parents emigrated, and I had this feeling for quite a lot of my early adulthood life: "I could go back and live in Europe. I've got a passport and every-thing. I've got relatives there. Where do I belong?" I'd worked out that I pretty much felt like a New Zealander but this was confirmation, utterly. And I've often thought that, genuinely, the interesting thing about New Zealand is its indigenous culture. And the more I know about it, the more interested I get. And because I've taught myself a little bit of the history and had to learn it because of working in journalism and just doing those stories you have to cover – you know, "Fallout from Waitangi", dah dah dah, all that stuff – the more I've come to realise I agree with Maori. I agree with everything they say about breaches of the Treaty and the rip-off, the whole bit. So we don't disagree about that stuff at all.'

Finlay points out that many Pakeha New Zealanders can still live through most of their lives without really knowing any Maori people. He says that's particularly possible in the South Island.

You can't have a sensible perception or perspective on these things if you're not intermingling a bit in your daily lives, either in work or your relationships.

'Contact just takes all the steam out of those arguments, particularly when you're intermarried. But if you work with Maori people, or something, these things become less abstract and less dramatic. The anxiety levels drop because you realise "Oh, they're human like me, and they've got their own valid opinions."'

Carol is in agreement with Ranginui Walker about the value of cross-cultural marriages to New Zealand society. 'Being the product! I advocate it because, with Finlay, there's no doubt about it, our differences are a great strength in our relationship. I look at our kids and I believe that's reflected in them as well. Those children are so lucky, they have such wonderful bloodlines. They have so much to fall back on. I feel the same way when I look at my own family tree and the fact that I have a German/Jewish surname. Because my height for example, all that comes from my great-grandmother who was Augusta Hirschfeld née Geister. She was six feet tall, as were all her daughters. And I love that aspect of my own family.

'One thing I used to notice when I was younger is that people, when they asked me what race I was, made an assumption that anything they found attractive about me came from my Pakeha side, not my Maori side. I think things have changed over the years, and maybe people's ideas of beauty have changed as well. But I knew the gifts my mother gave me in terms of my physical appearance were many. Both my parents gave us all in my family so many gifts. I'm lucky to be a product of a cross-cultural marriage.'

CHARL *Hirschfeld (junior) is an Auckland barrister who works on*

criminal cases and Treaty claims. He is the eldest son of Charl and

Ngawiki and when he was 26 he decided to find out what that mixed

ancestry was really about, through whakapapa and reconnecting

with whanau.

Because Charl was 15 when his mother, Ngawiki, died he believes he was more influenced by her than his two younger sisters were. He says his mother was a tough, violent woman who was always beating him. After her death, it was more than 10 years before he went back to the East Coast to sort out that 'unfinished business' and learn about Ngawiki's story.

As a child of a mixed marriage, Charl says he saw himself as both Maori and Pakeha and didn't distinguish one from the other because it all seemed very natural. He first became aware that he had brown skin when he was about five years old and started school. 'It didn't matter much to me but the differences seemed to matter to other people.

Charl Jnr

'There was a funny episode once when I was at school. My detractors, such as they were then at six or seven years old, decided that the best way to insult me was to call me a "Nazi" because I had a German name.'

Later he realised how bizarre these insults were in view of the historic persecution by Nazis of the Jews. 'I didn't understand it then, but it's a Jewish name. They were simply repeating their parents' prejudice and using that against me in trying to be offensive.

'There was always a feeling that we were different, because my sisters and I were the only brown-skinned kids at school for a while, until another Maori family moved into the area and then there were three more.

'I remember that when something Maori did come up – it might be to do with a place name, for instance – the teacher, and the rest of the class, would look at me for guidance on pronunciation or perhaps some admonishment for mispronunciation on their part. But I felt uncomfortable about those sorts of things because I simply wasn't brought up that way.

'I just pronounced it like everybody else I went to school with. Mum didn't really go down that path. She followed the mainstream as it was then. That was the high tide of assimilation in New Zealand. I was really aware that I was a Maori, but from a point of not really understanding that fully, because Mum had rejected it for various reasons that I now understand.

'My mother had been part of the diaspora from the country to the city, and she and Dad had decided early on that the best approach for the children was to get as good an education as possible. So they really emphasised that. From a really early age I looked forward to going to university.'

For a while Charl's chances of getting higher education seemed at risk. At 17 he was forced to leave Penrose College. He says it had nothing to do with being a brown-skinned kid. It was more that he wanted to have a good time with his fellow prefects, play sport all the time and go out with girls. He was neglecting his school work.

'At the end of the sixth-form year, the teachers were sick and tired of us wagging and so I was selected as lamb to the slaughter and I got the boot. I wasn't expelled but it was made clear to me that I couldn't come back to school. I tried to a couple of times – I was quite contrite then – but I realised the writing was on the wall. It was at the end of the year and I had really done nothing to deserve staying at school. So I moved on and became an apprentice chef the following year. It wasn't something I wanted to spend the rest of my life doing, although I'm glad I did it. A lot of people seem to like my cooking and I still enjoy it.'

When Charl was 19 he decided to sort out his education. In 1977 he re-enrolled at a different secondary school, Selwyn College. His father, who was in Indonesia at the time, gave him a small allowance of $25 a week; $17 went on rent in a flat and Charl had to live on $8 a week for a year.

'My sisters were in Australia, so I had no family support, but I certainly learnt a lot about myself, and self-reliance, and how to live frugally. I did seventh form and sat bursary to get UE.'

Charl's next step was law school. 'And it was during my time there that I became more aware of myself as Maori. I took advantage of the Maori Education Foundation offerings. They gave small book allowances. I had to state my tribal affiliation.

I knew Mum was from Ngati Porou and that's all I knew, nothing else. Then when I finished law school I decided to find out what my mother's story was.

'So I got in a Morrie one day and just drove there from Thames.

'I had no idea where I was going and what I was going to do once I arrived. So I managed to get to Tolaga Bay and I said, "I'm looking for the Kaa whanau." That's all I knew, that my mother was a Kaa. An old kuia said, "Oh, the person you'll have to see is Sophie Kaa at Rangitukia." So I arrived there on New Year's Day 1983 and, once I found where she lived, I walked through her kitchen door. Two of her daughters were there, Keri Kaa and Arapera Kaa, and one of my aunts said something to this effect: "Ah yes, we've been expecting you." She's like that, though; she's very presumptuous. I think there was more than a hint of irony in that.

'From that point, that completely changed my life. Suddenly I'd found a place where not only my mother had come from but also a place where I felt entirely comfortable because, after I started meeting my long-lost relatives, they made it clear to me that my place was there too, if I ever wanted it, which I did. There was no question about belonging, so there was this huge sense of existential fulfilment, and as I got to know my long-lost relatives I was able then to ask them questions and as a consequence piece together my mother's story – which was an uncomfortable one, a sad one, possibly a tragic one.

'She had lost her father when quite young, and the loss of her father was also my grandmother's loss. As a consequence Mum didn't really live with her mother. I heard that she suffered physical and sexual abuse. From the age of 14 she began trying to run away from home and was caught by the local constable one time. But she wanted to get out of there. She went to Hukarere School in Napier and as soon as she got through she really turned her back on that life. I understand that because, in putting together my mother's life, I've heard many unhappy stories.

'So, on the one hand, what's talked about is "happy families", if I can put it this way, this romantic view of what Maori life was like in those days, say before 1960, but the reality of it was that it was very hard.

There was a lot of physical abuse, a lot of violence, a lot of poverty. There wasn't very much to look forward to and my mother was deeply affected by not fitting into that context.

'She didn't like, for example, all the tangis that went on because she wasn't adjusted into it, I suppose. In the end my mother forgot how to speak Maori. So that's how significant that all was for her, and how alienated she had become.

'My mother was very, very unhappy. She left and unfortunately she never really resolved it, and I think that part of her frustration in life, about what remained unresolved, was then taken out on me. But I forgave my mother for that. When she was alive I was too young. We couldn't have talked about it. I lacked the maturity to understand the complexities of all of that baggage.'

The situation in Charl's extended family had moved on a great deal by the time he reconnected with them. The way of life his mother experienced had come to an end. The East Coast he found in 1983 was nothing like the isolated place it had been in the 1950s. 'That sense of isolation was long gone and people were much more worldly, much more outward-looking.'

Charl is fascinated by whakapapa and has become an avid collector of it. 'I've always had an interest in the past. I have a number of different lines of whakapapa. It's a wonderful thing whakapapa because it's quite varied as to what it is and what it can mean to you. It puts you in touch with your ancestors because whakapapa is a long chain of names of ancestors and you can see it go all the way back. I collect my European genealogy too. I'm intensely proud of my German side as well.'

Charl believes he has a really 'neat' Christian name because it is unique to his family (he shares it with his father.) The name was devised by his grandmother, who was trying to anglicise the Germanic side of the Hirschfeld family by using Charl instead of Carl. It has proved to be a great 'conversation-opener' all his life.

With such a background it seems almost natural that Charl's first wife was German. They met after he became a lawyer and five months after their marriage they went to live in Germany. Ironically, Charl, a Maori from New Zealand, came to learn the language of his other ancestors, becoming fluent in German and studying at the University of Frankfurt.

'So, Carol and Linda speak Indonesian and I speak German. One thing I really like about our family is that we're all bilingual. Learning

German was the most difficult intellectual exercise I've ever undertaken in my life. It's very difficult to speak grammatically correct German and you have to really discipline yourself.'

It was in Germany that Charl really felt the bite of racism. 'Because I am of racially ambivalent parentage, people really don't know where I come from. I don't have a neon sign on my forehead saying "I'm a New Zealander." They think that I am Arab often, southern European possibly. Anything! I was a lot thinner in those days.

'I remember, even in New Zealand, I used to go to dinner parties and people would say, "Oh, where are you from?" and I'd say, "Where do you think I'm from?" "Oh, you must be from Morocco," "No, keep going", and of course it would never dawn on them that I was Maori. They wouldn't even entertain the possibility.

'My racial ambivalence really dawned on me the first time I went to the United States in 1976 and was standing at the Greyhound bus station in Los Angeles and this woman came up to me and just started speaking Spanish. I realised that I looked like them and they looked like me. On that same journey, when I was in Hawaii on my stopover, people asked me directions!

In Germany, at the university, guys would come up to me and speak Arabic; Turks would come up to me and speak Turkish; when I was in Portugal people spoke to me in Portuguese.

'I've been to Argentina recently, and when I was there I look like them and they look like me. It's very pleasing to have that racial ambivalence.

'A lot of people don't think I'm Maori. When I put on a suit, when I'm a barrister, it's the last thing that they would think of. The moment that I put on my jeans and my black jacket and walk down Otara then I'm probably Polynesian, you know, more than Maori. Although, in Otara I can be a Maori too.'

In Frankfurt, Charl became confused about his identity and where
he fitted. 'I really wanted to become German but at the same time I felt
terribly homesick. At first I couldn't practice law in Germany, because
the Germans didn't recognise my professional credentials, so I had to
study law.

*The racism in Germany upset me and caused me to have this
identity complex, because there's no resonance there as a New
Zealander, let alone as a Maori. I was just 'foreign'.*

'The funny thing is that when Germans do find out you're from New
Zealand they go all starry-eyed about it, saying, "Oh, New Zealand. So
nice to be there. Nice to meet you." But before that I'm just another
brown-skinned *Ausländer,* they call them: foreigner. They're not very
welcoming to the *Ausländer* in Germany. So I came back and started
practising as a barrister. And that really resolved my identity complex.
It was partly to do with engaging in what you want to do, and for me
that was to practise law.'

Charl and his German wife, Tina Engels-Schwarzpaul, argued
sometimes about race issues but not in the sense that she was
prejudiced. Charl says she would question him about the degree to
which he was committed as a Maori. 'Which I found very strange
for her to raise. She is deeply interested in things Maori. She wrote a
doctorate which included a lot of reference to things Maori. She had
a very brown perspective, so that was a very important part of our
marriage.'

Charl had no intention to be involved in Treaty of Waitangi legal
issues but in the end the work chose him. 'Twelve years ago somebody
I knew rang and said, "I've got this Treaty case in Napier," and I said,
"Oh, I can't do that. I'm a criminal lawyer." And he said "No, no. They
want to meet you because they know that you're Maori."

'When I started, there were only three Maori barristers in the whole country, although more are coming into the profession now. Anyway, he insisted and I finally agreed and said, "I'll do it with my cousin, Caren Wickliffe." She had done some of this work before; she's a judge now. So we met the clients and it became probably the best and most important case that I've ever undertaken. Since then I've had 50 Treaty cases. They're all big pieces of litigation. I find them immensely satisfying professionally.'

The work has led Charl to mix more with other Maori and hear their stories. However, he says since law school he's had firm political views on Maori issues. 'Maori were portrayed in the media in a poor manner – if they were portrayed at all! So I used to collect newspaper cuttings and take an interest in all things Maori, even though I didn't have the language and didn't know much of the history. I've built up quite an extensive knowledge of the Treaty, for example.

'I like to assist using my professional powers as much as possible, no matter how hopeless the case might seem to be. I started doing water cases 12 years ago. That Napie r claim, for instance. I was doing foreshore and seabed cases long ago, when people used to laugh at the audacity of Maori to say that they had substantial interest in the foreshore and seabed.

I don't get involved in Maori politics but I see a lot of these cases as fundamental justice issues.

'There's a picture on my wall of Pania of the Reef. My mother was one of the models for that in the early 1950s when that statue was made. I mentioned the Napier case . . . Pania is actually a reef, it's about 400 metres off-shore near Napier, and it's in the shape of a woman spread out. And when the decision came out last year from the Court of Appeal and Helen Clark went on television and said the Crown owns the foreshore and seabed, I was very concerned on behalf of, amongst others, my Pania of the Reef clients, because that's not the way they look at it. They used it as a resource. That underwater reef has belonged to them for 600 or 700 years at least.'

Charl and his German wife divorced after 17 years; they had no children. And now he has a Maori wife, Tahei Simpson. He says marrying Tahei brings yet another aspect of symmetry to his life. 'I was never going to get married again and I'd never contemplated having children so I thought, "Oh well, at 47, it's too late now." Then, of course, one of those surprises in life came along and I am going to have twins in October 2005.'

To add to the symmetry, Charl is to have Maori children with another person from his own tribe, Ngati Porou. Tahei and Charl are distantly related. Tahei has Ngati Awa ancestry too.

Charl is aware that his cousin Caren would like to see Ngawiki's bones taken back to Ngati Porou. However, he plans to follow his father's wish for both his parents to rest at Mangere.

'If Mum had really shown that she was interested in where she'd come from, if, for example, she'd taken us there as children (we only went there once as a family during her lifetime) that would be different. But she had rejected that place. It's a factor that needs to be taken into account. I know why my cousin wants to take Mum home. She wants the tradition to be maintained because my mother was the tuakana, the eldest, and I'm the eldest of five generations now. There's this kind of continuity of having people together rather than buried all over the place. The more you can bring together, from a Maori point of view, the better. It's about mana and the wairua and all that sort of thing. On the other hand, I would prefer my father to be buried with her. It would be contrary to the cultural practice for him to be buried in an urupa on the coast. It's not impossible but . . . I don't think he would feel comfortable about that. So overall my preference is that she stay where she is and that he be eventually buried beside her – even though he says he wants to be cremated.'

Charl is not certain where he would like to be buried himself. 'See, I'm really a born-and-bred Aucklander. This is my city. To be buried at Rangitukia would be to honour tradition and that's my place and all that sort of thing . . . I will leave it up to those who succeed me to decide that and not really express a preference one way or other.

'I like Rangitukia. I belong there even though my relatives are unruly and I don't always get on with them nowadays. That romantic phase I spoke of before is long gone! But that's okay. Members of my whanau are strong-willed and also incredibly egoistic. They're hopelessly jealous; they're prima donnas. But they are bright and good speakers.

'What came out of Mum and Dad, for me, was a feeling that I could enjoy ultimately two quite distinct worlds. I see that as a strong part of my identity. I identify with the Maori side, I identify with the German side, the Pakeha side and to some lesser degree Dad's Australian side. It's a pleasure for me to have that. You don't have to cut it one way or the other. And I don't.'

GWENDA *Paul is a Pakeha who works on an organic kiwifruit*

orchard at Ohope with her Maori husband, Maanu. She also writes

articles and has an historical novel awaiting publication. She's

involved in research work and has a Masters in Social Science

from Waikato University and a Diploma in Freelance Journalism.

Since 1981 she's been actively involved in anti-racism and Treaty

of Waitangi workshops. Gwenda has four children, an adopted

daughter who is Maanu's niece, and 14 grandchildren.

PHOTOGRAPH:

Gwenda and Maanu Paul. Circa 1980

Gwenda Monteith was born in Otorohanga in 1939. Her father's job maintaining old generators took him to Kawhia when Gwenda was eight and then to Kaingaroa Forest when she was 14. Her father was English and Scottish, her mother Welsh, Scottish, Gypsy and Cornish.

'I am a fifth-generation New Zealander. My great-grandfather used to call New Zealanders of mixed heritage "pig-islanders". It was an old word, common in those days. We heard such sayings as "Don't bring the tar-brush into our family."

I think my parents thought Maoris were fine but there was a certain line you drew. They certainly didn't come into your families.

'There was always a barrier, which was strange because we were brought up in places where there was a majority of Maori people.

'In Kawhia, at one stage I was the only Pakeha girl in the class and I was made aware of it only when the new headmaster arrived with a large family. My mum said, "Oh, that's nice, you won't be the only Pakeha girl in the class." Until then I had no idea that I was any different. I went back to school looking at the other kids and trying to figure out why.

'We used to play a lot of Maori games, using stones with Maori names, stick games and hand games, and I had no notion that everybody else could not do that. However, at the end of the day, particularly in Kawhia, the Maori people rarely came in the door of our home. A Maori girlfriend called me from the gate. My mother thought that was quite okay. She didn't invite her in.

'In Murupara I went to Rangatahi Maori School, which included a few Pakeha kids. I had some Pakeha mates but, in general, I decided to join the majority and my mother used to get angry with me because sometimes I'd come home talking like a Maori kid. I learned two ways of speaking, one for school with my mates and the other for home. If I forgot to change over I would get slapped around the ears.

'At Ardmore Teachers' Training College, although I roomed with another Pakeha girl, I associated more with the Maori students. It was easier to relate to them. My parents thought this was unfortunate and as a result they actually moved from Murupara to the city so that my younger siblings wouldn't "fall into the same trap".

'I don't think my parents thought Maori were bad. It was just that my father, in particular, thought one of the worst things that could happen to me was that I would marry one. In those days there weren't many Pakeha women who married Maori men and the few examples that we saw were, for want of a better word, "white trash". They were women who had no self-esteem.

'I joined the cultural club at training college because I could sing waiata. A lot of Maori people still sang waiata koroua in those days. I didn't understand the words but I could sing them. I get brassed off now when I sing waiata koroua on the marae. People say to Maanu, "You have taught your wife well!" I grind my teeth because it's the other way around – I have taught him. I was very lazy about learning Maori language, though. I understood a bit, common key words, but I never bothered to really learn it.

'I went out with a few Pakeha blokes, but I found them a bit strange. The Maori boys and girls I'd been brought up with were all mates together. You couldn't just be mates with Pakeha boys.

'I met Maanu when I was 20. I saw him holding up a post at the Maori community centre in Auckland. I knew who he was because he came from Murupara, and I knew he was a policeman. It was the country thing in those days – if you met someone from home, you always greeted them.

'I thought he was pretty good-looking. There was a physical attraction and I knew the family. I thought he had a few problems that needed sorting out. I'm a rescuer and he needed rescuing. I thought he had a lot of potential.

'We both went back home to Murupara. I was teaching for a while, and he left the police force for a job in the Ministry of Works. We had a stormy relationship. It didn't work out well and I left Murupara and went back to Auckland. We got back together later on and eventually married about two years later.'

The time in between was traumatic for Gwenda. She found she was pregnant to Maanu. It was the early 1960s when social attitudes were cruel to unmarried mothers. Gwenda and Maanu also had what she describes as 'a period of great misunderstanding'. She says it was nothing to do with her being Pakeha and him being Maori. 'I had left Murupara, so Maanu said he wasn't quite sure if Alan was his child. That made me angry and I would have nothing more to do with him.

'A friend of mine got us back together again later. It's strange the way life goes.

The whole experience of getting pregnant was a tragedy. My parents refused to have anything to do with the baby, with the best of intentions. I placed Alan with a Maori family so I always knew where he was.

'I knew he would get a good upbringing, however if I'd watched them bringing him up I knew I'd be dissatisfied – it wouldn't matter how good they were. So I left them to it. That's how it was done in those days. You were selfish if you wanted to keep the child.

'The terrible thing was that, after it was over, I found that Maanu's family had been searching for us. I had cut myself off completely and made people swear they would not say where I'd gone. Maanu's family wanted me back, Maanu wanted me back, and Maanu's sister and aunties wanted me back and had been looking for me. Finally a friend of mine gave way to Maanu's family and told them where I was. It was a bit of a tragedy but it was too late. Alan had been adopted. Fortunately he's very much a part of our family now because we came together many years later when he was an adult.

when Maanu and I decided to get married neither of our parents would come to the wedding. My father said, 'You had to find the blackest one you could find, didn't you?'

'He was very distressed. The only time in my whole life I saw my father cry was when I left home to get married. It was all to do with children. "They'll be half-caste. You are not giving them a fair go. Life will be difficult for them. They will neither be one thing or the other."

'My mother thought it was dreadful and spoke of the "shame". "How can we tell your grandfather?" Actually my grandfather didn't give a damn.

Later, when my sister, Maida, married they didn't even want us to go to her wedding because the rest of the family would see us and the shame was so terrible.

'Then Maida and the chap she was marrying said, "If Maanu and Gwenda don't come to our wedding, there won't be any wedding." So of course my parents had to relent. Funnily enough, the grandfather everyone was so fearful of offending invited me, Maanu and our baby, Aaron, to come and stay.

'My grandfather knew I'd married this big black Maori chap, so my father was shocked that he'd invited us. I told Maanu that my grandfather was a very gentlemanly gentleman from a very Victorian time – the sort of Pakeha person Maanu might not have met before. So we get to Grandpa's house, and he shook Maanu's hand and said, "Good evening, sir." He called everybody "sir". He made us a big plateful of toast and tea, and then said, "Now I will show you to your bedrooms!" Maanu had one bedroom and I was to sleep in another room with the baby. That was my grandfather! Maybe he thought that he would recognise us but he wouldn't have us sleeping together under his roof. God knows. I wasn't anxious about it. I had long since learnt to live with all this nonsense and if people wanted to be silly, they could be.

'My sister's wedding itself was amusing. Maanu drove us to the wedding, but parking was difficult, so he dropped Grandpa, the baby and me off at the church. Grandpa and I go in and we are sitting up the front as part of the family, and I was keeping a space for Maanu. Finally Maanu was the last to arrive before the bride and groom, and as he walked in, the whole church turned around and watched him walk down the aisle.

It was funny! All my aunties going into a flutter, because it was their first chance to see this big black man who'd married into the family.

'I don't think Maanu noticed. He was quite used to Pakeha people, although not in the context of being the only Maori there. He didn't feel out of place. They all fell over themselves to talk to him. They wanted to suss him out and see what made him tick.

'Until her dying days my mother had difficulty telling people a Maori was married into her family. To add to the problem, Maanu became a controversial, well-known character. People saw him on TV and my mother, all her life, thought she had to defend me and defend him. She had this thing: "My daughter's married to Maanu Paul and they have a lot of land at Ohope, you know." That was her way of giving us "normal" status.

'Once they saw our baby, Aaron, it made a huge difference, particularly to my father. There was no way he was going to keep away from this child because my dad always loved kids. At the end of the day it was his grandchild and he adored all our children.

'I was brought up in a very politically minded family so I encouraged Maanu into politics. He got switched on to Social Credit. Maanu's good at numbers and I thought he had the ability to do it. He had the gift of the gab and he comes from a family of talkers. Maanu stood for Social Credit in Eastern Maori three times and did really well. Then some of the elders at that time encouraged him to join the Mataatua District Maori Council and Maori politics.

'As a mother I was interested in what colour my babies would be. I hoped they would be a bit brown and not blond and green-eyed like me. They all came out as typical half-caste kids. Some look more Maori than others. Eddie, the youngest son, is the most Polynesian in appearance.

'All my children see themselves as Maori. That could be partly because of where they've been brought up – among their father's people, rather than mine. My sisters and my brother and I are close and our kids do all mix, although I can remember my mother saying, "How would you like it if your sisters' children didn't want to have anything to do with your children?" That hasn't happened. Quite the opposite, in fact.

'When I left home my father said, "In 10 years you will have 10 snotty-nosed kids hanging onto your skirts and a drunken husband." So, being conscious of this, I went to the extreme to make sure that my children were the cleanest scrubbed kids and they had the neatest clothes. I wanted to be sure that nobody would point a finger at me for letting the side down.

'We did strike racism, though. The anger comes when things happen to your children. When Rachel started school in Hamilton it was a bad winter and my kids had been quite sick. On a lovely spring day Rachel was running round the backyard in a cardigan, and I said to her, "Take it off, darling, and get some sun on your arms to get rid of the bugs from your system." She wouldn't take it off, she said, "Because my friend doesn't like Maoris and if I take my cardigan off I'll go brown like a Maori." Well, I was so enraged! I went to the school and I spoke to the teacher, and she said, "We'll sort this out." So she got us to tape a song in Maori for Rachel to teach the other kids, and she actually brought the Maori thing into the classroom.

In Hamilton I realised I could write out a cheque in any shop and it would be accepted. But Maanu could write out a cheque only at the local grocery shop or garage where he was known.

'Once he went in to buy something but couldn't because he didn't have enough money, and I said, "Why didn't you write out a cheque?" He said, "Because they won't take a cheque from me." It hadn't dawned on me! It's things like that that make you mad and bring it home to you.

'Going to a bank, I could draw out as much money as I wanted, but when Maanu went into the same bank, they would let him draw out only $200. This sort of niggly stupid thing happens.

'Maanu had never been aware of this discrimination. It's only when you are in a mixed marriage situation that you become aware that there's a difference. Otherwise you go through life and never know. It amuses me when Pakehas say, "I've never seen any racism." I think, "Of course you bloody haven't!" And a lot of Maoris don't either, because they're not aware they're being treated any differently.

My greatest difficulties in this mixed marriage were to do with my children. All of them go through a crisis of identity at some time or other, and I remember Eddie at 17 saying to me, 'You know, Mum, we all have to make a choice, but really there is no choice. We have to be Maori.'

'And it was a matter-of-fact realisation for him. They have all consciously at some stage, through some experience, had to say,

"Maori is what I am." It can't really be anything else.

'It's not that the Maori side always makes it easy for them. For Maori kids at school, there is always the thing of pulling each other down. If they're doing well at school the others say, "Who do you think you are? Do you think you are better than the rest of us?"

'Aaron was very good at the haka. But by the sixth form there were few other Maori kids in his class and so he pulled out of the cultural group. When I asked him about it, he said, "My mates give me a hard time. They say, 'Why do you want to be part of those brown monkeys? You're not really one of those.'" That's the kind of thing that makes you really angry.

'I think there were different pressures on them depending on how they looked. Aaron is much more Pakeha-looking. He was almost pressured by his Pakeha mates to be like them. Then he would get a hard time from his Maori cousins. Where our kids went to school, half the Maori kids were their relations. Eddie, because he's so obviously Maori-looking, nobody ever treated him as anything other than Maori. He didn't have the same kind of problems that Aaron had.

'We adopted our daughter, Teresa, because her birth mother, Maanu's niece, couldn't care for her. She needed ongoing medical care and we were the nearest of the whanau to the hospital. Teresa has two kids now and lives with her second partner.

when I'm among other Pakehas, they'll say things they wouldn't dare say if Maori were around.

'It's quite a valuable place to be sometimes. It's like a spy in both camps. I don't have any difficulty now in understanding and holding a Maori viewpoint. When I was younger I did. There were a lot of things I had to come to grips with.

'I can understand why Pakeha feel threatened by some Maori views. Through my life I've done a lot of work in the anti-racism and Treaty of

Gwenda's 60th birthday, 1999.
Back (l to r) Lusiana, Eddie, Deborah, Atawhai, Solei
Seated (l to r) Rachel, Gwenda, Maanu, Aaron
Front (l to r) Lania, Haimona, Huriana, Kahu

Waitangi movements. I thought my experience was a valuable one
to share because, over time, I have managed to understand both the
Maori and Pakeha point of view. I saw where the difference lay and, as
an educator, I felt I had a valuable role to play bridging those gaps.'

Being in a Maori whanau, Gwenda found that the death process took
on a new significance. 'I had been to tangis when I was young. When
you're brought up as a Pakeha kid in a Maori community, you think
you know them well, but when you become a part of a Maori family, it
really is another dimension altogether, another awareness. Going to a
tangi as a member of the family is completely different from just being
a Pakeha going to a tangi. There are new expectations on you. Nobody
puts anything on you, but you become aware of things that you maybe
should be doing.

'Different women in my position make different choices. There are some Pakeha women, married to Maori men, who don't involve themselves in the marae situation, but I do. I have made a point of singing waiata with Maanu. I like singing anyway, so it hasn't been hard. You learn your role as your husband's partner, which of course changes over time. My role, because Maanu is a whaikorero person, is to stand beside him at tangis or functions at the marae. I go to the marae or do my bit in the kitchen, cook or whatever. I don't *have* to do any of that. I just know that is the traditional role you play. You choose. Nowadays, lots of *Maori* wives don't play any role in the marae.

One reason why I fulfil these roles is to make it easier for my kids. I know they're Maori. They have all had to make that choice, so it makes it easier for them if I play my role as well.

'I don't pretend to be a Maori. But I do the things that are good for me to do as Maanu's wife.

'When there's a tangi I go down there to Wairaka, if I can, and spend a day or two at the marae, and I enjoy being there. I have known the women for years. You are all mates and part of the whanau.

'I wouldn't rush out and encourage other people to get involved in a cross-cultural marriage, because I don't think everyone is suited to it. I think some people are happier with their own people. In a sense it was inevitable that I married a Maori man, because, in spite of my family's best efforts, I was just always more at home with Maori.'

❈

MAANU *Paul is a Mataatua kaumatua and an organic grower of kiwifruit, pigs, sheep and cattle who lives at Ohope in the Bay of Plenty. He's been a Justice of the Peace for 30 years. In 1986 he was awarded a Fulbright Scholarship. He received his Masters degree*

in Sociology and Maori in 1993 from the University of Auckland.

During the 1990s he appeared often in the media as executive

chairman of the New Zealand Maori Council. Maanu is also known

as an orator and writer in the Maori language and has been involved

in researching Treaty claims for his iwi. He and his Pakeha wife,

Gwenda, have been married for 41 years.

Maanu Paul was delivered by his father at home in Murupara in 1938. 'My father did all the birthing. Ngati Manawa are the river people, the fish people, Ika Whenua, and it is part of our tradition that the father and mother would go to the river, build a little manuka shelter for themselves a couple of days before the child was born and the father would do the birthing. The new parents would stay there for a couple of weeks, and if you were in the middle of 13 children, like I was, the other kids looked after you from then on.'

Maanu has a string of tribal affiliations. His father was Ngati Manawa and Tuhoe. His mother's ancestry was Ngati Mahana of Waikato, Tainui and Ngati Pikiao of Te Arawa. 'Our father helped plant the Whaingaroa forest and then he went out on his own working in forestry part-time and on the family land. We milked cows and raised pigs and planted big areas of potatoes. We had live eels in boxes in the river and we lived on wild pork preserved in fat in big cabin bread tins.

'My mother died giving birth to her tenth child. My father sent me to live at Oputea with his mother who was half-Scottish but could speak only Maori. She was also looking after four of my cousins. She used to pound up hinau berries and fern root and tawa berries and make us bread. So my job was to gather the berries and soak them so that the poison would go out of them.

'When I was born, my koro had already died. So I didn't know him but everybody, including my father, used to say I looked like him because I was black like him. The rest of my whanau are quite fair compared with me.'

Maanu learnt English only when he went to school. He won a scholarship there, which enabled him to go to Whakatane High School. 'At the end of my third-form year I got a certificate for the most improved English speaker! In Whakatane, I lived with my mother's mother. I learnt how to go muttonbirding and crayfishing with my uncles. I've been very fortunate that I had both maternal and paternal grandmothers instil in me a sense about tikanga and what was Maori. I knew very little about what was happening in Pakeha society.

'When I was in the sixth form at Whakatane High School there were six Maoris in the class of 13. But when my sons went, the proportion of Maori was far less in the sixth form. I believe Maori had better chances to succeed in my time. We were streamed into professional classes and the expectations on us were high. We Maori boys used to stick together because we played football and we chased girls together. I never went to a Pakeha home. Only once did I go in a Pakeha car, to go to a football game in Rotorua.

'I was never conscious of any racism when I was a kid, except within my own whanau, because I was always called a "black fella". I had a brother a year older than me. My father used to introduce us to Pakehas as, "This is my Pakeha son, this is my Maori son. That's my black boy." Black was a bad thing to be. It was bad in most cultures. Black is equated to evil and all that sort of thing. The crook is always dressed in black, you know? I wasn't hurt by the comments but it registered in my psyche.

'When I got my University Entrance exam accredited, my father called me home to milk cows. Then I did some sheep shearing and deer culling. I decided to become a policeman for a while and later I trained as a surveyor.

'One of the things I remember about my father and others of his generation was the way they wooed their women. When we ate kereru our father would wait on our mother and our sisters and they had the best parts first, which was the head and the parson's nose. As I got older my father explained to me that it was a "token of love".

'Actually, I'm a bit pissed off about the Jake Heke, *Once Were Warriors* image given to Maori men because I wasn't brought up like that. The way I treated women was totally different to the way my Maori mates treated women. They saw women, like typical Pakeha fellas, as images of conquest and satisfaction and all that sort of thing. I always wanted to woo women. It was the Errol Flynn style. So by the time Gwenda and I met I was a real wooer of Pakeha girls as well as Maori ones. I was a policeman at this stage. I don't know if it was the uniform or my wooing talent!

'I was very sorry about our first baby being adopted so I was determined to put things right. I think that came from both my kuia, who had high moral standards. I was taught the place of the Maori woman – he rangatira. Not like the models we've got today of women being chattels.

'My father didn't like the idea of me marrying Gwenda. He believed that I was weakening the blood.

My father would not come to the wedding and would not have anything to do with our marriage.

'He said Gwenda had no whakapapa. "Ko wai o nga rangatira – where's her chiefs?" he said. But when you're wooing a woman you're not too bloody worried about the chiefs, are you?

'Gwenda was beautiful. She still is beautiful. She was a woman I could talk to. That was one thing I found as a young Maori. You had very little intellectual discourse with the opposite sex, whether they were Maori or Pakeha, because most young women didn't go to higher learning and weren't too bloody interested, from my experience, in discussing what was going on.

'I admired Gwenda's intellect and we believed in what each of us was capable of doing. I believed that she would be a very good mother. She believed that I would be a very good father and we both had rebellious streaks.

'My father's objections to the marriage just made me more determined. When I was surveying on the Motu power scheme, on Thursday nights I used to leave the camp on my motorcycle, ride to Gisborne, do all my office work, and by midnight I was off to Te Atatu in Auckland to see her.

'Gwenda's parents didn't want us to get married either – probably with good reason. I used to own this bloody big Thunderbird and I used to turn up at her place with a crate of beer in the front and I'd stand outside going "vrrooooom, vrrooom". I was the stereotypical Maori to them.

'Although our parents boycotted the wedding, my sister hosted it for us, and all my brothers and sisters came. Eventually, my silly old father changed his mind and then Gwenda was his "best daughter". And he always thought the world of our kids.

'When our son Aaron was born, my father wanted the child but Gwenda wasn't having anything of that. My father wanted to whangai a child from each of his children but only two allowed it. In our case, he wanted this mokopuna because he was as hurt as I was about our first boy going into a strange family. He was a great guardian of the blood.

'It didn't mean anything to me that Gwenda was Pakeha. I'd had enough experience with Pakeha women by then and of the

Pakeha world in terms of employment. There weren't a lot of cultural differences that I noticed.

'One cultural issue was when we were visiting whanau. Gwenda would say, "Oh, we're going now," before the rapport between me and the whanau we were visiting had been completed. But that was more of an accident on her part. At one time she would make me eat my kina in the shed but then our doctor told her the kids were anaemic and needed to eat kina for iron and iodine. Now I have to fight for a share of the kina when I bring it home. There's bugger-all left for me. It's the same with fish heads. She thought it was bad manners once to suck on fish heads but now she eats them like that too.

Back (l to r) Brownie Rewiti – late MP for Eastern Maori, Gwenda, Maanu
Front (l to r) Eddie, Aaron, Teresa. Circa 1968

'When I started to get a high profile in the political world she decided to keep herself removed from that life. Some people are surprised when they meet her. "Oh, the bugger's got a wife!" But Gwenda was totally supportive. I would come home from Wellington or something and she would have a bottle of wine open and we would sit in the spa. I'd tell her everything and she'd criticise me. I'd get bloody upset about it and then I'd recognise that she was right and so I'd have to swallow my pride. Then we'd hop into the sauna and sweat it out and have a leisurely supper. We'd generally unwind. We were very fortunate. We'd spend time to talk to each other.

'I like material stuff but Gwenda is into relationships. She's a woman of high morals, great integrity and honesty, and fearless when she's challenged. Gwenda would be happy in a two-room shack as long as the relationships were right, whereas I would be bitching. I like my home comforts.

I was arrogant about my own ability in my youth so I didn't recognise racism until I met Gwenda and she showed me.

'In the police force I always thought it was competition that was the issue. But looking back I can see that I met racism there. Even after I had passed my inspector's exams I was given the shittiest jobs to do.

'Once, Gwenda and I were looking for curtains and I was in this furniture shop in Hamilton by myself. I was there for 25 minutes and no one came to serve me. Then Gwenda walked in and they were over to her in a shot. So we just blew the assistants apart.

'Another incidence of racism happened with our son who was at Marist in Hamilton. The Father rang up and told me to take my son away. I asked why and he said my son had bloodied the noses of three boys. So I asked my son what happened and he said they called him a "black bastard". So I gave the Brothers a blast about the need to make their school bicultural. It was at that time that Gwenda convinced me that I had the ability to be an educationalist. So that's how I went to Waikato University to study.

'I had the courage and confidence to do those things but Gwenda gave me the nous. She gave me the Pakeha thinking. She showed me how the processes worked. I had no experience of the social inter-actions that went on in Pakeha circles. I didn't know the politics. I very quickly learnt.

'I've made a few unilateral decisions in our marriage – like the decision to sell our lovely home in Whakatane and buy our present property in Ohope. It was just lupin and gorse then and we had to live in a little shed and caravan. We nearly got divorced over that. It was an economic decision I made because I could see the potential. We had to put up with camping for a while but now Gwenda loves it here.

'I think in any marriage, cross-cultural or not, you have to be prepared to accommodate the differences or it won't work. The cross-cultural thing is just another layer of difference. Gwenda and I live by the moral values of both our cultures and they are very similar. Honesty and integrity are cross-cultural. We have a great working relationship. She tempers my exuberance.

'Gwenda and I have cocked a snook at both sides and said, "We want a better world for our kids." I think my children will tell you they identify as Maori. I am only surmising but I think they can't find the surety and safety in the Pakeha world that they find in the Maori one. Part of it is that they are indigenous and they belong here if they are Maori.'

X
_____

RACHEL *Paul, at 34 years old, is the youngest of the Paul children. She's a lawyer who works in Opotiki. She's a Maori speaker and proud of her Maori heritage but also likes to wear the Monteith tartan in recognition of her Scottish ancestry. She says as she grew up she realised that her background was special.*

Rachel says she was brought up with the best advantages of both cultures. The only bad side came from society and its perceptions of her family. 'Mum and Dad created a home environment empowered by information and knowledge. We were very proud of who we were. I knew my whakapapa from a young age – I knew my mother's genealogy too – to reinforce in us that we were special and that we were different but not lesser than others.

'Lots of people called me "half-caste". I didn't appreciate that because I felt that if it was half of something, you weren't really fully anything. The way Mum approached it was that we were privileged to be moulded by two cultures. As I grew older and had to deal with negative perceptions, I thought, "I can see two sides of everything. I can see two worlds. I live in two worlds and you've only got one. How limiting!"

'I don't think all mixed-heritage kids get as good a grounding as we did. My parents were intelligent and thoughtful and empowered us to deal with the outside world.

when I was about five, and didn't understand racism, I took on board the comments around me. I remember putting white powder on my face to make me whiter.

'I was already getting pressured by other people's perceptions of how I should or shouldn't be. It must have been upsetting for Mum and Dad that I thought I needed to be white like everybody else in order to be accepted.

'Mixed-heritage children don't fit in the right box. When we fill out a form we are expected to be one thing or the other. Our society is making us choose to be one or the other and we can't. My brothers can't either. We've always had to deal with that from when we were young.

I have chosen to have a Maori identity because that's the face I see in the mirror.

'And that's how others see me. Society says to be successful you must be Pakeha, you must take on certain attributes and push aside anything that is not mainstream. I can't do that. That's not who I am. I have taken a stronger stance on my Maori identity because I have to. I can't reject it.

'Three years ago I came home to live with Mum and Dad to learn Maori. With second-language learners I can converse well but with first-language speakers I have difficulty. When we were growing up Maori language was not prized at all so my father didn't speak Maori in the house then. In order to be fulfilled I need to have Maori as well. I need to be able to express myself and be able to participate in both my worlds.

'I am lucky that my father is an orator and that he has such a wealth of tikanga Maori knowledge. Sometimes I just feel like getting into his head and saying, "Can you just download all of that and put it in here?"

'At school I used to hear comments like, "Oh, those Maoris, they're dumb. They're fat. They're always in trouble. Why can't they look after their kids? But you're not like that, Rachel." When I challenged them they would say, "Oh, but it's not personal. I'm not talking about you." I would say, "How can you not be talking about me when you are generalising about the whole group of people I belong to?" But they couldn't see the connection.

'My parents' marriage worked because Mum was raised in an environment where there were a lot of Maori people. She has a high sense of justice and morality. Mum always had an open mind. She is great on the marae, too. She's the waiata queen! She's a great singer. She never wanted to lock herself off from our right, as Maori children, to participate in and practise our culture. So she pushed us so that we would be strong in who we are – rather than rejecting it as lots of mixed marriage children do. I belong on my marae, in my Maori culture, and

I also feel empowered with education, both Maori and Pakeha, that allows me to walk into any situation and feel strong.

'I think Dad made some compromises in the marriage, too. They both had to be respectful of each other's differences. I don't think he would have run the household in the way that Mum runs it. This house is run with her rules, expectations and standards. He has to go along with that. But I think it was easier for him to walk in both cultures than it was for her. Maori have to live in a Pakeha world because they are the majority. He had to. Whereas Mum could make a choice to participate and join in.

'Despite their happiness, I am not sure I would advocate for cross-cultural marriage. I've had a number of relationships – both Maori and Pakeha. Both offer cultural challenges for me – for different reasons.

I have been looking for a Maori husband but I haven't found one. The Maori men of my age avoid marriage and commitment.

'They are quite selfish and egotistical. Other professional Maori women, the same age as me, have these discussions. What is wrong with these Maori men? Also, there are not many Maori men who are my peers. They may not have the same education. And I'm not a typical Maori woman. I am not a typical Pakeha woman either. But that's fine. I'm me and that's fine.

'I actually find that men from outside New Zealand are less likely to have hang-ups and perceptions about Maori/Pakeha things. Strangely enough, my brothers have married a League of Nations. One has a Fijian wife, another a Greek wife and the third a Pakeha. Their children are all colours of the rainbow.

'When I have children I want them to have a strong Maori identity in the same way that my parents did for me. They may have two or three different groups of ancestry and cultures. That's fine. I would love my children at seven years old to be trilingual. That would be awesome.

(Recently Rachel began living with a new partner, Ferenc Schmidt, who is Hungarian and the couple are expecting a baby. Her view that a man from outside New Zealand might be easier to settle down with is proving prophetic.)

※

Edwin (Eddie) Paul was born in Kawerau in 1964 and is the third

son of Gwenda and Maanu Paul. He was a solicitor in Whakatane

for 10 years before he became a deputy public defender in Manukau

in 2004. He is responsible for an office of lawyers providing criminal

legal aid services to the public. Because they are at Manukau, his

clients reflect the community of South Auckland: many Maori and

Pacific people. Eddie and his Fijian wife, Lusi, have three children,

Solei, Lania and Haimona.

Eddie Paul was exposed to taha Maori when he was growing up, although, despite his father, Maanu, being fluent, he didn't learn much Maori language. 'I used to go to all the hui with Dad and stay at the marae, without really participating in what they were doing – just going along for the ride. I learnt the kawa of the marae and the various formalities, but I'm not really good at languages, so even when I learnt Maori at school, I was really poor. At times it's a regret. I just get on with what I do best.

'I identify as a Maori. You can't help but be a Maori when you look like me. You are always going to be treated like that. Partly it was because other people defined me, but the other thing is that Maori are more inclusive and will accept you as one of them, whereas Pakeha won't. That's a thing you learn early on in life.

'The defining moment was when I left high school and went to university. That's when you have to be one or the other. I left my comfort zone where everyone knows Eddie Paul and what I look like and my background. When you leave home you've got to accept what you are and be comfortable with that.

'I know I am half-Pakeha but that side can't be equal because I don't look like a Pakeha. I am very comfortable with our extended Pakeha family – as they are with us. We participate as much as we can with family things with our wider family but, of course, because we were brought up in Whakatane we spent more time with the Maori relatives.

'I had lots of Pakeha friends through school because I was in a group which was achieving academically. There weren't so many Maori in the sixth and seventh form but I played football so that was another group of mates. I feel comfortable in both Maori and Pakeha company. I have some Pakeha friends I would trust with my life.

'I think it's not usual for Maori to be comfortable in both worlds. Some are very uncomfortable with Pakeha and very aggressive and antagonistic towards them because of that. As a deputy public defender, I have clients who would never ever be comfortable with Pakeha because of the way they've been brought up. I don't think Pakeha would be too comfortable with them either.

'At home I wasn't very aware of cultural differences. Mum looked after us most of the time and Dad was always off doing things, so it was very much a Pakeha household. I am aware of the problems Mum had with her parents when she first got married. Her mother was quite a snobbish old bird, a bit of a battleaxe, probably a bit racist, but she loved us. We were closer to my Pakeha grandparents than to my Maori grandfather. He was a hard man – not like the old koros you hear about who awhi their kids and mokos. Not him.

'I became aware of my Pakeha grandparents' attitudes as I grew older. They made no effort to say Maori words correctly and said certain things. It was petty stuff but it was a demonstration of how they viewed things Maori. They didn't openly criticise but you can sense things. They were not positive. But I don't think it impacted too greatly on our relationship.'

Eddie went to Otago University for his law degree and that's how he met his Fijian wife, Lusi. They were on a bus to Dunedin, from Christchurch. 'My first impression was that she was nice and a pretty-looking girl – not culturally different.'

Eddie found himself mixing with a group of Pacific Island students at the university because his best mate was a Fijian Indian and his new girlfriend, Lusi, mixed in that crowd too. In general, he can see an affinity between Maori and Pacific peoples.

I am a bit new to South Auckland, and I don't have an identity wider than being Maori, but my kids may see more homogeneity between Maori and Pacific people emerging in this area.

'I find that I do have shared views with the Pacific Islanders I mix with. They are lawyers and judges who want to advance the interests of Pacific people as against anyone else. They want success for their families and their children – Pacific people in general. They are critical of various New Zealand organisations – like racist aspects of the police. There have been recent examples of that in South Auckland which are very upsetting to a lot of Pacific people. No matter how successful Pacific people are or what position we hold, there will always be institutional racism and people who want us to fail. That's not to say that Maori aren't as bad to each other at times.

'With Pacific people I find they have similar group dynamics and we

Eddie and Lusiana's first wedding in Aotearoa. (They later had a traditional Teuuteuu, gift
exchange, in Fiji).
Aaron, Rachel, Lusi, Eddie, Gwenda, Maanu. 1987

have the same sense of humour. They are very respectful. I don't know
about the ones that are born and bred here.

*Being married to Lusi I've found that Fijian women don't overtly
show affection. Like, Lusi won't hold hands or kiss in public.*

'I found it unusual at first. She's mellowed now but when we
started going out she used to push my hand away. Another thing is the
wearing of dresses. Kiwi girls rarely do. I think it is an endearing thing
about Fijian women because they act like women. They are polite and
quietly spoken. They are religious, too, so if you go to their islands their
observance on Sunday is quite strict and you are expected not to work.
Even here, her mother finds it irksome that I work around the house
on a Sunday. She thinks it's wrong.

'In this cross-cultural marriage we've had some family stresses. We've had adult family members living with us. Lusi's brother was here for nearly two years and that was hard – supporting another family member when I didn't think it was necessary. My values are that you support yourself. I recognise that's a Pakeha view. But Maanu's brothers didn't come and live with us for any long periods. Lusi's mum comes to stay and I don't mind that. She's retired and can't support herself. But having another fit young person live with you doesn't work for me. Lusi's brother is really easy-going and is a really nice man but it's just different.

'In our marriage we have mutual interests – we are both lawyers and go to the same church, and enjoy the same group of friends. I think we see each other as equal. I know she's brighter than I am and I accept that. Our families are very different. Mine are "blow bags" basically, they talk about themselves all the time. You wouldn't get boo out of her family. There is a lot more humility. That's one of their attributes. Some of Dad's older relatives were like that but Maanu has learnt not to be too humble. I think that's less and less a feature of Maori these days – families who are rich in their Maoriness to the extent that they practise humility.

'Our children, with their mixed heritage, will have challenges along the way but I think they've so much more going for them because they have a wider family base than other people. They have quite a mix of aunties and uncles and nannies and koros. And they have all those attributes mixed into their genes. Lots of advantages.'

Lusi joins the conversation here to talk about how the children identify. She says when the children were in Auckland and mixed largely with Fijians they said they were Fijian. 'When we went to Whakatane they continued to say they were Fijian for about two years and then they changed: "We are Maori." So now they are Maori. I think they're more likely to be Maori from now on.'

Eddie doesn't believe his children have struck much racism in their lives, although his nine-year-old son, Haimona, probably fits in better now they live in South Auckland. 'He was more the odd-one-out in Whakatane at the local Catholic school because he was the big brown boy in his class and all his mates were little white boys or little white Maori boys. Here there are lots of big brown boys at his school. The girls' school is multicultural and multiracial, too.'

Haimona went to kohanga reo and kura kaupapa until he was eight. He was fluent until the move to Auckland but he doesn't practise now. 'When Maanu has the time, he talks to him, but it is difficult with the distance. I think Haimona has the basis and he can recover that easily. He has probably got his mother's skills in languages, unlike me, so he'll be able to pursue that later on.'

Lusi says Haimona is a year and half behind in his English at his mainstream school but they expect him to catch up. She's glad Haimona can speak Maori but she wishes that the education system was such that children didn't have to miss out on either English or Maori.

She says although the two girls haven't had the language, they have a good strong knowledge of their culture and their place and where they belong. 'They know where their marae is and their whanau and also their Fijian family and who we are. I don't think they will be lost. I think they have got all that to fall back on.'

Eddie believes interracial marriage is going to happen more and more. But in my view, if watering down occurs, without some sort of cultural carry-through, then all you are going to be left with is brown people who are Pakehas, really, and that's probably no good to anyone.'

'I think in some respects I have been watered down myself. But I think that you have got to be *something*. You can't be just a Kiwi. And if you're brown, you are always going to be something different. So it's always better to have something to hold on to and say, "This is what my brownness means," rather than, "I'm brown and that's about it." That's very empty and sad, really, especially when you think that maybe two generations back you were quite an identifiable person and your family was. To end up two generations down the line being brown but nothing more is pretty sad and probably doesn't leave you with much soul.

One of the reasons I married a brown person was that I saw with my parents that it's harder for kids of mixed marriages, brown and white.

'You have to face things that you wouldn't necessarily have to face if you were one or the other, especially when you are younger. As children you don't understand that you don't have to take on the responsibility of the failings of all Maori. You see Maori criticised and you feel it and it hurts. You can't differentiate that it is their problem and not yours. Sometimes Pakeha don't necessarily think that you are Maori, or Maori enough, to feel hurt and they think you will just play along with their racism or that you are accepting of it. However, when they belittle Maori you feel it. Those memories stay with you and you don't want it for your own children.

LUSI *Paul was born in 1961 and brought up in Nadi in Fiji by a solo mum with the help of an extended family. 'We were raised with Fijian values, which are respect, humility, sharing, lots of love and whanau.' She was educated at a boarding school and came to*

New Zealand to take her seventh form year at Prince High School in

Dunedin. She became a lawyer in 1994 and works at Child Youth

and Family as a legal adviser. She and Eddie have an eight-year-old

son and two daughters of 12 and 16.

Lusi had Maori teachers when she was at school in Fiji and it may surprise many to discover how much she was taught there about New Zealand and Maori. As part of social studies she was taught a little about Maori culture and how to sing Maori songs. She learnt the names of the various Maori tribes and where they were located. She also studied some New Zealand history, including the land wars.

Lusi believes Maori have much greater opportunities here than her people have in Fiji. However, she can see that Maori have valid grievances about their colonial history. 'I think Maori experienced much worse colonial exploitation than Fijians did because this is where the English wanted to live.

'In New Zealand I prefer to be called a Fijian, rather than lumped in as a Pacific Islander. I am always being made conscious that I am different because I have an accent and people often don't catch what I am saying.'

Lusi's first meeting with Eddie was nearly enough to turn her off him for ever. She was getting on to a bus with a large suitcase. 'Eddie was sitting on the first seat with a very grumpy face. In Fiji, men would come and help you but he just sat there. When we got to the train station he started following me around and trying to make conversation. But I wasn't interested in him. He had no manners and I wasn't very impressed.'

Eddie told Lusi he was new to Dunedin and Lusi, being polite, helped him to find a taxi. She continued to carry her own bag and

Lusi and Eddie Paul

had no expectations of him. She was in the seventh form at school and had decided that she wanted to marry a white man for stability in her life. Lusi says Fijian men are 'waited on hand and foot' and she had decided she did not want that sort of man for a husband.

'I didn't think he was good-looking because he wasn't my ideal. But he persevered. He started bearing gifts like wine goblets and bringing chicken around to cook. He had a lot of grovelling to do.' The courtship continued as Lusi began her studies at Otago University and she and Eddie mixed in the same student circles.

Lusi says Fijian and Maori cultures have many similarities; however, from her perspective, Eddie did not embody traditional Maori customs and values.

I think he is more Pakeha in his way of thinking and that is where the clash is for us.

'I think he is successful because of his Pakeha side. He wants to achieve. His Maoriness just adds to who he is.'

The couple married and studied law together in Dunedin. When Lusi became pregnant with their first child, they stayed for a while with Gwenda and Maanu at Ohope before moving into their own home in nearby Whakatane. After she graduated, Lusi worked as a solicitor in a general practice while Eddie ran his own business.

Lusi enjoyed going to the marae with Eddie and found herself able to understand Maori very quickly because she has an aptitude for languages. She already spoke Fijian, English and conversational Hindu. 'I can speak Maori but I found I was intruding on them and felt that I should not do it.'

She was keen to see her children learn about their culture and about who they were, but she had hoped for more whanau interaction. 'I was used to the extended family get-together in Fiji every Sunday for lunch. We lived in Whakatane for 10 years and we would see Maanu and Gwenda only once every six weeks. I thought it was sad. They lived just over the hill in Ohope and I tried to encourage Eddie to go there most weekends, but everyone gets caught up in their own world here. Everyone is in their own nuclear unit.'

Lusi and Eddie are happy together now but they admit their marriage had its problems initially. After four years they both went off in different directions. Lusi was in the final year of her law degree. 'I wanted to finish my degree but we had our daughter, Selena, to care for. I thought it was best to send her home to my mother in Fiji. And that's where the difficulty was. Maanu and Gwenda visited Fiji for a holiday and formed the view that it was no good for the child there. So I had to write them a letter telling them to mind their own business. I felt Selena was well cared for, but there was a cultural difference. I am used to the extended family and they are not.'

When the couple came back together after two years, Lusi says their marriage became stronger. 'Now we meet in the middle. We got over our teething problems.'

Lusi and Eddie talk easily about their cultural differences.

With money, Lusi says the differences are marked. 'I share my money and he doesn't. His money is for the nuclear family. My money is for the extended family.'

Eddie and Lusi's three children
(*l to r*) Solei, Lania (*front*) Haimona

'He has come to accept me for who I am. I help my mum with her mortgage because she is not earning and there is no superannuation in Fiji unless you work for the government. I see it as my role to help my mother.' However, she can see the benefits of Eddie's approach. 'If Eddie was the same as me, we wouldn't have bought this house in Papatoetoe.'

Lusi sees parallels between marriage and the Treaty of Waitangi relationship between Maori and Pakeha. As a Fijian, she respects that Maori are tangata whenua and that they have a unique position in New Zealand. 'I don't feel excluded from the Treaty relationship but I think it is more of a Maori/Pakeha thing than anything to do with me. The Treaty is about working together as partners and that's what life is all about. I can see the positive things that Pakeha bring to that and the positive things that Maori bring. I wish there was a middle ground where people got on better. I think the cultural appreciation of both sides is really poor. If Maori and Pakeha appreciated each other's cultures they wouldn't experience such fear – because the problem is fear of the unknown.'

She would like her children to acknowledge all their bloodlines. At present they say they are Maori, but she would like them to acknowledge that they are Fijian and Pakeha as well. 'How does Gwenda feel if you don't acknowledge her side? And she is still alive!'

'Sometimes Haimona says to me, "Why am I so black, Mum?" And I say, "Because you have a black koro and you have my Fijian side who are black as well." Sometimes it bothers him – mainly in Whakatane. Now he's in South Auckland he seems to worry less. When he goes to Fiji he fits in.'

Lusi, and more especially her relatives in Fiji, find it hard to accept the way teenagers dress and behave in New Zealand. She didn't want her 16-year-old daughter to have a boyfriend at such an early age and Lusi's mother was offended when the teenagers kissed in front of her. Lusi says this has meant more compromise. 'This is where my kids are brought up so I had to find a middle ground where both Eddie and I are happy. We need to have rules. The good thing is that Eddie and I have similar values and that's why it works. We can talk about it.'

JACKIE *Taylor is the British-born daughter of Tom Harrison, a former mayor of Marlborough who was accused, by some politicians and Maori leaders, of racism at the height of the foreshore and seabed debate. Jackie is an entertainer who makes a living singing at gigs in the Marlborough area. She has four children from a previous marriage and one child with her new husband, John Taylor. Until she met John, of Ngapuhi, she harboured many fears about Maori people, but he's gradually helped her to modify some of her views.*

PHOTOGRAPH:

John and Jackie (holding baby Gabby) and their combined families

Jackie Taylor came to New Zealand at the age of four when her father joined the New Zealand Air Force. At school in Ohakea she soon lost her English accent after ribbing from the other kids. Her first contact with Maori was in the primers. She was 'absolutely petrified of them', because she hadn't encountered people with different-coloured skin before and the boys, in particular, appeared so big. 'They were quite intimidating to me because of my pommy accent.'

It wasn't a good start to her view of bicultural relations in New Zealand. But by the time Jackie reached standard four at Bulls School she had a number of Maori friends. 'You didn't notice after a while that they were different, that they were Maori.'

When the family moved to Blenheim, Jackie cannot recall learning anything about Maori history or culture at Marlborough Girls' College. 'The only thing I remember about college Maoris was they were bullies. Again I was terrified.

For some reason I attracted the bullies. The Maori girls used to pick on me all the time.

However, Jackie says she can laugh about it as an adult because a ringleader of the bullies from those school days is now a mate.

Jackie's first husband was a Pakeha and she moved with him to Australia where her first three girls were born. Her only son was born back in New Zealand. The first marriage ended in divorce.

Jackie's eldest daughter, Alison, was to introduce her mother to Maori things from a new perspective. 'Alison went to Whitney Street School in Blenheim and they have a bilingual class. She was curious about Maori culture and when she went to Bohally Intermediate School, she joined the kapahaka group.'

Alison continued with kapahaka at college and took part in competitions. Jackie found herself meeting Maori people when she took Alison to these events. 'Her weekends were Maori Culture Group.

She absolutely loved it. She still does. And they made her kaiarahi when they were competing – which is the leader. She knows basic Maori and wanted to learn all about the culture and stay on maraes and she got quite heavily into it. But my other children haven't.'

Some of the cultural differences became obvious to Jackie at school plays or prize-givings. 'Every time a Maori child got awarded something they'd all get up and sing. I thought that was quite strange. It made it a very long presentation, I tell you! Even when my daughter got up, they did it for her, and she's not even Maori! They just loved Ali.'

About the same time, 1995, Jackie met John Taylor and married him five years later. Her first moment of attraction to John did not involve any awareness of his racial background. 'It's quite hard to explain but I didn't think, "Oh, he's a Maori." Although he looks Maori, for some reason it didn't come into it. He's not a black Maori, if you know what I mean.'

Jackie's impression of John was that he was 'such a nice guy' and interesting to talk to. He had travelled a lot and she thought him very well educated. However, she soon realised that she and John had had a very different upbringing. 'We did a lot of talking when we first met, until the wee hours of the morning. So I found out a lot about his family.'

Jackie had come from a tight family unit without other family in New Zealand. 'Whereas in the Maori culture it's very extended. John went to live with aunties at different stages. He tells me it's what they do. It was so different to the way I've been brought up. And I was struck by how well educated the whole family were. All his brothers and sisters have degrees and have done really well for themselves.'

The scope of John's family struck home recently when John's daughter turned 21 and all his brothers and sisters came, from around New Zealand and Australia, to Blenheim for the birthday. 'I thought it was awesome. Basically I didn't do anything for a week. They all just took over.'

John and Jackie put up 20 family members in their house. There
were also caravans and a big tent for the food. She says John's family
is very close, although they all 'fight like cats and dogs'. 'I can imagine
if anyone crossed one of them, it would be the whole lot sticking up
for them. John's mum is Maori and she's just a lovely, lovely lady.
She holds herself beautifully. Got a lot of mana. JT tells me when she
was growing up she used to get the cane across her hand if she spoke
Maori. They had to speak English at school and she doesn't speak
Maori now. She can. He's heard her speak fluent Maori. And he can,
too. He's done it at funerals. But I've never heard him do it.'

Jackie says John has spoken only a few words of Maori in their home
and she's never attended a tangi. She says her views, on Maori issues,
are influenced by her father. 'I remember, growing up, that Dad had
a lot of respect for Maori. But in saying that, he had no respect for
dole bludgers. That wasn't just Maori, it was anybody that wouldn't
help themselves. But he had a lot of respect for the older Maori – the
people with mana who were polite. What I am trying to say is that a lot
of the young Maori these days, that I've met, have got no respect for
anyone, property or anything. Whereas the older Maori, they're just
lovely people.'

On Treaty issues, Jackie shares her father's view that some claims
over the last few years have been absurd and gone much too far. 'The
next thing's going to be the air that we breathe, and the rivers, and it's
just going to go on and on.'

John (listening to this conversation) interjects, 'They've already got
river rights,' and Jackie looks surprised.

*I just think that my children are Kiwis – whether they've got
Maori blood, African, whatever, running through their veins,
they're Kiwis.*

The child fathered by John is called Gabrielle, or Gabby. She, of course, is the only one of Jackie's children who has Maori ancestry and Jackie says her daughter is really funny about it. 'She'll go, "I've got Maori blood in me." She's knows she's the only one of my five children who has. Or she'll say, "Me and Dad have got Maori blood in us." She thinks it's important.'

Jackie was asked by one of John's cousins, when Gabby was three or four, if she would take her daughter to kohanga reo. 'I said, "No. If John wants her to do that, he can take her to pursue that avenue."' Jackie says the cousin was quite upset and advised her to tell Gabby about her culture. 'And I said, "Well, I do. I tell her about my culture. And her dad can explain his culture because I don't know anything about it."'

She says John wasn't bothered about whether his daughter attended a kohanga reo or not. If Gabby wanted to take up the culture in the way that Alison did, she would back her. But Jackie would not like her to feel forced into it by others. She says one of John's other children, his third daughter, Katrina, is very strong in identifying herself as Maori although her mother is Pakeha, too. 'If Gabby wants to go that way, that's fine. My other daughter did and she's got no Maori blood in her!

'Gabby gets treated like all the other children because as far as we're concerned she's just our daughter. We've had hot debates in our house, because JT's oldest girl – she's the 21-year-old studying tertiary – has managed to get the Maori grant and all the rest of it. And she doesn't have to pay it back. One of my daughters was a bit upset that she can't get the same treatment because she hasn't got any Maori blood in her.'

During these big debates Jackie says all the kids, from both families, think it's unfair. Even John's daughter agrees. 'But she says, "Well, I might as well get it if I can." And I'll be saying that to Gabby, too. "If you can, you may as well."

I think all Kiwis should be all treated the same. Everyone in
New Zealand is an immigrant. It is quite hard when you've got
two different classes in a house. You've got the privileged class,
and you've got the one who is treated normally.

Jackie has seen her father, Tom Harrison, in the headlines over
issues like the foreshore and seabed, criticising Maori claims to customary title.

She says she and her husband basically agree with him. 'Dad actually
rang JT and said, "Look, this is where I stand and the media will be
saying these things. I just want you to know that." And JT said, "Look,
I totally agree with you." So I thought it was nice of Dad to forewarn
him. If Dad thinks something, that's it. He stands by his beliefs.'

Jackie is not sure what John's family think about the foreshore and
seabed controversy. It hasn't been discussed with her Maori in-laws,
but she believes they would probably accept Tom Harrison's views
too.

One cultural issue that's prompted arguments between John
and Jackie is the matter of what will happen if John or Gabby
die.

'He tells me that when he dies all his family from way up north
will come down to get him. And if anything happens to our daughter
Gabby, they'll take her back there, too. And my answer to that is, "No!"
I've got my beliefs as well, and I don't think they have any right to do
that because she's only got a little trickle of Maori blood in her.'

Jackie says John's whanau would have a bit of a fight on their hands
if they tried to take her daughter's body away. 'She's got English blood
as well. Like, I often say to JT, "Why do people who've got a sixteenth
or a thirty-second of blood go with that instead of the rest? Why not
stick with their English part?"

'John says we don't have the same spirit (wairua). I don't understand all that spirituality. That's totally foreign to me. I can't imagine my family from England coming over to get me when I go. I don't understand it because I haven't lived it. My daughter Alison, she understands why, because she's been taught about their spirituality and how important it is to be on your ancestors' marae.'

Jackie has not visited John's marae, partly because it's so far up north and partly because she says she's not really bothered with going there or learning about it. While she believes John would accept that his daughter should be buried as Ngapuhi, she says he's not strict about any other cultural values in their home.

'We have come across things, like a friend of mine sat on a school table and this Maori lady said, "Don't sit on that table! I'm a Maori and you're not meant to do that!" and my friend turned around and said, "Well, in my culture we're allowed to sit on tables!" John will say, "Stop sitting on that bench. We've prepared food on that bench," and I agree with that. Just little things. But he doesn't ram it down the kids' throat.'

Some Maori customs really appeal to Jackie. As an entertainer she's often asked to sing at functions in Picton where a lot of Marlborough Maori live. An elder might say a prayer before they have supper. 'You don't have that at a Pakeha twenty-first. And one of the other things that I've found about the Maori culture is the way they treat their older people. I think they've got it right there. We're quick to put them in a home, whereas the Maoris seem to look after them, from what I've seen.'

John tells Jackie to explain how he changes when he goes up north to his family. 'Yes,' she says, 'he gets the walk on, and he gets the talk on when he goes up to Hamilton where his brothers and sisters live.

And when all his family came here for the twenty-first, it was quite amusing. He got the walk on and the talk.

'I thought it was quite neat, actually. He started wearing his jandals with socks and all the clichés. When he met my ex-husband for the first time, the bugger came down the stairs and went, "Oh, kia ora mate. I'm JT, eh?" Did the Maori talk. Normally he doesn't talk like that at all, unless he goes down to Picton with all the Maoris.'

John becomes such a different person she's not sure which one is the real John. She believes he's a bit of a chameleon. He can fit into both worlds, sliding from one into the other. She doesn't believe he makes an effort to be different for her. 'I don't think so because he was pretty much like that with his first wife, too.'

Jackie believes her cross-cultural marriage has succeeded because culture hasn't been an issue in their relationship. 'He's a good fella, and that's probably why I didn't notice he was Maori when I first met him because he doesn't act like the typical Maori. He was well educated and travelled, just an interesting person. His dad is Pakeha and a schoolteacher and a headmaster and I think he influenced their life a lot. His mum was a teacher, too. Both his parents are well educated. So education was important in their family and John's like that with our children as well. He's got quite rigid views on that – that education is important.'

JOHN *Taylor comes from cross-cultural parents himself so he knows a lot about what it takes to make such a marriage work. He's nearly 50 and has been with Jackie for about 10 years. They married in 1999. John has two degrees, in food technology and chemistry, although he hasn't worked in those fields for about 17 years. He has his own transport/distribution business in Blenheim, employs several staff,*

and works in rugby development.

John Taylor was known as 'Wee John' by the many aunties, uncles and cousins of his mother's whanau. His Pakeha father, John senior, or JT senior, was a teacher from Australian, English and Irish stock. His mother, Vivian, is Ngapuhi and hails from Kaikohe. The family moved a lot but lived mainly around the Waikato.

In the holidays, John went home to Kaikohe with his brothers and sisters. 'We either stayed with aunties and uncles or on the family marae.' He learnt Maori because it was spoken all around him. 'Especially by my grandmother, who was a beautiful old kuia. She spoke it to us all the time. She spoke the old Maori – where we learnt our wairua, our spirit, and what it meant.'

John is adamant about where he wants to be buried. 'It's about 12 kilometres inland from Kaikohe at a place called Rakatau.' He has attended many tangi there, every time one of his family dies, and some in the 10 years since he met Jackie. 'She doesn't know them so she doesn't come.

She gets a bit spooked by those sorts of things. It's because the casket is open and people sleep in the wharenui, the main meeting house, next to the body and things like that. English don't do that.

He's not concerned that Jackie is reluctant to attend a tangi. He says he would never force her to do anything she was not happy with. 'It would be a very different thing if I died. People change when things like that happen. And if my parents or brothers or sisters died she would come along. I don't think she would want to know much about it. She'd just come along and be an observer. I have said to her that I won't force anything foreign onto her that she doesn't want to learn. It doesn't worry me if she doesn't understand. I just love her the way she is. She's beautiful.'

John met Jackie over a drink with friends at the Criterion in Blenheim. He was smitten as soon as he saw her. 'I'd gone through a separation, basically a bit of an upheaval, and I wasn't really looking around for anybody, I can assure you. Especially someone with four kids! But, yeah, it was instant, for me and her, when we saw each other.'

He didn't know about her four kids at first. But he met them all the next day. 'And I starting thinking to myself, "Whoa! What's going on here?" But as we got to know each other I went from having three girls to having six girls and a boy. My kids are a bit older. My eldest is 21. The youngest is about the same age as Jackie's eldest.' John's middle daughter has a Maori partner and a baby, so John is a grandfather, too.

He works fulltime for the Marlborough Rugby Union as a rugby development officer, which means he's mixing with other Maori all the time. 'I'm coaching at the moment and I've got 25 in my squad – and only four of them are Pakeha boys.'

John says Jackie is also mixing with Maori people on a regular basis. 'She's an entertainer so she's got no choice. She sings two to three gigs a week. There's always Maoris in the audience. She's bloody good too, mate.

'I'll tell you something funny. When I first met her, I said I was coaching down in Picton and she said, "Ew, ew, all the Maoris!" She just had a preconceived idea. She hadn't mixed with them very much. And then I got her a few gigs down there in the pubs, the rugby club and everything else. She goes to Kaikoura and there are a lot of Maoris down there as well. And now she's perfectly at home with them. She doesn't feel out of it at all.'

John believes Jackie's attitude was influenced by the bullies she met at school and what he calls the 'Maori gang culture', which was prevalent in New Zealand during the 1970s and '80s.

I showed her 'once were warriors' and she thought it was too far-fetched to be true. I said, 'You've got no idea, girl. It's not far-fetched at all.'

'*Once Were Warriors* and *What Becomes of the Broken Hearted* is exactly what I have seen in my own lifetime. And with my extended family. I've got cousins who've been in gangs. Just didn't have the same opportunities I had. I could have quite easily gone that way if I didn't have the father I did.

'It blows Jackie away because it doesn't matter how rough they look, I just go up and talk to them. It doesn't worry me. I don't feel negative about Maoris at all. Mind you, I feel negative about Maoris that keep holding their hands out. But I feel negative about Pakehas that do that, too.'

Racism is something John experiences himself occasionally. 'Oh, I've been called a black bastard quite a few times. Nigger nuts, hori, black arse, blah blah blah. Jackie's heard people call me that. But it goes just straight out of my head – water off a duck's back to me. Just depends what your disposition's like. I've got cousins, and if somebody said that to them they'd turn around and smash 'em. Racism is a bitter thing.'

He doesn't believe people these days would deny him services because he's Maori. 'Not so much now, no, because I'm pretty well educated so I just won't put up with it. If I think I'm being got at racially, I'll just tell them. But if somebody calls me black arse or nigger, or something like that, I don't have any time for them. If they're friends I just don't worry about it.'

John is not always in agreement with his father-in-law, Tom Harrison, on Maori issues. He says they have debates over such matters, often when Tom comes for a Sunday roast at their house.

'A lot of the time I agree with him because he's just a good, decent man. But sometimes he's got some radical views. I just go, "Nah, nah, Tom. You're out left field there for me, boy." That's what it's like with his wife and daughters too. The thing about Tom, though, is he's a highly principled man, a man of integrity, and what I like about him is, even if he's wrong, if he believes in something he's prepared to stand up for it. He's not prepared to be intimidated or bullied. He's a man of small stature but he casts a big shadow, Tommy does.

'He doesn't intimidate like Rob Muldoon did. He doesn't use that sort of rhetoric or language. He just knows what he stands for and most of it is just good, decent things that most New Zealanders want – a decent standard of living, a space for their family, health and education, things like that. He's quite a political man, Tom.'

John is not inclined to share his father-in-law's strong criticisms of the Waitangi Tribunal. In particular, he doesn't agree that there was no such thing as a 'holocaust' in Taranaki and that the Tribunal discredited itself by making such a finding.

'Well, he's lying there cos there was a holocaust – at Parihaka. I'll have a talk to him about that. I don't think he understands things like the confiscations. It's hard for somebody coming from England to understand Maori thinking. From a European perspective they'll try and protect their property, their chattels, their money, right? From a Maori perspective they're trying to protect their lands, their waters, their customary gathering rights, things like this. They're not really things that are in single ownership. They're collective ownership.

'It's hard for half of the Maoris to understand, let alone Tom, because we Maori have got so much English blood in us now. You're talking about a spiritual thing; it's wairua. If you don't understand the concept it's hard to explain to people. And it's why these Maori people are driven, because it's something intangible passed down from generation to generation by word of mouth. It's not written down as a statute or law.'

On the foreshore and seabed issue John agrees with his father-in-law that it's a non-negotiable right for all New Zealanders to be able to use coastal marine areas. 'I want to make one thing clear. I'm proud to have Maori heritage, no doubt about that. I'm proud to have English heritage, and Irish. Probably the fiery part of me comes when the Irish blood mixes over in the Maori bit. You've got to be proud of all the places where your blood comes from and learn from those cultures. If we're ever going to solve these issues we've got to think of ourselves as one people, two cultures – or three cultures, or four cultures.

what Maori people have got to think of is that they're not just tangata whenua (people of the land) by themselves. It's all the people here now.

'It's going to get worse too, because we're going to get a lot of Asians here soon and what are we going to do about that?'

John's family have land up north in a whanau trust. 'Some of my stupid cousins were trying to hock it off and get it put into Pakeha land deeds so they can sell it! We've got forestry up there and they were milling that illegally!' He believes it should stay as Maori land so it is safe from alienation. 'But as the Maori blood's filtering down, it's getting weaker and weaker. Another 40 years and just about everybody born in New Zealand will have some Maori blood. Yeah, it's just going to be too many people that have to sign to get the land changed over.

'There's a lot of people that have got really, really sad and legitimate claims and grievances. You only have to look at Eva Rickard with the

Raglan Golf Course. That was a legitimate claim, and in the end she won. But if nobody got off their arse and complained they'd still be playing golf there, wouldn't they? It's a horrible piece of land anyway. It means something to them, though. That's what I was just saying. It's a spirituality thing. It's the wairua. I can't explain it unless you feel it. If you come to our marae up north and you went on there, even if you're Pakeha you would feel it all around you – what it means to these people.'

John decided that he wouldn't push his Maori heritage onto his children. He wants to leave it to them to decide what they want. If they choose to identify as Maori and want to know about their ancestry then he'll tell them. He says the cousin who told Jackie that Gabby should go to kohanga reo is an activist. If he had heard her say it he would have told her 'to piss off' and mind her own business.

John says this particular cousin has not twigged to the fact that Tom Harrison is his father-in-law. Neither have some other members of the family. When Titewhai Harawira, another relative, was coming down to Blenheim for a hui, John's mother rang up to warn him. 'She said, "If Titewhai finds out that you're Tom's son-in-law, she'll be marching around." And I said, "Well, don't tell her."'

Remarks made about Tom by the deputy prime minister, Michael Cullen, in Parliament infuriated John. 'I wrote him a letter of disgust, and I never got the decency of a reply. It was just an ignorant comment.'

John says some of the more radical people in his family would find Tom Harrison very challenging with his views on the foreshore and seabed and other issues. 'They wouldn't be as accommodating as I am. But my immediate family of brothers and sisters, mother and people like that, they take the same view. They're like me, quite pragmatic. We're not into sensationalism. If you look at it in the clear light of day, to me it's just a storm in a teacup.'

while some of John's relatives would find Tom's views 'inflammatory', John says Tom might also find some members of his whanau too radical.

'I've had a lot of occasions over the last nine or so years to sit down and talk with Tom. He's conservative but, as I've got older, conservatism is a good thing a lot of the time because we have the benefit of seeing what has worked and what has not. All the old values that we always talk about but we don't see nowadays, of decency and respect and all these sort of things. Jackie and I bring our kids up with all those old-fashioned values. And there's a breakdown in society at the moment in families with a lot of kids just not being exposed to these sorts of things so they have no real moral viewpoint of what is right and wrong.'

John believes cross-cultural marriages can be very successful. 'I don't know if you've noticed but there are a bloody lot of Maori boys marrying Pakeha girls and lots of Maori girls marrying Pakeha boys. What we're finding nowadays is that the world's such a small place, things happen so quickly and that's what I think is happening with this interracial marriage. It's just happening more and more and more. Exclusivity doesn't happen any more.

'My driving force is Jackie and my kids, all eight of them. But anybody who gets into a mixed marriage, you've just got to be thick-skinned. Some people get real upset about nothing. It sounds like Jackie and I agree on everything, but we don't.

I don't understand fully her English heritage. She tells me she doesn't understand Maoris, so we've learnt through trial and error just how to talk about it.

'That's the main key; you've just got to talk about it. Not get too excited about it.'

John believes Jackie would not survive up north where his Ngapuhi whanau come from. She is 'too English'. However, he knows he would survive well in England, because he makes more compromises than she does. He'd just fit in.

'But it doesn't worry me. That's the way it is. I love her and I understand that that is the way it is. I don't want to go and live back home so why the hell would she? Don't get me wrong. I had an absolutely wonderful childhood and we learnt everything there. Until I was about 16, we used to go up north to be with our cousins. We ran wild, raided orchards and everything was on horseback. Typical little country Maori kids we were. No electricity, everything was cooked on the stove and water from the creek. Washing was done in a copper outside and the food's different, everything's different there. Jackie wouldn't last a day. Doesn't matter how many of my family were there to reassure her. So I can't see the point of taking somebody into an environment where it's going to be totally foreign without them wanting to do it.

'There are a lot of good things the English have brought here, too. We've got to remember that. The English, by and large, are a fairly decent race. They might have had colonial and expansionist views but I think they're not a bad race overall. English people don't like cultural change much. They go to Spain and want English food and all that. I've seen it happen. Complaining because they can't get baked beans, bacon butties and things like that. They're a different race, the poms.

'They're delightful sometimes, though. I've got a good one here. She's lovely. I didn't think it could be like this. It's even better now than when we met!'

※

TOM *Harrison was the mayor of the Marlborough District Council*

until the 2004 local body elections. He came to national prominence through his outspoken comments on the foreshore and seabed issue.

Eight Marlborough iwi made a claim in the Maori Land Court

for customary title to the foreshore and seabed largely because

they complained that the Marlborough District Council was

discriminating against them when approving marine farms. Tom

says he wasn't the mayor during the time they complain of. Tom's

daughter, Jackie, is married to John Taylor so he has a Maori

granddaughter, Gabrielle.

Tom Harrison has a strong English accent because he was born in the Lake District in the north-west of England in 1937. He trained as an aircraft engineer in the Royal Air Force and served in a number of countries. He married Anne in 1960 and found he couldn't settle down back in Britain after his service ended. When the New Zealand Air Force advertised in Britain for tradesmen, Tom signed on.

Tom, Anne and their two babies went to live at Ohakea where Tom met Maori people for the first time. 'I had heard of the Maori people through the All Blacks. And in England we used to look forward to the All Blacks' comings – and of course the haka. And I'm so proud now of being a New Zealander. The haka strikes into the heart of all New Zealanders.'

The family made friends with Maori and they were

(l to r) Jackie, Tom, Anne, Gillian. Circa 1969

taken to the marae at Bulls. 'I never thought of them as Maori. And I still don't. You just didn't think of any difference, you know.'

The air force sent Tom to Singapore and to Malaya on exercises. 'They would say when we were there, "Sing us some Maori songs." And the guitars would come out and all of us on that squadron were so proud. We would sing the Maori songs with gusto. "Pokare kare ana", the usual ones. And we would just pull together. We were one people.'

Tom is now 67 and has put his roots down in the Marlborough Sounds. His son was born in Blenheim and he has eight grandchildren. 'So this is our country. We've lived here most of our lives.'

Before he became the mayor of Marlborough in 1998, Tom was a candidate in the parliamentary elections for the New Zealand First Party. He became disillusioned with the party but still agrees with many of Winston Peter's ideas. For instance he supports the New Zealand First leader's criticism of people who 'hijack the Treaty for their own benefits'.

'I hear from my Maori relatives [John Taylor and his family], that there is now a group of people who *have* hijacked it and do very well financially. Some call them the "brown table". I go to Wellington quite a lot and I see these people, and quite frankly I feel quite sick. You will see them in the Koru lounge and driving BMWs. Some people have done very, very well. I think Maoridom has been very badly let down by its leadership.'

He admires the generation of New Zealanders who have recognised that there were wrongs in the past and want to settle Treaty claims. However, he believes the Waitangi Tribunal and the Maori Land Court have lost all their mana.

'When the Tribunal makes recommendations to the government and it talks about what happened in Taranaki as a "holocaust". And when you get Tariana Turia using the same word . . . Hey, you know what happened there? There was no holocaust. That type of terminology is what upsets non-Maori New Zealanders. And when you hear Tariana Turia saying, "unless you've got Maori blood in you, you're a visitor here", I get quite upset. I want to be inclusive.

And by the way, I don't accept the word 'pakeha'. 'pakeha' to me is a derogatory word.

Waitangi Tribunal claims are becoming more and more outrageous and never-ending, in Tom's view. And before the foreshore and seabed – which has Tom fuming – he disapproved of claims for the airwaves, oil, and gas and mineral reserves.

'Also, you've got a claim before the Waitangi Tribunal, which is being heard in secret, claiming ownership of the flora and fauna of this country. I get a bit annoyed because, as a New Zealander, my heart is the flora and fauna. It's the rivers, the streams, the mountains and the foreshore and seabed of this country. That goes to the very heart of being a New Zealander. That's why we mustn't divide it on ethnic grounds, because I can never overcome that. I can never jump that void.'

Tom says some Treaty claims are genuine and some are not. He believes the public has had enough. 'People are saying let's clear the genuine claims out of the way and put a time limit on it. And then move on as one people.'

Tom believes his own family has shown how this can work. He's enthusiastic about his Maori son-in-law, John. They get on well and he says racial differences are not an issue. 'In my family we are Celts and my son-in-law is Ngapuhi. It's an amazing mix of the two bloodlines and we are so proud of both lines.'

Because John is from Ngapuhi, Tom has formed some strong views about various events at Waitangi. He says it's another example of the Maori leadership letting people down. 'You know my Maori family tell me that the marae is sacred ground. When visitors go on to that marae they are treated with respect and dignity, especially if they hold a position in the community. But we are seeing that sacred ground desecrated by people who are demanding privilege. The Queen of England was attacked with a wet T-shirt! I would never think of doing that to the Maori Queen. And when I see Tame Iti on that marae spitting at the Governor-General, who represents the Queen, and stamping my New Zealand flag into the mud, and when I see Titewhai Harawira making our prime minister cry on that marae, and when I see the Opposition leader having mud thrown at him, I begin to wonder. Hey! This isn't what my Maori family is telling me a marae is about. And Waitangi, of course, is my marae – Ngapuhi, through my son, my son's marae. And we're proud of that.'

When the deputy prime minister, Michael Cullen, made a statement in Parliament about Tom Harrison being racist, it was a shock to the former mayor and his family. Tom believes Dr Cullen was referring to remarks he made about some Maori activists getting better opportunities to talk to the government over the foreshore and seabed than the Marlborough tribes. 'I issued a press statement asking why the government was talking to the ugly face of Maoridom, the bully boys of Maoridom, and I identified them as Titewhai Harawira, Tame Iti and Ken Mair. They are the ones who have done the damage in this country. And my tribes, who were the ones at the centre of this, weren't even consulted by the government at the time. Neither was my council.'

Tom also denies allegations that his council discriminated against iwi over applications for marine farms – either before or after he took office. 'I can assure you that being a Celt and having spiritual values myself, I look very carefully when the Maori comes to me (under the Resource Management Act) and tells me, "That has spiritual significance to me." I feel that deep down inside.'

Tom was touched when his Maori son-in-law wrote to Michael Cullen and told him that his father-in-law was not a racist. 'You know,

I've got an amazing son-in-law. He has made my daughter very happy. He would be the best barbecue cook ever in the world.

And we've got an amazing granddaughter with a lot of talent. And we as a family, we don't expect that granddaughter to have any privilege due to that little bit of Maori blood she has got.

'John's father is a non-Maori. He was an ex-school principal. And his wife, Vivian Taylor, is our matriarch. She's an amazing Maori lady. And all their children. We are just one big family. We don't even think of ourselves as Maori or non-Maori.'

Tom says he felt no reservations about his daughter, Jackie, marrying a Maori. In his view, the Harrisons have embraced Maoridom completely through the marriage. 'We are one country but we are different cultures. And all our cultures are important. That's why I am proud of the haka when I see it.'

Generally, Tom says he doesn't discuss his views about such things as the Waitangi Tribunal or the foreshore and seabed with his family. However, he admits that some Maori family members poke fun at his political incorrectness.

All the family were down here for a big party and there were a few jokes made about 'promise not to talk about the seabed.'

'But it was all done humorously and we respect each other's opinion. And that's how it's got to be – rational debate, respecting each other's opinion – because we've got so much going for us in this country.'

Tom admits that some of his views might cause discord in the family if he discussed them. 'We know each other as people. We respect each other, and that's what we've got to do as a whole New Zealand people. The family must be strong. In any family you have disagreements but you have to try to overcome them and look at what the goal is we are aiming for.'

He says the question of Maori scholarships has been a sticky topic in the family. 'And, of course, my granddaughter has got very little Maori blood in her, by the way. In fact, you wouldn't tell that she had any Maori blood. But she's got the best of both bloodstreams. And, by gosh, she's a talented little girl. I don't think she'll need a scholarship. But if there's a Maori scholarship there, you do take it, don't you? However, my other grandchildren haven't got access to that. Who helps the non-Maori child?'

Tom agrees with the premise that cross-cultural relationships will be resolved in the bedrooms of the nation. 'Because I hold my immediate Maori family in the highest esteem and respect. I know the deep-down values and feelings of my immediate Maori, my Ngapuhi family. And by golly they are great people and they've got some fantastic values. They want what's best for their children. But they also want what's best for this country. And separatism is not the way to go. As far as family is concerned, we are one. And it's a great blend. A great mixing of genetic genes. It really is!'

The Prime Hapu

MARGARET *Prime was born in Waiuku in South Auckland in 1952 and raised as a Pakeha, with her twin brothers and sister, in a predominantly Pakeha community. Her father, Ben Ross, is English and her mother, Waina (née Henare), 'half-Maori' but Margaret knew only European ways in her childhood. That changed when her parents moved to Motatau in Northland and Margaret married Kevin Prime of Ngati Hine. She plunged into a traditional Maori lifestyle on a farm with no running water or electricity. She's now*

PHOTOGRAPH:

The Prime Hapu with new baby Samuel. Circa 1995

the mother of 13 children ranging in age from nine to 32 and has

six grandchildren.

Margaret says her mother, Waina, chose to do things the way her English husband wanted them because she loved him and wanted to please him. 'I don't think my father actually expected her to stop expressing anything of her Maori background. But there were so few Maori in Waiuku where we lived and those few did not speak the language or follow the traditions. There was just no drawing on that culture.'

Later Margaret was to learn that her iwi was Ngati Hine and that her mother was a cousin of the Maori leader, Sir James Henare. But, with her fair skin, light brown hair and green eyes, she looked like her English father and people in Waiuku assumed she was Pakeha.

'My second name is a Maori one and when we had to say our full names at school I was so ashamed, because in our area Maori were looked on as being on a lower level than everyone else. In a silly way, something lodged in my head to think that Maori was something to be ashamed of.'

At school Margaret says she learnt little about Maori things. 'That was the pre-Maori renaissance era. It wasn't in vogue. From school I went to university for a couple of years. I've never really had a job or career. I left university intending to travel and ended up pregnant with twins at 20, and since then my job, more or less, has been a mother.

'I was a solo mother for two years until I married Kevin and he's been a dad to my son and daughter, rather than their Pakeha father. I met Kevin when my parents moved to Motatau where my mother had land. I wanted a change of scene from Auckland. I came up to live with them for a while. Kevin was a few miles up the road and we had common sport interests.'

The move north brought Margaret into contact with a heritage and culture she knew nothing about. 'It was a total change. Maori is still the everyday language here. It took me a while to adjust. The marae kitchen was run by the kuia. They had a very strong arm on the kitchen activities and you couldn't just bowl in. You had to be invited or be there long enough so that you became familiar and could lend a hand at doing dishes or peeling veges or whatever. Gradually I became phased in. The locals thought I was very Pakeha-looking. They all knew my Maori roots, so that was okay. But the initial reaction was "Who's this Pakeha?"

'After I'd been in Motatau a few months, I had my first experience of a tangi. My mum's uncle had died and it's normal for everyone to go to the tangi. I'd never even seen a dead body until then, so I went halfway up the hall and asked if I could just stop there. And I was allowed to. I found it really hard to get my head around how people could go up and cry with the grieving family and then get halfway around the hall and laugh like anything with somebody else. For me, if a loved one's died you're crying for them. It took time to get used to the openness of expression, but also the change happening so quickly from absolute broken-heartedness to joking. I can be like that myself now, even though it seemed so hypocritical at first.

'I was going carefully at the marae. I didn't want to do anything wrong. It was all new – kissing everybody and rubbing noses. My father got into it but it took him a while.

If there was a hui for three days, my mum was a full-on person, and she'd be there to support the family from go to whoa, helping with cooking, everything.

'There were times when my Dad resented that immensely. "You and your marae", he'd say. But it was such a generalisation what he was saying. It wasn't the marae that was holding my mum. It was just her aroha for loved ones and that.

'In the Maori environment it seemed to him she was very different. That side of her was always there but she'd left home in her mid-

Kevin on his horse, Steel, with his very faithful and clever cattle dog, Don, about to move stock

teens and gone nursing and left it all behind. She'd married and lived away from home. It took her a wee while to get back into it, the language especially. But the ways were still the same and she was able to slip back in.

'She loved it when Dad would come along with her, but there were times when maybe a close cousin had died and her love would draw her to be there, helping all the time she could. That was when Dad wouldn't understand. She could be strong-willed. She knew she'd have music to face when she got home but she would face it. Her loved one would be buried in two days, that'd be the end of that, and she could chew things over with Dad later on.'

Margaret says her attraction to Kevin wasn't a physical thing. 'He had Afro-type hair and an unkempt beard. But I was drawn to his lifestyle. He was living on his family farm without electricity. That, and the character of the man, I found really attractive. I fell in love with the whole package.

'I didn't know I was taking on such a change of life and one that would be such hard work for me. I'd been used to modern comforts. I didn't go to Girl Guides, so I had no idea about lighting fires and washing by hand or anything like that – or only going to town once a month.'

Margaret says her father didn't like Kevin initially because he didn't want his daughter to be caught up in such a simple lifestyle. In his eyes it was primitive and backward. 'But after a while he saw that I loved it and he was happy if I was happy. They have great respect and love for each other now, my Dad and Kevin.

'Kevin's family farm was about five kilometres from my parents' farm. My folks had power at their place but the Prime house had been sited three miles inland because it was central to the activity of milking cows in the days of Kevin's father. By the time I arrived it was just dry stock and pine trees. In recent years we've moved to the front of the farm. Kevin's mum wanted to come back home, so they relocated a house from Auckland to here and got the power on.

'We had eight children before we moved down and got electricity. It was a lovely, beautiful lifestyle at the old house. But I was ready to move. I had sporting interests and things like Maori culture taking up my time, as well as the children. So I was getting sick of how long it took to do hand-washing and things like that.

'At the old house, we had a 500-gallon rainwater tank for drinking and cooking. There was the long-drop toilet, and the bathroom and laundry was the creek down the hill and that was that. In summertime we'd have to cart water up in buckets because our tank water would run out. It made you appreciate everything, that sort of living.

'I'd come home from netball and because where we lived was only a summer road, I'd leave our

Margaret with three of her young ones in front of fairly new planted garden

car about four "k"s down the road at the front of the farm and walk home. By the time I got home I'd be quite hot and slip into the creek, in the middle of winter, and it was nice. Very refreshing.

'When the babies were little we'd boil up water at the house in a little baby tub and wash them in that. Once they got a bit older they went to the creek, too. But we called it a swim. A bath was a chore, but going for a swim was never a problem.

'Until I married Kevin I used to get all my fruit and vegetables from the supermarket. But Kevin and I grew all our own vegetables – and some for the whanau in town who didn't have big gardens. We grew sweetcorn, Maori potatoes, Pakeha potatoes, kumara, tomatoes, capsicum, watermelon, beans and peas. Lovely!

'We had pigs, sheep and cattle. Kevin was very good with the gun and sometimes a little cluster of quail would come around the house. We had a cat that used to bring us eels. He would just eat the head and we would have the rest. We did our own eeling as well. They were plentiful in those days. Of course there were chooks. We had fruit trees, too, like apples, macadamia, pears, plums and peaches, until possums became pests and ate the fruit before it was ripe.

'Apart from the huge lifestyle change there were cultural differences between Kevin and me. Things we would've done at our home as young people, like sitting on the kitchen bench. You'd never do that here. You just don't sit anywhere where food is eaten or prepared.

we had an old cream can that we put the flour in and to me it was an ideal height for a seat but a no-no for Kevin and his family. Sitting on it just was not done.

'Food things were a big cultural difference. In our upbringing, you were allowed two biscuits maximum when you had a cup of tea. That was totally the limit. Whereas Kevin's way was that you eat as much as you like. Their family was ultra-generous. If it's there, eat it, and if it's gone, well, something else will come on the scene.

'We didn't have much money in our earlier years, because we were managing the family farm, and the wage they could afford to give Kevin was less than the dole. But he wouldn't go on the dole. He would work for whatever they gave him and that was that. However, we were never short of food.

'We still go down to the marae and it's an integral part of the area. Once people would take three days off work to go to a tangi, but these days not many jobs will allow an employee to do that, so only immediate family will be there for the duration. Before, life almost stopped when someone died and everybody went and helped. But people don't have the same amount of time for the marae that they used to. At one time, one small family would go down and decide that windows needed fixing and lawns needed doing and they'd just do it. These days it has to be more of an organised effort to get a working bee and fundraise for things like repairs.

'When people ask me why I have 13 kids, I say, "No power, no TV!" That did have a bit to do with it. Kevin was one of 12 so my husband is a real children person. He wanted them. I'm not such a great one with the children, but he couldn't have them so that's where I came in. And I loved him and that's what he wanted. But after our last one it was like, "Honey, I'm tired! Can we stop, please?"

'The youngest is now nine and he wasn't supposed to happen. It's a bit embarrassing when you've had 12 children and you still ask, "How did he happen?" But he did and Samuel's a real joy. But once we'd had him it was: "Please honey, no more!"

we have brought the kids up with the idea that their identity is half-and-half Maori/Pakeha.

'Kevin has maintained his reo and so on and he has been useful in a lot of areas because of it. It's because of his knowledge of Maori that he's in his present occupation as a commissioner in the Environment Court. It's very useful to have a Maori there who understands Maori perspectives. Whilst he's benefited in a number of ways from being fluent in Maori, he's always been of the view that our children need English, and so we've really pursued the English side more than anything. He was never ashamed of the Maori side. Certain relations come here and you always converse with them in Maori, on the phone and so on, but his underlying thing is that the children need English. Maori is okay, useful even, but English is essential.

'I encourage him to speak Maori at home but it doesn't last. It's a bit of a shame. You miss so much, speaking only English. There're words in Maori without an English equivalent and it can be quite expressive in a way that English isn't.

'All our children have gone to the local school and they've done well there. Four of the younger ones went to kohanga reo, but kohanga relies hugely on whanau help and I'd find myself down the kohanga two or three days a week, and it really was very demanding with the other children and all our other activities. I couldn't do that for all of them.

All my children so far have Maori partners and I think it's a good thing to have like marry like.

'There were a few difficulties with my parents because of cultural differences, and if couples are from the same culture it's easier. Being married is hard enough, I think, without extra challenges. It's nothing that we've pushed or anything, except to say that it's been my own view that it's good that you marry your own kind. And that's what has happened.

'Nowadays, I think of myself as the same kind as Kevin. I am one-quarter Maori and Kevin and I are distant kin. He's definitely more Maori than me in every way. But I forget sometimes that I'm not dark-skinned. Living this life, I think as if I'm a Maori. I just feel that way. It's not like the days when I was ashamed of my middle name. I love my Maori side.

'All of Kevin's kids are olive-skinned with dark hair and dark eyes. They look like Primes and people recognise them as Primes. Sometimes they growl at me, "Why haven't we got light-coloured eyes like yours?" And it can be a bit embarrassing for me when I meet the children's friends and they say, "This is my Mum." The friends say, "Your mum?" I think they expect Kevin's wife would be more Maori just because *he* is so Maori. I feel sometimes that I'm a bit of a disappointment . . . not to myself but to others. He knows Maori ways and traditions well enough to even break them and get away with it.'

Margaret's mother, Waina, died about 11 years ago and her father, Ben, now lives in Kamo, near Whangarei, with a friend. 'He is still very much a Pakeha, living a Pakeha lifestyle. We don't always agree on Maori issues but I don't get wound up about it. He has a mixed stand, my dad. He sees a lot of Maori unemployed and in jails and looks down a little on Maori because of that. But he's not so one-eyed that he can't discuss things and be persuaded to, what I would call, a more balanced point of view. He's never had a racist bias at all. Sometimes his views are against the Maori perspective but he's not always against things Maori.

'Our family have been sheltered from racism here. At the moment, Motatau Primary School is 100 per cent Maori. And Bay College is about 70 per cent Maori, so it's weighted towards the Maori, really. Our children are quite confident in who they are, so if anything crops up they'll handle it.

'During one of the Aussie/All Black games there were 32,000 people there and when they sang the Maori anthem the television showed a close-up of one of our sons because he was singing the anthem in

Maori. Obviously the camera picked up someone in the crowd who knew the words. My children are all proud of their Maori side.'

✗

NINETEEN-*year-old Peter is one of the Prime children who is still at home. He says that except for some European traditions like 'manners' his upbringing was more Maori than Pakeha. He says he was taught respect for elders and other Maori values so his Maori side is stronger than his mother's side.*

'I have a good time with my Pakeha granddad but I tend to mock him more than anything because he's so English. He's always joking around with us, too. He's never really been into the Maori side of things. I think he *gets* the Maori side but it's not really him.'

It doesn't surprise Peter that he and all his siblings so far have preferred to have Maori partners. 'If you're brought up in a culture that's Maori then you identify with someone who shares the same characteristics as you. Our partners understand the mechanics of our family. If we had European partners, I don't know if they'd understand the way that Maori work.

'I've been going out with my girlfriend for about three and a half years now. Both her parents are Maori and she was brought up in a largely Maori-influenced family, speaking Maori. If you can identify with your partner you are more attracted to them at first.

'I can see how it might benefit race relations if Maori and Pakeha intermarry. It would help the Pakeha families to understand the way

Maori think. In a way that's like my grandfather. He does understand Maori and respect them but doesn't necessarily live like them. I think he's sort of bridged a gap, so to speak. So being married to my grandmother let him understand the ways of the Maori and what they do.'

Although Peter can see the value of bringing cultures together through marriage, he says, with wry smile, that *he* won't be putting the theory to the test. 'As long as I don't have to do it, then it's all right!'

✦

KEVIN *Prime of Ngati Hine is a farmer, forester, conservationist and company director from the small settlement of Motatau in Northland. He was appointed as a commissioner of the Environment Court in 2003 and is the chairman of the Auckland Savings Bank Trust. For more than 20 years he's been involved in community matters with marae committees, Maori committees, runanga, Maori development, school boards of trustees, charitable trusts, health trusts, community trusts, forestry trusts, forest companies, health companies, health boards, conservation boards at local, regional and national levels. He's also served on ministerial advisory groups related to health, forestry, conservation, Maori affairs, environment, Crown Research Institutes, lands and sport. Kevin has found time among all that to raise 13 children with this wife Margaret.*

Kevin Prime was born at home in Pipiwai, west of Motatau, in Northland in 1944. 'My mother had all her babies at home, except for one of my sisters who is called Hohipere (hospital) because she was born in hospital. My mum said hospital was traumatic because Maori got treatment below second-class citizens and the staff were blatantly abusive. She wouldn't go back again. There were 12 of us kids. We also had whangai and other children who were looked after by Mum and Dad for people who couldn't afford to care for them.

'Dad had a rule that we had to speak English to him all the time. It was to try to improve our education and improve his English, too. Mum learnt English at school but couldn't speak it that well. We spoke English at home, until visitors came, because Maori was spoken in the community. When my father was angry he always spoke in Maori, and if he had to explain to us how we should use a wire strainer on a fence or something he had to speak Maori to find the words.

'We saw the benefit of speaking English when we went to Motatau School. The Prime family did best in their lessons because we knew what the teacher was saying. This was in the 1950s and '60s, which is not long ago, and we weren't allowed to speak Maori at school.

'When there was a death or a wedding, we went to the marae and we often went to work there to do things like putting on a new roof. It was a typical Maori community, mainly dairy farming. We milked more than a hundred cows. Dad was an innovator. He planted pine trees well before it was fashionable. He experimented with dairy beef and he invented farm equipment. For a person with limited education I thought he did really well. He had huge gardens of vegetables. We ate beef and pork – and that generation didn't waste anything. The leather was treated and made into saddles and bridles and belts, all the fat was rendered and used for cooking, the intestines were eaten and the rest cooked and given to the dogs. If they cut a tree down for firewood, they'd chop it all up and get all the brushwood, and the stump was demolished, and the roots. We were brought up with that Maori culture of "waste not, want not".

'A lot of the so-called traditional cultural foods were common. They didn't have fridges so everything you didn't eat fresh was either salted or stored as huahua – sealed in jars with fat. Wild food was available like watercress, puha and dandelions. There were eels in the creek and freshwater crayfish we called kewai. Our upbringing was predominantly Maori.

'Everything focused on either the school, the marae or the post office.

'There were few Pakeha in Motatau. The first Pakeha we ever saw were Dallys [Dalmatians] who came up home. We were down at the creek having a wash and they were laughing when they saw us with no clothes. We didn't see what was funny about people just washing.

My dad didn't like Pakeha and he made no bones about saying so.

'One day in the 1950s we were down the road because someone had dropped off some discs for the farm. We had our big tractor and trailer there to load them on and these Pakeha people went past and called out to ask if we wanted a hand. You would think that Dad would say "No, thanks". But I suppose he didn't know what to say, because he literally swore and abused them! He had people there already to help him, but he needn't have been like that to the Pakeha. It was really embarrassing for us as children because we knew these strangers were being helpful and offering assistance, but Dad didn't see it like that. He always saw Pakeha as trying to get one over you and not to be trusted.

'As the years went by, Dad mellowed a bit towards Pakeha but we still didn't mix with them. It was the culture and upbringing of that time. As time went on, we found that Pakeha weren't all that bad and weren't all out to get you or rip you off. But my oldest sister came home from training college with stories about Pakeha customs. Our people are generous and buy things for people all the time. But she said Pakeha would just let her carry on buying things. In their culture, Pakeha are saving themselves money, whereas for Maori the culture was that you always offered your best.'

Kevin had his first major interaction with Pakeha at Bay of Islands College in Kawakawa in the sixth form in 1962. 'It was the first time I'd seen so many Pakehas and yet half the class were Maori. Even then we still tended to mix with our own. I continued to play rugby for Motatau and we used to beat the Bay of Islands team. The culture of distrust meant that you went hard out to try to beat those largely Pakeha teams. They were athletic and very competitive, but we had a natural fitness from running four "k"s to catch a bus every morning.

I remember my older sister, Janet, telling me about the first time she visited a pakeha home. She said they didn't have enough food.

'They just cooked enough for those who were there and if more visitors came you either didn't feed the visitors or you divided the food up so they actually starved! Later I visited the same Pakeha home with a friend and it was the same thing. We didn't get enough to eat either.

'It's so funny because, just recently, our daughter in the fourth form wanted to stay at a Pakeha mate's place. And she said they starved even though they were visitors. They had to go and buy takeaways. It was a total cultural shock for her.

'At home we have visitors just about every day. We cook regularly for 20 or 30. We have a room at home where we have meetings, like a marae, that will sleep 20 people with its own shower and toilet. We call it Mo Tatou (which means "for all of us"). Mo tatou mo nga mana pukepuke rau – for us, the important people of the sacred hills of Ngati Hine. Over a long period Margaret has prepared the food for

Four of the Prime sons and a niece putting down a hangi

all these meetings. I cannot remember her complaining and she'd be embarrassed if there wasn't enough food.

'I suppose if you added it up it's really quite costly, and she has to do most of the work. I've got a lovely wife. She's really supportive. She asks, "How many people are coming?" I say, "20 or 30," and she cooks for that number and the younger kids will help her serve it.

In Maori culture, food was always part of the expectations. I would never ever dream of doing what a pakeha might do; they would have no problem about asking the visitors to bring a plate or contribute.

'We would never ever do that. If people choose to bring a koha that's fine. However, my dad would have been highly insulted if people brought food. That was the Maori way of showing their love for the visitors, to manaaki the manuhiri.

'I stay a lot in hotels in my job and I get fed up with the hotel food. I really miss my Maori foods. Sometimes I ring Margaret and say, "Can you find me some watercress, some pork bones or muttonbird or fatty food?" Just for a change.

'I met Margaret in the late 1970s. Our oldest was born in 1978. I was the only one with a rotary hoe at Motatau and all the local Maori had gardens, so nearly everyone got me to prepare their soil for planting. Margaret's parents had just come back to Motatau and I rotary-hoed their gardens and that's when I first saw her.

'We played tennis together. She already had two children and I loved children and I still do. And now I'm on to grandchildren. We have six of them. Twelve of our kids were planned. Only the last one wasn't.

One of the differences I noticed with my wife was that Pakehas bath or shower every day. We used to wash in the creek at night if we were dirty.

'But if we did nothing to get dirty I didn't see any point in washing – unless we were sweaty and that. On the other hand, Margaret religiously felt that the kids should be clean. I actually thought it was good for them to get dirty, playing in the mud – as long as they washed it all off afterwards.

'She would always be wiping their noses. I would be more inclined to teach them to do it themselves. Whereas Margaret would dress them and fix their food. I would be saying, "Let them get their own." So that was one of the differences: a Pakeha mum would always dote over her children, where I believed they should learn how to cook early, wash themselves, dress themselves. That was how we were brought up.

'She had a totally Pakeha upbringing, so things that we wouldn't bother about, like farting, did bother her. In her culture, you never ever do that, especially at the table or anything.

'Margaret is someone who doesn't complain so when I told her we did the washing in the creek she didn't object. The first time, she put the washing powder in the creek and it floated away! I said, "You have to put it in the tub and clean it with those washing boards." We did that for years until the 1980s when we shifted to where we are. Now she has a flash washing machine. We can afford to do those things now but in the early days we couldn't.

'Margaret understood. We had our own garden and we always had lots of food. We could kill a cattle beast. I knew how to make corned beef and bacon, how to pawhara eels. We had enough to share with others in our family. I think it was the culture that Dad taught. You give once and you receive twice. And Margaret is still like that. She's overgenerous to other people. I think she learnt a lot of that from her mother and it was reinforced by me.

'Although she had some Maori ancestry, I thought of Margaret as being Pakeha. She couldn't even say "Motatau" properly and they made her captain of the Motatau team and she had to practise and practise to pronounce the word. But she was willing to learn. Margaret would walk the four kilometres from the middle of the farm where we lived to get to the road and then down to the marae for the culture practice, twice a week. I wasn't keen on that so I would stay home. So she learnt Maori waiata and all the action songs.

'Margaret's first two children were treated the same as the others. When they were young I used to go up the farm and we'd sit them on the scrub bar in front of the tractor with braces and brackets to hold them there, and they would go to sleep. And when we had more children, we had Margaret sitting on one mudguard and children on the other side. If you had them on the tray they would go to sleep and fall off when we went over a big rut!

'When I look back I would attribute a lot of my own success to having a Pakeha wife. I think they're supportive of their men. Margaret is intelligent and has a very good academic understanding of everything. She's very good at numbers. We complement each other well. I couldn't care less about detail. Sometimes I have been treasurer for various organisations and Margaret is meticulous about the books. If there was one cent missing she would want to find it, and I would say, "Look, I'll give you the cent." She'd say, "That's not the point."

'In a community like Motatau, I was always secretary or treasurer, or both, on our committees because I was better at looking after money and the better one at writing. Even so, my writing was atrocious and Margaret used to do most of it for me. I would dictate and she'd write all the minutes up and the letters. When we got a typewriter she would type them up for me. It was easier when we got computers. Our children were all brought up to be computer literate.

'When I travel anywhere, Margaret says, "How long are you going for?" and "Are you speaking? You will need a tie and a suit." If I am on a field trip she'll pack walking clothes. She knows what's appropriate. Whereas I would wear a Swandri to a meeting and it wouldn't make any difference to me.

'I was a trustee with Ngati Hine Forestry and most of the people on the board had Maori as their first language. It was still my first language then, too. But because I was the best English speaker, the old people used to make me be the spokesperson. That's how I ended up unwittingly becoming a spokesperson for Ngati Hine.

'When I was appointed to the Bay of Islands College Board in 1984, that was the first time I had ever been on a real Pakeha committee and the following year I became chairman of it. I am still chairman. That was before our oldest started school there. Now I have had seven children through the college and I have four going there now and one more in primary school, so if I wait till the one in primary school finishes, I've got another eight years to go!

'I liked Pakeha meetings. At Maori hui people would turn up late and do a mihi that could go from 10 minutes to two hours. Pakeha meetings start on time, there's a quick welcome and then you're into the business. At Bay College I make sure we get through our business in an hour because we have good administrative support. On Maori committees there are rarely the same resources to back you up.

'In 1986 Sir James Henare asked me to chair a Maori Health Service development group for the Northland Area Health Board. My spoken English wasn't good. It was shocking, really, although my written English was okay. But exposure on all these boards meant that I was hearing English spoken around me all the time. I was often put off by the formality of "Mr Chairman" this and "Point of order, Mr Chairman" and so on. I wasn't much good at debating things, so if people opposed what I said, I just backed off and didn't push my ideas. Just the same, most of my life I've been in the governance area. I've never been the worker. I've always been on boards.

'Margaret was never prepared to go on committees herself. She talked me into accepting the treasurer role at the kohanga reo providing she did all the work. She didn't like being the front person, she was always one to support others. The children were supportive, too. They used to do photocopying for the marae and the runanga etc.

'At first we had one van, but as our family grew, the cars had to get bigger and bigger. I wanted to buy an 18-seater because Mum used to come out with us as well and she had some whangai with her and that was extra. My eldest kids said they wouldn't ride on a bus if I bought one! Now they are big enough so that we can travel in convoys.

'All the children are individuals, of course. When you have 13 you really notice their individuality. Some are quiet, some are helpful, some are comedians and some have a clear direction about what they want to do. We have the whole mix. If I started over again, I don't think I would change anything. I would like to have that diversity within the family again.

'Margaret's first two children understand the Maori language. The boy, Michael, mixes more with Maori mates, yet he's blond-haired with Pakeha features. Annette has always preferred Maori boyfriends and her girlfriends are also predominantly Maori because of the community she was brought up in.

From very early on, I used to tell my girls, don't blinking marry a Maori! Get a Pakeha.

'At least you won't get a hiding all the time because I felt that a lot of the Maori men were quite violent and didn't look after women properly. That was my advice to the older ones. It's changing now. My daughter in the army has got a lovely Maori man. I probably wouldn't give the same advice now because we have a new generation.

Ironically, I have never wanted to teach our children to speak Maori. And the thing we've argued about the most, from when I first met Margaret, was over the fact that I wouldn't talk to them in Maori.

'It's only since the little ones went through kohanga reo that I've changed. I used to think that speaking Maori was a weakness. But I've come to realise she was right. In our time there was Maori all around so it was easy to learn. But now you have got English all around and it's totally different.

'Margaret said Maori language would open doors for the children. I used to argue that it was my knowledge of Pakeha things that helped me in my life. But it turns out my Maori background has proved very useful too.

'Margaret and I never ever argue about race things. Funnily enough she's far more Maori than I am in a lot of ways because she realises what she lost through her Pakeha upbringing. I often have too much of a business approach to issues. I like to see if things stack up financially. However, I am all for doing things for social reasons, too – if there is a clear objective. For example, with our farm our family don't want to make millions of dollars. All they want is the land to be kept in the family so it's there for them to come whenever they want. They love the forest and we have a bush camp. We have got our own marae, and that's what they are happy with.

'Margaret thinks more about lining the marae walls and painting and all those other things. She makes sure there are proper cooking facilities, that the sanitation is okay. She thinks of the details. She does everything, like the wages, taxes and bills for us and our company, Prime Holdings.

'It is great having someone like Margaret with her culture and upbringing around. She'd never argue with me publicly or growl at the children. She will in private, of course. I have no trouble growling at the children in front of others if they are disobedient and I threaten to slap their ears, too, but she's very discreet.'

LOSARIA *Harimate McGruer is a teacher in a kura kaupapa Maori.*

She started adult life with limited education but now has a Diploma

in Teaching, a certificate in bilingual teaching and a degree in

Maori performing arts. Her Pakeha husband, Paul, has embraced

her culture and language in a way that makes her proud of him and

happy for their three children.

Losaria was born in Invercargill in 1963, although both of her Maori parents hail from the North Island. Her father, Hori Waho o Te Rangi

PHOTOGRAPH:

(l to r) Nikita (6 years), Paul, Losaria, Renata (5 weeks), Jamal (10 years)

Harimate, is from Tainui (Ngati Haua) and her mother, Hiria, is Ngati Porou, originally from Whareponga near Ruatoria. Hiria's father is a Pohatu from Mahia, but she was raised as a whangai by her aunties on the East Coast. Hori grew up at Ratana Pa so he lost contact with his Tainui whanau.

Life for the Harimate family was nomadic and dependent on the seasons. Losaria's father made his living in freezing works and shearing sheds. Her parents met while they were both in seasonal jobs and they moved to Invercargill together in search of work.

Losaria is one of seven children. 'Two of my oldest siblings were born in Te Puia Springs but the rest of us were born here in Invercargill. For six months of the year my father would work in Southland at the freezing works and for the remaining six months he moved us to the North Island to do the sheds there. So we grew up in the shearing sheds.

'My parents didn't really talk about different cultures. They didn't drink or go out, so everything to my dad was his family – and work. And my mother was the same. My dad worked with a lot of Pakeha but didn't mix with them socially. Outside the family, I didn't see the crossover between Maori and Pakeha. The only time Dad spoke to other Pakeha people was when the vehicle needed to be fixed or he was at the petrol station.'

The impact of changing attitudes in Maori society, and the wider community, to Maori language are very evident in the Harimate whanau. The three eldest children (including Losaria) were brought up without hearing Maori language spoken in the family, but as the years went by and the Maori cultural renaissance burgeoned, the reo was restored to the home.

Losaria is sad that, because of the social climate of the times, her parents did not teach her to speak Maori, even though they were fluent speakers.

'I left home at 15 to live with my nanny, and when I returned as an adult the reo was back in the home. The youngest brothers under me were brought up with the Maori language. By that time my mother was really hard and fast in the kohanga reo movement in Southland. She was one of the ones who supported the kaupapa in Invercargill. The movement would have changed her view of how her tamariki were brought up at that time. I felt a bit let down then that we older ones missed out, but I have found my own way to take me to my Maori side.'

Losaria tells a story about how her father came to learn the language in his forties to please his in-laws. Hori was not allowed to wed Losaria's mother unless he could speak Maori. 'So my father had to spend a bit of time with my grandmother and learn how to korero before they married. Learning the language in his forties made him stronger in his Ratana hahi [faith/church]. He was an Apotoro Wairua [unpaid minister], as my father would say, so my four younger brothers were brought up through the hahi. That's where the reo was introduced into their young lives. They all went to kohanga reo in Invercargill.'

Losaria's first opportunity to learn about Maori language came when she stayed with her mother's relatives on the East Coast for nearly two years, from the age of 15. 'I went to live in Whareponga with my nanny, a native speaker of the reo. Out of all my siblings, I am the only one that has actually followed the Ngati Porou side. My cousin influenced me. I went with her one time back to the Coast with her husband and whanau to visit her mother. My grandmother was there, too, and for some reason I wanted to stay and live there with my nanny.'

The seeds were sown for her love of the environment and language, even though she didn't converse with her nanny in Maori then and has been a speaker for only the past five years. 'Something must have clicked and was instilled in me when I came away from the coast. I had the reo around me and when the right moment arrived, it just seemed to come. Nowadays I can confidently korero to someone for most of the day if I have to.'

In Ruatoria, Losaria was at Ngata College with other teenagers from her whanau so she fitted in and was very happy. However, on returning to Invercargill she felt lost. Most of her old friends had left school and she saw herself as out of place. 'There were that many Pakeha in the system around me I felt uneasy, so I wagged school.' She lasted about a month and then quit college.

'Before I went to stay with Nanny I didn't feel different. It was, to me, a normal upbringing. When I was growing up I couldn't see the difference in the colour of people's skins. I didn't see any racism. It wasn't until I had gone away and come back that I saw it.'

What made Losaria most out of place was the way she spoke. 'It was the lingo thing. I'd lost that Invercargill dialect where you roll your "r"s, and people would say it was like someone coming from the bush and back into the city.'

Losaria headed north, first to Wanganui, then Otaki and Levin. Her first jobs were as a machinist and babysitter. In Levin she found work at the hospital as a kitchen hand and it was there that she met her future husband, Paul. He was her first Pakeha boyfriend.

'We got on easily and worked well together. He was tall, blond and blue-eyed and I thought he was a very shy guy. Paul wasn't like some Maori guys I'd dated. He didn't ask for anything and treated me like a lady. I'm still treated like a queen today. I'm very, very lucky.

His father wasn't very happy. He didn't like me at the beginning, because I was Maori, I think.

'My husband and I used to go out drinking once a week and meet up with his dad, but he'd ignore me. So we came to a bit of a clash, him and I.'

Losaria says Paul's father mellowed towards her after they had their children, but she still felt Paul's parents did not make the most of their grandchildren. 'We were living there and we were disappointed that they didn't really spend much time with us. And I thought, "Well, they have had their time to come and get to know our kids. So we will move back down to my family and my family will treat our kids differently."

'Before we were married, I took Paul back to Invercargill to meet my parents. He was the first man and also the first Pakeha that I'd brought home. So my dad opened his arms: "Whatever is ours is yours. You just help yourself." I never got the same respect from his parents. They are totally different. I thought they were a bit strange.

'Paul would probably say they are not whanau orientated. They didn't welcome me with open arms. I didn't let it get to me. I shrugged it off. In the end they probably did come to like me, although they never actually told me that. They told Paul.'

Losaria says Paul's mother shows much more interest in her grandchildren now. 'His mother can't talk enough about our kids. We send photos for Christmas and she has them plastered up, and when visitors come and say, "What beautiful children!" she says, "Yes, those are my little Maori grandchildren." We have been living down here for 10 years, and out of those 10 years she's been here once. It's hard for her to leave the North Island. Paul's father always said he would, but never did. He passed away in December 2002.

'The difference between our families was that my parents loved children and Paul has always slotted in very well with my whanau. My mother still enjoys all the grandchildren.'

Losaria and Paul have three children. The eldest, Jamal Paneta, is 11, Nikita Anahera is seven and the baby, Renata Paora Neil, has just turned one. All the children have been to kohanga reo and the eldest are in a kura kaupapa Maori.

'We speak half-and-half Maori and Pakeha to the kids. Paul's level of reo is the next step up from a beginner. He goes to Te Ara Reo classes and is doing well with talking and writing. I don't think I would ever be what you would call fluent. But I converse confidently. I teach students in te reo Maori at the kura kaupapa Maori. Paul is training to be a teacher in bilingual education.'

Losaria had a very unpleasant experience of racism not long after she, Paul and their baby boy moved to Invercargill. She went into a shop and outside were two skinheads, from a white racism group, waiting for a Maori boy who was inside. 'The Maori boy wanted to use the shop phone to ring the police. That poor boy wouldn't leave the shop until those skinheads had disappeared, but the shopkeeper people didn't really help. I was that scared that I bought what I needed and got into my car. I took off because I didn't know what to do. That was the first time I had ever seen that sort of thing.'

She's had one experience of racism in reverse within her own family. A relative, who dislikes Pakeha, once called Losaria and Paul 'white trash' during an argument. She doesn't have any contact with that relative any more.

Apart from that incident, Losaria hasn't been aware of any cultural gap between Paul and her whanau. 'In his job at the hospital back in Levin he was working with a lot of Maori. He had his first taste of Maori culture through that, and going to marae for birthdays and stuff. And when he met up with me, we went to marae quite often. When we had our first child we took our baby to kohanga reo and had turn about looking after him because of our jobs.

'I observe a lot of tikanga and that, with my tamariki, and with Paul. Sometimes he sees Maori people doing things that I have taught him not to do, and I say, "This is our whare and our tikanga."

I have taught him about tea towels – that they must be washed by themselves. Not wearing potae in the house, no brushes on the table. He learnt these things quite early and used to question a lot of them.

'But it's really only common sense in the end. He's coped quite well with the tikanga of things that I have taught him.'

Losaria says Paul has a good understanding about racism in New Zealand. 'He has learnt a lot at teachers' training college. He has been researching the Treaty of Waitangi and New Zealand history. He realises now that Maori, back then, were wronged. When Paul reads negative stuff about Maori in the paper, he sees that as Maori-bashing. He didn't like what Don Brash had to say about Maori.

'He has always thought he might have a bit of Maori in him. If you researched back, he may have. Who knows?

A lot of Maori men, and some of my colleagues, actually envy him for the things he does for Maori education and the input he has.

'He's very dedicated, especially on Maori education and anything that will benefit our tamariki. He enjoys it and says it's for our children at the end of the day. He goes to lots of Maori hui with Maori kaupapa. Everything he does is kaupapa Maori. He is driven for our kids.'

Although Losaria's whakapapa connections are in the North Island she feels she belongs in the Maori community of Invercargill. When there are Maori events of importance, she and Paul go to one of the three local marae. 'The main marae Paul and I go to, and are registered with, is Nga Hau e Wha in Invercargill. If someone in our whanau dies, we will go to Nga Hau e Wha for the tangi.' When it comes to a burial place she expects all her whanau will end up in the Invercargill city cemetery where her Dad's body lies.

Her father had been uprooted from his Waikato connections so it suited the family for him to be buried in Invercargill. It may be a departure from tradition but Losaria's mum will be buried there, too – in the city where she has lived for more than 40 years. 'Her Ngati Porou whanau would like her to go home but she's written it in her will that she wants to be buried here. Our children's whenua are buried in the gardens of our houses in Levin and Invercargill. I see it as going back into Papatuanuku, wherever it is. I don't see the need to go back to my tribal land for that.'

'We don't eat a lot of Maori food because the children are fussy about what they eat. Paul doesn't like seafood much unless it's fish and chips. I like rotten corn but Paul doesn't like the smell, so I don't have that unless it's at a marae somewhere. When we were growing up Dad used to go out and pick puha and watercress and go floundering. But today we get it from the shop. Kai Maori is not so plentiful as it was when I was growing up in this area. Just occasionally we'll have a boil-up but we don't get much Maori kai unless we go to a marae.'

The identity of the McGruer children seems to be well established as primarily Maori – while acknowledging their Pakeha background, too. 'Our children are Maori-looking. They are not dark but they look Maori rather than Pakeha. Our son is actually just beginning to learn English as an 11-year-old – making the transition into English – so he's enjoying that. Our daughter, who is seven, can read well, and for some reason she is able to read English even though she has not been taught to do so. She's quite forward for her age.'

Losaria has a vision for her children that they can walk in both worlds with their heads held high and understand both their Maori and Pakeha ancestry.

She says they need to be educated in both aspects of their cultures 'so they can confidently stand and korero about who they are and where they come from'.

'People in Invercargill might call us radicals because we put our children into a different sort of school. We don't see ourselves as radical, though. It is just giving things to our children that I didn't have when I was growing up. And the reo is here and it's free – or so-called free.'

Losaria is proud of her academic achievement in recent years in view of her early departure from secondary school. 'I now have a Diploma in Teaching from Rangakura at Whanganui Polytechnic and an 18-week bilingual teaching certificate and I recently completed a degree in Maori performing arts from Massey University with distance learning from tutors in Hastings. I did the learning through block modules.

'Since we left Levin we don't have best friends like we had before. So it's just our family. We still keep in touch with our old friends from Levin, where it is interesting that all Paul's friends are Pakeha and all mine are Maori. Down here, our world is us and our children. A lot of the kids think Paul is the best teacher and coach on earth and that our children are so lucky to have a dad like Paul.

'I think he needs a gold medal every day. He does everything. If the baby is crying he picks him up. I can switch off to the crying but he can't. I am happy to have a bit of a mess in the house because it's lived in. He likes to tidy everything up. I think it's because he had a short time in the army, things have to be in their place. He cooks and cleans, feeds the children, does the washing, hangs it out. And you wouldn't find a lot of men today doing all that.

'Paul is my rock. He is my everything. I would be lost without him.

I don't think there would be many Pakeha men who would be so generous and willing to embrace the Maori culture.

'A lot of my women colleagues say that. Even my mother thinks the world of him because his heart is in education for our tamariki and the Maori kaupapa. He is one of a kind. He has always said our marriage is fifty-fifty. I don't see differences between us. I just see love. I love this man so much I don't see any other culture but him and the children.

PAUL McGruer has been with Losaria for 19 years. They were married

in 1993. He's currently on study leave from the kura kaupapa Maori

where he taught NCEA cooking, while he studies fulltime to become

a qualified teacher. He holds positions unusual for a Pakeha, as a

trustee on the board of the kura and a member of the Maori arm of

the School Trustees' Association, Te Koru Puawai.

   Paul McGruer believes he is a Pakeha but is a bit hazy about his

racial background because, while he knows his mother is European,

he's uncertain about his father's paternal ancestry. Paul's father

was placed in a boys' home because his mother was unmarried. 'The

day my grandmother married my grandfather she came to collect

Dad. He was eight years old and he took on another name from

his stepfather.'

Until Paul's grandfather died, Paul thought he was descended from the McGruer family. But at the funeral he learnt his father's real name and that his grandfather by birth came from Wellington. Paul has not bothered to follow up on it further because he also learnt at the funeral that his dad hated his birth father. 'Dad's real father never contacted him. My real grandfather had nothing to do with my family and when he left my grandmother he didn't want any ties. He didn't even bother to contact his son (my father), so why should we make the effort?'

Paul was born in 1966 in Levin. He has an older and younger brother. For the most part he had little to do with Maori as he was growing up. 'My dad had a few Maori friends that he used to meet down at the Working Men's Club. Dad was mad on cricket and played the game for 20 years for the same club. So we three boys all played too. It was a really good childhood. We never went without anything. We always went on holidays and they were really good parents.'

At school, a high proportion of Paul's fellow pupils were Maori. He guesses it was something like 60 per cent Pakeha and 40 per cent Maori. Levin was flourishing in those days. He remembers that there were jobs at 'the Kimberley Hospital, the horticulture centre, the main caravan industry in New Zealand was in Levin, a licorice factory, the Nuthouse chippie factory, the eel factory. It was a big industry town, a lot of work. All the schools were full.'

Paul says there wasn't much offering in the school curriculum if you wanted to know anything about Maori things, unless you took it as an option in the fifth form. 'I had a couple of half-caste Maori mates. I had no problems or racist tendencies. I used to play cricket in Levin and there were a couple of Maori in my team, and one night we all went out for a drink at the Working Men's Club. My dad was there and this particular Maori guy, who played in my team, had had a scuffle three years earlier with my older brother, and my older brother was banned from the club. My father blamed this Maori fella for that altercation. I don't know whose fault it was. After we had had a few beers, my father and this Maori fella had an argument and my father said racist remarks to him in front of my wife-to-be, Losaria. He made comments about colour and Maori and that wasn't nice at all.

'My father was always a person who would have the last word and he would always nit-pick if he didn't like somebody.

A lot of Pakeha when I was growing up would say things like

Yeah, typical Maori!' That type of thing. Dad was that kind of person, although he never said anything really nasty.

'It was unfortunate that Losaria was there. It brought her to tears and we ended up leaving. She told me, "He obviously doesn't like Maori!" and that was three years before we got married.'

Losaria, Paul and their first son, Jamal, born in 1993, left Levin in 1995. 'Dad was the one who visited us the most, but even though my parents lived in the same town we didn't see that much of them. Losaria and my father got on quite well after that altercation in the club. I went around and we talked about it and he said it was nothing to do with her, just that him and this guy never saw eye to eye. He said, "I just didn't like what this fella did and I told him so." But he said he didn't mean it to apply to Maori in general. He said, "I've got all these Maori mates," and tried to make excuses. But Losaria and I both felt the things he said were hard to take.

'Dad and Losaria got on quite well in the end, when he was dying. Mum used to ring me up and say, "Dad might not say much, but he is proud of you and proud of Losaria, what she has done with her teaching and how you have brought up your kids and your move to Invercargill and how you have both got good jobs." He never said it to me or Losaria. It always came through Mum.

'My parents had grandchildren who were full Pakeha and ones that were half-caste. When all the photos of the kids are taken, you can see my son stand out – a little darker one.'

Paul is sorry that his late father did not really know his Maori grandchildren. However, he doesn't think it had anything to do with race and he acknowledges that Invercargill was a long way away for his parents to visit.

'My mum came down for Christmas 2003. It was the first time she had been down in the nine years we have been here. My kids just loved her and she loved being here. Our new baby was only six months and his being Maori never came into it. It was good as gold. The race thing was more my father. But over the years he had mellowed out. We would ring each other up every weekend and he would get on the phone and talk to my son and my daughter about sports. It annoyed me that he never came down here, but Mum came down only after he passed away.'

Paul's interest in Maori things began before he met Losaria. At 17 he started work in the kitchen at the local hospital. 'I used to deliver the food to the wards, and there was a large number of Maori staff, especially ladies in the canteen and the kitchen hands. My best friend's aunty married a Maori guy, and his wife worked there at the hospital. My friend used to make a few jokes about "They're all bloody Maori", or "bloody Horis", and I used to say, "But your uncle is one."

'The daughter of one of the ladies I worked with died while I was there so she had a Maori funeral, a proper tangi. And we all went there as part of the staff, and that was the first time I had seen a dead body open in the coffin. I was really quite scared. Luckily we went with Maori people we knew, but I was really nervous and didn't know what to do. I stayed and had a cuppa tea and went home.

'Before I met Losaria, I went to another couple of tangi and had a few social get-togethers and the guitar would come out and all the songs, and I felt quite at home. They were quite a good bunch of people to have a good time with. Once I met Losaria and her friends, we would go to other hospital functions over the years. She had a lot to do with Whanganui. Her father was Ratana and she took me there and showed me about her religion and all the Maori culture she is into there at Otaki and going to the marae there.'

Paul didn't think of Losaria as being different. 'We just got on really well. I was the cook, she was the kitchen hand and race never came into it. She met my mates and got on well with them. I was flatting with two other guys and she would come around and clean the house and they thought she was wonderful. They would drink with her and we would go out. My other two mates had girlfriends so we used to go out as three couples. Nothing about Maori came into it at all. We all keep in contact today, too.'

When Paul and Losaria went house-hunting for their move to Invercargill they experienced what they believed to be racism, although they could not prove it.

Losaria would apply for a flat to rent and was always unsuccessful. 'She thought it was because of her Maori name, so I decided to apply and I got them. It might have been a coincidence, but I don't know.

'I think New Zealand is a bit of a racist country. I don't think the Don Brash comments in his Orewa speech helped. The Waitangi Day things, the foreshore and seabed issue and the hikoi show we are a racist country because we can't agree on things. I think we have changed recently. Some days it's like New Zealand is moving along biculturally, but another day something comes up and the country is divided. Although I think we are a little bit racist, it's not as bad as what it could be.

'Everything Losaria and I do is involved with Maori.

I feel more comfortable in Maori culture than in my own. I notice that we have more Maori friends than Pakeha friends here in Invercargill.

'Nowadays I feel more comfortable going to a tangi than to a Pakeha funeral, or going to a noho marae where you spend the weekend at a meeting – sleeping, eating and talking with people.

When I first met Losaria's parents in 1988, after going out with her for two years, I got to her home in Invercargill and saw that her brother had dreads and they looked really rough and I thought, "Shit!" . . . but they really liked me and, from that day onwards, I have never met any

Maori that I have ever had a run-in with. Losaria spent a bit of her childhood in Ruatoria and even when I went there, about the time of the fire, with all the Rastas, and we went into the local pub and I was the only white person there, and they came over to me, and would buy me a jug and ask me if I wanted to play pool and I'd get on the pool table and win a few games, and it was awesome. Any Maori I have met has taken me in and been really nice to me. I just felt comfortable with anything Maori and I didn't know hardly any Maori language or culture. Over the years Losaria has taught me, and I have found things out for myself at kura, and going to the Ratana church, and through her parents and friends we have here and other close friends of hers that are now friends of both of us.'

From Paul's perspective the move to Invercargill in 1995 was difficult at first, but in time it opened up new opportunities. They moved at the request of Losaria's mum because her dad was dying. On arrival they found themselves with a child and no jobs, plus a mortgage still to pay on their house in Levin, which proved hard to sell. They moved in with Losaria's parents. Eventually Losaria began working as her mother's secretary on a training course. Paul took a job as a kitchen hand and two months later was promoted to head cook. In that same year Losaria began training for her new career in teaching. She was lucky to have part-time work for her mother while she was a student.

'I lasted at the hospital for 18 months and then Valentines restaurant opened up and I got a job as head chef. At the end of '98, the kura my wife was working at went away on school camp. They wanted parent help, so I offered to go and ended up being the cook. When we returned home the principal said, "The teachers were raving about you," and I was offered a job at the kura because of my hospitality experience. The kura job gave me more time with my wife and family and better hours.' Paul started teaching at the wharekura in early 1999 and also ran the canteen there. Over the years he got involved in NCEA planning.

If it hadn't been for Losaria I wouldn't have got into further education.

'When I left school I never thought of being a student again. Now Losaria has a teaching diploma and performing arts degree and I'm going for my teaching degree. We sold the house in Levin in '98 and ended up having enough money to buy a car and started saving for another house. I am really glad we made the move and it was the right time for us.

'My father-in-law lived for another couple of years after we came here, which was good. He got to know my son really well. He died early in 1998 when Jamal was four. They had a really good bond there. He would talk to him in Maori because my kids had been to kohanga. It is the same with my mother-in-law. They can have a conversation in Maori, no problem. My in-laws just loved being able to talk to the grandchildren. When my in-laws were at school they used to get whacked for speaking Maori. My mother-in-law was a big supporter of the kohanga movement here in Invercargill about 20 years ago. So with her mokos going to kohanga with the other kids, it's fantastic.

'I have just completed my level 2, Te Ara Reo. It's a free course one night a week. I watch Maori TV when I can. I learnt a lot when I was at the kura. There were a lot of fluent speakers there and they said, "The best way to learn Maori is just to listen to it, even though you may not understand. After a while you will get to know what people are talking about." So I used to go in the staffroom and just listen and ask them if I was getting it right.

'I've never been a person for public speaking. When I was a child I used to dread the thought of doing speeches. But my shyness disappeared after I'd been teaching at the kura for a year or so. I started with a class of 20. Earlier this year I took part in a Treaty of Waitangi symposium with the local NZEI [New Zealand Educational Institute] and I was asked to be a co-presenter and I said, "I will do it." Me and another lady actually presented this Treaty workshop. I was as nervous as hell but when I did it, people came up to me and said, "You did a great job. Would you like to do one in Bluff?" And a few times now at teachers' college we have had to do presentations and I did one, with PowerPoint display, about my life and my bicultural family. I got an "A". I was rapt.

I have even had to talk on a marae. You know how you go to a powhiri and you get welcomed on? Well, I found myself in a situation where I had to get up and speak in Maori, and that is one of the things I have always dreaded.

'It was only a short speech and just a basic introduction. There were probably 30 people there. I was really nervous. I have to do speeches at teachers' college, too, because I am in the bilingual unit. Me and the other guy had to do the korero for the whole campus to these manuhiri from Hong Kong recently. It's an honour but it's a real nervous one. Three years ago I would have refused to do it. But now I am prepared to take it on when I have to. And a lot of that is to do with meeting Losaria's friends and family, being in the school and teaching.

'I would not be speaking in public at all if I had not become involved in the Maori culture. I find myself so much more relaxed in Maori culture.

I was one of only two Pakeha at the kura and they called me 'Matua'. They don't seem to see me as a Pakeha.

'The kids always ask me what my iwi is, but when I say I am Pakeha they are quite shocked. A lot of Ngai Tahu are fair-skinned, so they assume I am Ngai Tahu.

'My kids are bicultural and you can't change that. I want to learn about their heritage as well as my own. So some people sort of admire me for what I do. You feel a bit embarrassed, but I'm happy and feel proud about how I am learning every day – things about the Treaty and other bits and pieces.'

Paul believes people in bicultural marriages need to compromise and make efforts to understand their partner's culture. 'Pakeha culture is all around you anyway. But we have talked about my family and their background. I can go back only to my grandparents with my Pakeha culture. But Losaria can track her whanau back many generations.

when our kids do their whakapapa at school and family trees, they will go to their Maori side. That doesn't bother me at all and I am quite accepting of that.

'If I didn't get to know the Maori culture, then the kids wouldn't be going to kohanga or kura. I think my kids are lucky because they are bicultural. They are comfortable in both worlds and can speak two languages. There wouldn't be many kids who can have a good conversation in two languages. Even though they go to an immersion school, they are brought up in a Pakeha world. My kids wouldn't have been that way if I hadn't supported my wife's culture. They can rattle off my in-laws' whakapapa.

'I know lots of Maori kids who have no Maori language at all and go to a mainstream school. They are really good with their Pakeha side, but one of the parents, who is Maori, told their Maori kids, "You are never going to get anywhere learning that Maori stuff," so they don't bother. My personal opinion is that the kids miss out on their own history. So I am all for biculturalism, I think it's important.'

Paul belongs to a Maori arm of the NZEI, Aronui Tomua, which represents Maori primary teachers and support staff throughout the country. 'I was a staff rep for the wharekura for the last three years on the school board of trustees. Now I am on the board as a parent rep. In New Zealand there is a School Trustees' Association based on 11 regions. About three years ago, another region started to support Maori trustees called Te Koru Puawai. I am a member of that national body. I think I'm the only Pakeha but I'm there because I'm on the board of a wharekura.

'I used to call myself a Jaffa – until I found out it has another meaning about Aucklanders, too. What I say is, a Jaffa is red, but it goes white when you suck it and then it's brown on the inside. That's like me – white on the outside and brown on the inside. So I am totally Maori in my heart and everything inside is more Maori than Pakeha.'

The O'Regans

SANDRA *O'Regan is a Pakeha spouse who knows what it's like to share the weight of tribal obligations placed on a Maori leader. She is married to Sir Tipene O'Regan, a potent voice in New Zealand and Maori politics. Sandra is little known by the public but her part in Tipene's influential career has been significant. She trained as a teacher and then as a nurse and has worked at many jobs, even through the night, to keep the family afloat during tough times.*

PHOTOGRAPH:

Tipene and Sandra O'Regan, 1994

She and Tipene (also known as Steve) have five children and

13 grandchildren. They live in Wellington.

Sandra was born in Wellington in 1943, a third-generation New Zealand of Scottish, Irish and English ancestry. Her father, from a West Coast family, moved to Wellington to train when he joined the army and that's where he met Sandra's mother, a clerk at the Reserve Bank. Returning from the war, her father joined the government, studied at night school and became a civil engineer.

'We lived in a state house in Johnsonville from when I was five. I suppose we were middle class in the sense of my father's job, but we were really quite poor. Our family had no contact with Maori while I was at home, although after I was married my father transferred to Rotorua with the Ministry of Works where he had a tremendous amount to do with Maori people.'

Sandra says there were only a few identifiable Maori families when she went to primary school and Wellington Girls' College. 'At primary school, one family met the stereotype. They were rough, you were scared of them, they were bullies with bare feet and runny noses and all those sorts of things. Another family I sort of knew was Maori but I didn't think much about it because they didn't fit the stereotype of that time. They were clean and well dressed and achievers.

'I must have had preconceived ideas about what Maori were like, but I'm not sure where it came from because my father never expressed those things.

My mother was a typical snob of that era. She used the word 'common' to describe just about everyone and I think Maori were 'common', too.

'I met Steve when we were both at university part-time. I didn't like him and I ignored him for a long time. On one occasion my girlfriend and I were walking along Lambton Quay, and this drunken creature staggered out from a pub and greeted my friend and asked to be introduced to me, and I just walked on in disgust. I didn't like drunk people. He'd been celebrating the birth of his friend's baby.

'I didn't know he was Maori, but he used to ask my girlfriend about me. She'd tell me he wanted to see me and in the course of that I learnt he was Maori and on the student executive.

'I was absolutely against racism. I didn't know really what it was, except I'd read lots of books on slavery and bad treatment of indigenous peoples, primarily American Indians and "Negroes", as we called them. My sense of justice was that everyone should be treated equally. It was a very immature and simplistic attitude toward racism but I held it strongly.

'Steve and I both worked in government departments. He was at the Parliamentary Library and I was at Industry and Commerce. He had a motor scooter and he stopped one day at the bottom of the Terrace and offered me a ride to my university lecture. I gave in to the temptation of a ride up the hill, and that carried on.

'It was not that I fancied him then. We were friendly but I was more interested in having my ride and just socialising for 15 minutes in the common room at the university to pay for it. I wouldn't go out with him, but I was in danger of losing my ride because there were others who were reasonably interested in him, so I finally agreed that I'd go to the movies with him – to protect my ride.

'Steve was very verbal and I was very inarticulate. I didn't know how people like him knew so much and were able to express themselves without sitting and working out for an hour what to say. After all, I was only 17.

'On the night Steve and I were due to go to the movies, I got home and found my mother was in labour, my father was at a conference, and I had to drive her to the hospital.

I rang Steve and told him I couldn't go because Mum was having a baby. He thought he'd had some pretty dramatic put-downs in his time but this beat the band!

'After that, I lost my ride and we didn't see anything of each other until my nineteenth birthday when Steve rang up and asked me to go sailing for the day. I agreed and we got engaged three weeks later.

'I didn't have a very good relationship with my mother but she liked the idea that Steve's father was a surgeon. In those days it was just about as good to have your daughter marry the son of a doctor as it was to marry a doctor. My father said I shouldn't marry Steve because he was a Catholic and a Maori.

'I agreed with his reservations about the Catholic side of it. But I was appalled that my father had seized on the Maori aspect and I reacted strongly to that, accusing him of being a bigoted racist. He also said that I was too young, which I was. But I just focused on the Maori side of it. Basically what he was saying, although it took me a long time to recognise it, was that I had no awareness of people from different backgrounds and cultures and because I was so young it would cause problems. He was absolutely right. So he wasn't racist in that sense. But of course I focused on that and it gave me the stimulus to do my own thing.

'Steve's parents didn't like the idea of our marriage because I was a Protestant. Steve had drifted from the church and he certainly wasn't behaving and doing the things a good Catholic should do – especially like marrying a Catholic. His mother was an extraordinarily gentle and gracious woman who could hold her own in the Pakeha world. She was socially adept and so on, but she had this Maori side to her, too. She managed to incorporate both. She'd had a tough time being a Maori married to a Pakeha doctor.

'Many in Wellington society thought their mixed marriage appalling. Once a year some disaffected person phoned his father at Christmas time to talk about that "Maori whore" or that "Maori bitch" that he'd married. She'd escaped from Bluff, a tough life down there, and come to Wellington and trained as a nurse – which is how she met my father-in-law.

'By the time I met her she was in her sixties and she had diabetes and heart problems so she looked much older. She had white hair with a blue rinse. She was very Maori in some ways, but equally she didn't look particularly Maori. Rather like Steve.

'After we married we both wanted to go overseas. We were booked to go in January 1964, but I got pregnant and had a baby at the end of the year. We still intended to go overseas and then there were complications with the boat bookings. We both ended up enrolling at teachers' college to give ourselves a qualification before travelling. My in-laws, who were keen on this idea, let us stay in a flat underneath their house rent-free and looked after the baby while we were training.

'We were the first married couple that went to teachers' college. Lots of people married while they were there, usually because they got pregnant, but we were already married so I was a mature student with a baby at the age of 20.

At teachers' college there was a Maori Studies elective which we both took and I have to say that, at first, my marks were higher than Steve's!

'We became interested in education and the Maori side of it. If you were looking at wrong or inadequate things in education, they were much more evident among Maori. So that's where our focus on Maori disadvantage and problems and the study of those things arose. It was the beginning of our real involvement in things Maori.

'Steve became passionately involved and at the same time he had contact with Ngai Tahu. They had sometimes asked him to do research and prepare submissions for select committees and so on when he worked at the Parliamentary Library. We didn't go to Ngai Tahu maraes. He was just a behind-the-scenes worker. So while there was contact, there wasn't much time for wider involvement. There was a baby and postgraduate study and work during the holidays to get some extra money.

'At teachers' college we made trips up the Whanganui River. So, even though Steve was doing things for Ngai Tahu, our real Maori contact was with people of Whanganui.

'At the end of our two-year course I had our second daughter and we built a house at Paekakariki with a State Advances Corporation loan and capitalised family benefit. Steve began his teaching there. He did his Honours degree part-time and took some more Maori-based courses, especially his postgraduate research papers. He was also a member of the Maori Graduates' Association, which was pushing for law changes and Treaty of Waitangi things, and the establishment of Maori language in the universities.

'In his second year of teaching he was seconded back to the teachers' college to teach in the Social Studies Department, focusing on Maori. He was there for 17 years. The Maori Studies Department was established and he developed and headed that. Still, Steve's main links at that time were with tribes like Whanganui, Taranaki, Ngati Porou up the East Coast and Tuhoe rather than Ngai Tahu.

'Then in 1976 Frank Winter died and Steve was co-opted onto the Ngai Tahu Maori Trust Board to replace him as the North Island representative. Steve was young for the job and it was a big responsibility with an ever-increasing family.

'People assumed we had a big family because of the Catholic name O'Regan, but it was really to do with failed contraception. I had four children when I was using contraception. I probably wouldn't have had any babies if I didn't use it. In fact, I was sterilised before I had Hana!

'Steve took his students on field trips to Rotorua and Ngati Porou, up to Tikitiki and Rangitukia, and up the Whanganui river, and he had to make trips down south, too. I never went because I was having, or caring for, babies and I also had to work.

We were so broke that I worked odd jobs, usually at night. I was never free to go with him. For many years I think Ngai Tahu thought I was a myth.

'I constantly resented the fact that he was spending so much time doing work for Ngai Tahu. I supported it, in that I thought it needed to be done, but there would always be some issue that needed to be worked on. One assumed that once an issue was over, one would be free to get on with one's life. It took me a long time to realise that that never happens. Thirty years later, we actually had to decide to disengage, because nothing stopped, nothing was ever finished and over. It just built and built and built.

'As Steve became more and more involved with the Ngai Tahu claim, I had to work longer hours to support our family. We were always broke, really broke. I worked in the toll exchange at night. At one point my sister was living with us for about a year and we'd alternate with the babysitting. She worked at tolls, too. We arranged our shifts so that someone was home to look after the children. Steve also did a lot of the babysitting, but because he was away a lot of the time, we had to be reasonably independent of his timetable.

'I decided I didn't want to go back to teaching and I would go nursing instead. So the day Hana, our youngest, started school I began my nursing training. During my training I still worked at the telephone answering service two nights a week. By that time my eldest daughter was old enough to babysit while I was at work if Steve was away. I had to work those nights because of the cost of Steve being involved with Ngai Tahu.

'Ngai Tahu didn't have any money, although they usually managed to repay his fare to Christchurch. In the early 1970s, he went by ferry to Christchurch. He'd go down overnight, or take the old car over to Picton and drive down. If it was school holidays, or there was something other than just a board meeting he had to go to, I made him take some of the children. As a result, they had much more direct exposure to things Maori than I did. I was at home looking after whoever was left and working to earn our living.

'It made me feel very left out of the Maori world the rest of my family were part of. My children, during their childhood, have been to far more places than I've been to. If Steve was away on a field trip he had to take a couple, if not all of them.

'As his involvement grew, I was less and less involved. We talked about the issues a lot and I believed in it all quite deeply, but I wasn't involved directly. I'd threaten divorce one moment, and then I'd get angry about whatever the current issue was and say, "Well, they can't get away with that. Go and do this!" I basically supported it, and because we'd talked about it, I was involved with things vicariously through him. I would give him my views and opinions on what should happen and, in that sense, we generally operated as a team intellectually.

'There were things that really brought the injustices suffered by Maori home to me. In the 1970s Steve was involved with the change to the law that allowed Maori land to be taken under the Public Works Act without compensation. We knew people that this had happened to, and we could see how wrong it had been historically. Most people didn't know it was happening and wouldn't have believed it anyhow. Steve would get calls from people or communities in different parts of the country and he had to go and fight for those things. The need to do something was obvious to me – like black and white.

'I was angrier than him about what was happening in the society that we were living in. It all seemed so hypocritical, so ignorant. He just felt that it was something that had to be dealt with and you got on and did it. I think for a long time he felt it was because of ignorance and he was in a teaching situation so he had a means of doing something about it. A lot of change did occur.

So many of the things that he was involved in were effective. The only trouble was that these issues took time and resources – especially the family time and resources!

'Tipene began to attract a lot of public criticism, too. He'd be on television or be quoted in the papers whenever there was some issue happening, and it was an era when people didn't want to know about things Maori because we had "wonderful race relations" . . . or so everyone said.

'He was the face that started saying, "It's not quite like that," and "There are problems in the future if we don't change things." People found that unacceptable. My family found it unacceptable, too. I became alienated from them because, once they'd gone to Rotorua, my mother found it very difficult in her new social milieu to admit that her daughter was married to that troublesome Maori on the television.

'Most of the criticism of Steve was racist and there were letters to the paper and other media stories. It fascinated me that, almost inevitably, they would focus on him having "changed his name". I still call him "Steve", but in a Maori situation I'll call him "Tipene". It just comes naturally. He's never changed his name. Tipene's just the word for Stephen. In fact I usually call him "Tiwi", which has been his family nickname since he was a baby, which I presume is the Maori for Steve rather than Stephen. I go between one and the other unconsciously. At a marae, people speaking in Maori would call him Tipene and so it would be reported as "Tipene O'Regan", at which point people would start getting upset about him because he's a "born-again Maori", or "changed into a Maori". We had to just ignore those things and learn to laugh at them.

'I've experienced prejudice, too. Steve's been told by various people in the Maori world that he really ought to get rid of me and get a proper Maori wife. These were people who either wanted Maori to only marry Maori or people down south who didn't believe that he had a real wife because they never saw me!

> *It struck me as pretty ironic when people started to talk about Tipene being on the gravy train after we'd had such a struggle with money and I'd helped to pay for so much of his Ngai Tahu involvement.*

'I worked for 12 years as a nurse, much of it on night duty. The only family holiday we ever had was when Hana was 11 months old. During the claim period our outgoings in salaries and office expenses and everything else were about $300,000 a year. Ngai Tahu paid $200,000 but we made up the shortfall.

'If Steve hadn't been earning decent money from the Fisheries Commission there's no way we could've done that. Part-way through I stopped nursing, which I loved, and worked with him. I was the only one, through years of osmosis, who knew what was being covered in all those issues.

'If there has been any cultural difficulty in our marriage it's the years of obligation that Tipene felt, and had put on him, to work for his iwi. If people are thinking of getting into a cross-cultural marriage it helps to know what they're actually going into. I was married so young I didn't know what path I would be heading down. It has been incredibly difficult. There hasn't been sufficient time for our children. That's my biggest regret.

'The children have all survived and done well in their own way, but they've certainly been subjected to an awful lot of strain and missed out because we didn't have the money or Dad wasn't around or Mum was at work or whatever. They weren't left on their own, but sleep has always been a prime requirement on my part as I worked at night. That's been my biggest regret – that surely you could be Maori or have a cross-cultural marriage without being involved to that extent. It was a great relief to me when he pulled back from most of his tribal involvement.

'The cross-cultural side has been difficult, too, because there's been so much antagonism towards him for being "Pakeha-turned-Maori" by those who choose to write off whatever he's doing on that basis. And that's come as much from Maori as it has from Pakeha.

'We were always very positive about our children being Maori. That was another dimension to their life. They had their own difficulties with it. We lived in the middle of Wellington and we were busy. They went off to marae and hui and whatever, but that wasn't all the time, so they predominantly had a Pakeha upbringing because of where we live and the schools they went to. I think they also had another difficulty, in that they were seen as the privileged children of a leader.

'All the children look Pakeha, some more than others. They've all had experiences of being put down for acknowledging their Maori heritage. It's worried some of them and others it hasn't. The four girls have Maori names that many can't pronounce. Rena gets "Rina", Taone gets a range of things, including "Toenail", Miria gets "Maria" or "Amelia" and Hana gets "Hannah".

'I think the two older girls probably had a more Pakeha experience than the others. They both live overseas now. Our eldest daughter, Rena, chose to teach in South Auckland in primary schools that were predominantly Maori and Polynesian, but she found that very difficult, too. Being Tipene's daughter, there was an expectation that she was culturally competent in every sense and she found that difficult. She

Back (*l to r*) Rena, Sandra, Taone
Front (*l to r*) Miria, Hana, Gerard. 1973

ploughed on and helped establish a marae at one of the schools, but she did it on her own terms. I think she was probably a bit like me. She believed that certain things were important and she did them, but all our children resented the expectations that were placed on them, by Pakeha and Maori, as Tipene O'Regan's offspring. Those expectations were usually negative.

'Our second daughter, Taone, went nursing and specialised as a psychiatric nurse. At some point, there was an expectation that she would automatically be knowledgeable about Maori mental health. She was, to a significant degree, but the expectations were unrealistic. She lives in London now, married to a Welshman with three little children. For the last seven years they've taken their children along on Saturdays to the kohanga reo at New Zealand House. Her children, who were all born in London, regard themselves as part-Maori, but of course if they came back here and proclaimed that they'd be laughed at.

'Our son did his BA in Maori Anthropology and he's worked at museums in the Maori area and as the heritage manager for Ngai Tahu. He's back at university in Auckland studying archaeology.

'Miria is the fairest of our children. She has white skin, blue eyes and bright red hair. People do not believe her when she says she is Maori. She has had a lot to put up with because we discovered only recently that she'd had a broken neck since she was about three. Now she has two big titanium bolts through her neck. She'd been suffering from headaches for years because a bone was hitting her spinal cord.

'When Hana was six she had her right hand cut off in a freak accident and had to have it sewn back on. She had years of physiotherapy and further surgery, and so the household revolved around that. Miria, who was four years older, was a bit neglected at that time. She had the responsibility of making sure Hana got home safely from school, or taking her to physio. I was working. As an adult, Hana has quite a high profile as a Maori speaker and promoter of the language for Ngai Tahu.

I think my father was probably right. I shouldn't have married a Maori and a Catholic. I've been able to deal with the Catholic side of it, but I sure as hell didn't know what I was going into on the Ngai Tahu side.

'But I must add that Steve's father and grandfather were involved in politics, so before we got married I made Steve promise that he would never go into politics. I've been spared that. He was interested and involved in politics and always has been, but promised that he would never formally go into it and he has stuck to that. I didn't know there was a back door called "Maori"! I think if I'd had the same view or knowledge about Maori as I'd had about politics at the time, I probably would have vetoed the Maori thing, too!

MIRIA *O'Regan was born in 1969 and is the fourth of the O'Regan*

children. Unlike her siblings, she inherited very fair skin and red

hair from the genes of both her parents. She has a Pakeha partner

and three children.

'In my family I feel different. I think every red-haired child does. It was other people who made me feel it because they always commented on how different I was. As kids we spent half the time trying to convince people Gerard was my brother and the girls were my sisters.

We had lots of arguments with other Maori kids on the marae, when we were little, about whether I was a Maori. I felt like I was defending myself all the time.

'It made my experience of the marae different from the others'. It was the feeling that I didn't belong as much. I didn't feel comfortable with other Maori children.

'I liked hanging out with the tauas [senior women] and being at the back in the kitchen. The old tauas gave unconditional love. They'd hug me and knew who I was and they treated me nicely.

'Nowadays, I don't spend much time on marae. It's not a place I go and feel relaxed. At one time we went away a lot to marae with Dad when he was lecturing at the teachers' college. Mum was working around the clock and he used to have to take us when he was taking his students away.

'I never related to my mother's family – only Dad's side. But on the marae I found it tedious. I couldn't usually understand what was going on. I remember sitting there wanting Dad to just be quiet. He was always the last to speak and usually the longest. As a very young child I knew the right thing to do and we would sit there patiently and listen, but it was hard. It was probably because I didn't feel comfortable in my colouring and lacked self-confidence. My younger sister, Hana, had this craving for the Maori language, whereas I was very self-conscious and I had very bad pronunciation and I couldn't roll my "r"s.

'Having bicultural parents meant we were different.

At Kelburn School I identified as being Maori and I had the same arguments with my pakeha mates. They wouldn't believe me either and I was defending myself from both sides.

'And at that period my father wasn't very popular with the public. It was during the Springbok tour era. We went on marches with Dad and I was the only one in the class who did and I had arguments with my classmates about it. I was called names. My father was a "radical" and it was always an issue. I always felt I was trying to stick up for him. I was very proud of him, but I was always on the defensive waiting for the attacks to come.

'My way of coping was to put my shoulders back and say, "Get stuffed!" to everybody and I was labelled as the mad redhead, the redhead with the shocking temper. I lived up to the stereotype of redheads.

'Even my name has posed difficulties for me. I pronounce the "r" in Miria as a "d", and can't roll the "r". I have a complex about that. I tell people my name and they say, "What?" Teachers would ask me how to say my name properly, and after the second or third time I would just say "Maria", because the next part of that conversation would be, "How come you have a Maori name?" Then the conversation would end up, "Oh, you're not related to that Stephen O'Regan, are you?" And so it would go on. I used to avoid those conversations.

'The demands of driving the Ngai Tahu Treaty claim made a big difference to our family life. Mum was always working to keep it going. Most of Dad's work for Ngai Tahu was unpaid and the wage he was on didn't fund the amount of travel he had to do around the South Island.

A few years ago I felt very angry towards Ngai Tahu. People in the tribe don't seem to realise what my father did and what we have all missed out on as children.

'He wasn't there for us for 80 per cent of the time. In the holidays we went away with him but he was always tied up with work. My mother has worked her whole life and brought up five children and done so much for Ngai Tahu. I felt they weren't grateful. I know many of them show their gratitude in many different forms, but I felt that they didn't appreciate my parents' contribution. Dad could not have done what he did without Mum.

'Looking back I'm just amazed at what my mother did at the time and the way she totally supported him. Considering where she came from and her background, I find that amazing. The other thing that used to peeve me off was the publicity around Dad and the "fat cat" label he carried for quite a few years as chairman of the Fisheries Commission. You feel like screaming at the world. He could have made 10 times more if he had gone out privately and looked after himself. My parents could have retired 10 times over – without huge mortgages in their sixties.

'We basically felt like we were poor. We lived in an old house in Wellington that wasn't done up, there were five of us, Dad was always away doing his Ngai Tahu stuff and Mum was always working. That's how I always remember it. Later their house became a lovely central city home because Dad did all the handiwork on it himself. I have seen huge job offers he received from overseas that would have set him up financially, but it would have taken him away from the tribe so he refused them. After the settlement, when the tribe didn't offer him a role, that really gutted him.

'There were gains for us five kids, of course. I remember we used to watch him work so hard and be very impressed by him. There were always interesting people in the house and we had our trips to marae around the country. The discussion at the table was always lively and Mum was involved in that.

'I had problems with learning, unlike all the others in my family. I had a broken neck for 30 years and no one knew. I didn't have a very long concentration span because it was too painful to hold my head up for very long and I would lie my head down and go to sleep in class. Nowadays, I have two huge bolts holding my head on. I am still in pain, but it's managed and I am lucky to be alive, because in theory a cough could have killed me instantly. I am able to understand my life better now that I know about my neck.

'I had a baby at 16. I left home when I was 14 and never returned

(l to r) Georgia, Miria, Jessica and Ana O'Regan-Gray

home to live. I went down a very hard path, but I managed to survive it and basically get through it. I've been in a relationship with my partner, John, for nearly 17 years. I met him when my eldest daughter was one and he has brought her up as his own. We have two other children. John is Pakeha and we live a very Pakeha life, although we have Maori friends, too. I live in Wainuiomata and it's very racially mixed. Maori things are still a part of my life, but I am most comfortable on a Ngai Tahu marae. Outside of Ngai Tahu I am on the defensive straight away. I am still not confident about myself because, knowing my family connections, I suspect people will tend to expect too much of me.

'Issues like the foreshore and seabed are openly debated in our house. John's information comes from what he sees on television and in the news, and his discussions with Dad. You couldn't put him in the totally ignorant redneck basket. Last time we went to Te Kaha he had to pay $10 to get on the beach to fish, so them saying they are not going to charge to get on the beach is a lot of rubbish. That's where John's views come from. My father discusses it with him, but they often don't actually understand what the other one is trying to say. It doesn't end up as an argument. I think they have respect for each other and I think Dad understands and knows the level of information John is basing his opinions on. They both give their views, then start talking about fish and how to cook it.

'When the whole family is around we get into big debates about such topics. I will tend to go and do the dishes. They are on another level intellectually and it goes above me. I *choose* to disengage, so I don't find it a problem.

'Our eldest child, Jessica, took Maori at college and my children have spent time with Dad and Mum going away to marae, so they feel reasonably comfortable in those things. Jessica received a scholarship from Ngai Tahu to do her chefs' course in Christchurch. She's interested in her Ngai Tahu background and I am proud of her. The others have also learnt some Maori and they all get help with their reo from their aunt, Hana.

Ana is still not totally sure and confident. Once, after being away with Hana, she came back and said her mihi and so on and then said proudly, 'I'm Maori.' I heard her own father say, 'No, you're not!'

'"What do you mean? You've got a bit in you. It doesn't make you Maori." And we started the whole argument over again with him! Even though he has heard bits of how I feel. It was like, "Oh, my gosh! Here we go again!"

'Being Maori is about whakapapa but it's also about how you feel. You are allowed to call yourself what you like. It's what you relate to and how you feel. But our girls sometimes get a different message from their father. John and I have talked about it. He doesn't understand it. He is from a blue-collar, suburban type of background and has had no exposure, apart from me, to marae and Maori identity issues. Lots of his friends are Maori and they grew up together. To him, there's no difference. He definitely is not racist. But he just doesn't have an understanding of the whole concept of Maori and how you don't have to be half-Maori or have the right colouring. Even being with me for 17 years he doesn't have an understanding of how his comments affect us.

'John has never been on a marae with us. If we went to a tangi, it would be me and the children. He has no problem with it but he doesn't feel like there's a place there for him. He thinks Ana, as a blue-eyed redhead, will make herself look foolish standing up and telling everyone she's Maori. He says she doesn't live that life, she's not involved in it, she doesn't speak it. I find the discussion quite disturbing. He couldn't understand why I got so upset and didn't want him to say such things to our children. We have had to agree to leave this subject alone because there's just no point discussing it.

'I still have a problem filling in forms which ask if you are Maori or New Zealand Pakeha. I tend to go for Maori. Sometimes I write Ngai Tahu. I always vote on the Maori roll. For my kids I always put their iwi on forms. I feel a bit divided but then, at the end of the day, if I had to say which side of the fence I was on, I would call myself Maori. That's just how I feel and what I have learnt as a child. When I die I want to be buried in the South Island and I always feel a strong connection to the place. To me that's how I feel Maori.'

✠

HANA *O'Regan is the youngest of Sandra and Tipene's five children.*

She was born in 1973, grew up in Wellington, went to a Maori

boarding school in Auckland for her secondary schooling and

was an AFS Scholar in Thailand for a year before completing a

Bachelors in Maori and Political Science at Victoria University and

a Masters with Distinction from Otago University. She specialises

in Maori language and identity politics and taught Maori language

in tertiary institutions for 10 years. She's now working for Ngai

Tahu Development Corporation championing the revitalisation of

the Maori language within Ngai Tahu and the South Island. She's

a member of the Maori Language Commission. Hana's Masters

thesis from Otago University, 'Ko Tahu Ko Au – Kai Tahu Tribal

Identity', was published in 2000. She has had severe endometriosis

since puberty, requiring five operations since she was 23, but she has

been able to have two healthy children.

One of Hana O'Regan's earliest preschool memories is going with the rest of her siblings to culture club practices and absolutely loving the Maori songs. She knew even then that this was something that most other people didn't do. And this difference was more in her consciousness when she had the accident which severed her hand at the age of six.

'My big worry in the hospital was about losing my Maori blood. In my six-year-old mind I was concerned that only a part of me was Maori and I was disturbed that I might lose it. This demonstrates that I already knew something about my identity as being of mixed descent. I knew people broke that into parts and I wondered which part was Maori.

'I remember my Pakeha grandfather breaking up my Maori ancestry into eighths and feeling that, because people did break it up, somehow it wasn't enough. At the same time I also had an idea about what it meant in terms of whakapapa, in terms of genealogy and also in terms of participation in cultural activites that went with it.

'The hand injury was a turning point in my life because a friend of my father, Te Aue Davis, became involved in my life and helped me to get my hand functioning again. She wasn't Ngai Tahu, but I spent many school holidays with her. I would traipse around the country with her and I was exposed to a wealth of different experiences. One of the things that struck me was going back to her people in Te Kuiti and meeting her aunties, who were very old at the time. That was when it really started to sink in for me that I was different. I was the honky, the white kid, and now and then they would call me "honky", but not in a hurtful way. I used to go around people at the marae and say, "Are you

Hana at Queen Victoria School for Girls,
aged 16 years

Ngai Tahu?" "Are you Ngai Tahu?" trying to find another one like me.

'I was so keen on learning Maori that I remember getting a buzz sitting through a powhiri as a little girl and I would annoy Dad trying to get translations of what I didn't understand.

'When I was coming up to 12 years old I was sent to board at Queen Victoria School for Girls so that I could do what I really wanted and learn Maori. At the age of 14, I wrote in my diary that what I wanted to do with my life was to work with my tribe and the language. I didn't enjoy boarding school.

I found it difficult being Ngai Tahu, because I was a white little thing who didn't look the slightest bit Maori in a piupiu up on stage or anywhere else.

'Ngai Tahu weren't very well known and there was still a belief that there weren't very many Maori in the South Island and so I couldn't be a Maori from there because we didn't exist. It was a pretty common perception.

'I was luckier in terms of timing than my siblings. My two eldest sisters didn't have the opportunity to learn Maori at school. My mother probably gave more active support to me in terms of my Maori language than my father. That's because she was around more. Often if she needed to get a message to Dad without anyone else knowing, she would get me to say it in Maori. Mum understood, better than Dad, my need to feel secure in the language, but he was very proud of me.

'My peers were a lot less forgiving about my fairness and my background so I often felt more comfortable with the older people, sitting and learning from them. I have to confess I still hate going to a hui alone. I have improved, because when I was a secondary school senior I was getting a particularly hard time, being called "honky" and "not Maori enough", and my father said, "Darling, you are Ngai Tahu. You have that whakapapa. No one can ever take that away from you. You don't have to try and be 'Maori'. Just be who you are."

'When things got tough I would always come back to that because I knew, at the end of the day, no matter how people were treating me, they couldn't take away the fact that I did have whakapapa and it was Ngai Tahu. Then I started investigating what that meant. I didn't have to talk rough or use the modern Maori slang at the time. I didn't have to wear hoods and trackies and act a certain way to be Maori. That was a phase I tried in my first two years at boarding school to try to fit in. My mother was shocked to see her little girl come back speaking a completely different lingo and having a fit at her for having matching cutlery in the house, because Maori didn't have matching cutlery! I was wanting to dress in a way that wouldn't make me stand out or make me look pretty. It was one of the hang-ups of the Maori youth that I was trying to be part of.

'I became more confident when I had a level of Maori language which allowed me to understand, to participate and to debate in a way that didn't make me feel excluded. That was at university. When people were talking about me in Maori, thinking I didn't understand, I could respond. I could defend my position irrespective of what people said to me and that's when I started to think, "I am what I am and that is me."

My mother has been an incredible support throughout this quest for identity and Dad pops in and gives some words of wisdom now and then, which always helps.

'Recently I went to Hastings for a three-day hui where I could brush up on my language. I haven't been able to go to places to develop my language in the last couple of years because of my two babies. My mother offered to come and look after my four-week-old son so that I could do that. That's just another example of the kind of things she's done for me throughout my life. She drove up from Wellington to Hastings, was up all night with me, and during the day she brought him down to class to be fed when he woke up. That's the kind of commitment I get from Mum.

'I am of two minds about the value of mixed marriages between Maori and Pakeha. I have had a very positive experience myself. I think that's because of the way my mother has been with my culture and the support she gave to me in my identity and as a person. Both my parents were supportive, but especially my mother.

'My parents have had problems themselves. I think it depends on how flexible people are on both sides, and how one parent embraces the culture and the choices of the other. My mother is not one of these people who speaks Maori, who's gone out and actively worked with Maori as a Pakeha. But she's accepted Maori culture as part of our family life and, as a mother of Maori children, has embraced what we want to do as part of that culture. In that way the mixed marriage hasn't really been an issue. The difficulty is that the offspring are going to have less Maori blood and are going to be perceived as "less pure" because of it, so, irrespective of how stupid those things might be, those feelings and perceptions still affect many of us today.

'I get a bit angry when I see that Dad and Mum are not being appreciated for what they have done for Ngai Tahu and other Maori people as well. People made comments, and still do, about our family, without having one ounce of knowledge about the reality.

'When Mum was struggling for money and working nights to feed her five children, Dad would send off a cheque to support some Ngai

Tahu issue without telling her. She was the one who had to figure out how they would pay it. We lived our life largely without our father because he was working for them.

'I've been aware of the challenges of mixed marriages in my own choices of partners. Early on, I swore I would always have a Maori husband and that he would be Ngai Tahu. That's not something I'm proud of now. I grew out of that. It just so happens that I fell in love with the father of my children who is Ngai Tahu, but by the time I met him it wasn't a paramount issue.

> *I wanted a Ngai Tahu husband at first because I was thinking about the whakapapa of my children, and that's quite an astonishing viewpoint, I think – from somebody who has come from a mixed marriage and somebody who has been so supported by the non-Maori partner.*

'My eldest baby, Manuhaea Rena Mamaru-O'Regan, is blond-haired and blue-eyed and the second one, Te Rautawhiri Mahaki Mamaru-O'Regan, came out looking Maori. People have said, "Hey, you've got a Maori-looking baby!" But I have to say, "Yeay! Yes, I have. But my girl is absolutely gorgeous and I wouldn't have her looking any other way." It's not like I was disappointed that she didn't come out brown, or overjoyed that my son looks the part. Maybe my son won't have to go through what I went through but I don't want them to have a certain appearance just so that I, or indeed they, can prove to everyone else they are truly Maori!

'I don't want them to feel they are any less Maori because of the way they look. But they will be able to speak Maori as they grow up, so that will be one less thing they'll be challenged on. And because of that, I think their identity will be a lot more secure from an early age. My partner, Peter, doesn't speak Maori but he's been learning. He grew up as a whangai in a Pakeha family from birth, so he didn't grow up with Maori language or culture. It's quite an interesting relationship. He's identifiably Maori and I am the fair one!'

✗

SIR *Tipene O'Regan needs little introduction to most New Zealanders. He came to prominence as an educator on things Maori and is known as the architect of the Ngai Tahu renaissance. For decades he battled to have the injustices to his South Island iwi recognised and he led the tribe's Treaty claim, which resulted in a $170 million settlement in 1997. He was for many years chairman of the Ngai Tahu Maori Trust Board and is now Assistant Vice-Chancellor Maori at Canterbury University and upoko of his Awarua Runanga at Bluff. He holds a variety of directorships and trust positions both in New Zealand, Australia and the UK, and is a former chairman of the Treaty of Waitangi Fisheries Commission and the Sealord Group. His has been a voice of reason in the New Zealand race relations debate while always being forthright in his advocacy for Maori and Ngai Tahu.*

Sir Tipene O'Regan was born in Wellington in 1939. His Pakeha father was a surgeon and his Ngai Tahu mother a nurse. 'My mother was quite noted in her day for her fine singing voice and my father admired that, as a house surgeon, when she was first sister-in-charge in the Casualty Department at Wellington Hospital.

'There's no evidence I know of that their families objected to their marriage but there certainly were a lot of negatives amongst the rather close-knit Wellington medical fraternity. I think there were three other doctors in Wellington, in my youth, who were married to Maori women and those women used to meet at our home quite a bit. Those meetings generally coincided with the arrival of Bluff oysters and titi from the south! I think it was hard for those women to have friends in medical society. There was a certain amount of nastiness about in that period, even in the late '50s.

'My father was the driving force behind the Citizens' All Black Tour Association which protested in 1959 about Maori being excluded from rugby tours to South Africa. The prime minister, Walter Nash, was quite widely reported as having observed that the only reason O'Regan was driving this cause was because his boy, meaning me, had "a touch of the tar-brush". That kind of language was pretty normal in those times.

'There was constant travel of Maori people through our home because Wellington was a place where people broke their journeys. My father had the phone put on at my taua's house in Bluff so that there could be regular toll contact between her and my mother. My mother's sister was here in Wellington together with one of my poua's sisters and a number of her Ngai Tahu cousins. They were all frequent visitors and there were regular contacts with her Ngai Tahu cousins who lived in the Wairarapa.

'I spent quite long periods in Bluff when I was small, with my taua and my uncles. I knew about eating mutton birds, oysters and scallops and watching my taua kill the chooks for the pots. I used to go to hui with her. She would come to the North Island and visit relations. My taua spoke Maori, but my mother used English with Maori terms and phrases blended through it. My own daughter, Hana, and her generation speak more Maori today than my mother's generation. I suspect more than my mother ever heard!

'My taua went to every Ngai Tahu claim meeting she could get to and spent hours discussing issues with my Pakeha father. He had a huge enthusiasm for New Zealand history and the law, so he was often more informed about my mother's people and their issues than she was. My mother and father may have had rough times as a cross-cultural couple, but I can remember them walking along holding hands not long before my mother died at 67. I think my father's professional life was developed almost entirely on the back of my mother's adoration of him. She had an extraordinarily generous disposition, she was always very much a woman and had a tremendous amount of personal charisma. She was seldom retiring, though. She had been a sister-in-charge so she knew how to command.

When I first saw Sandra I described her as 'whisky in a tall glass iced'. She was very tall and attractive and had a somewhat remote personality for someone rough like me.

'I met her in the city. I was a student and I lived in a very large duffle coat and drank more than I should have. She was, in contrast, a somewhat cool and sophisticated woman.

'I asked her out a few times and she routinely turned me down and then I thought I would have one last shot and she said yes. Then she rang me up with what I thought was a pretty lame excuse that her mother was having a baby and she wasn't able to come. I thought that was that, and I hung up. It was some time later that I discovered to my astonishment that there was in fact a baby!

'It was an issue for her family, to some degree, that I was of Maori descent. There was a bit of grumble there about our marriage, but it was more that I was from a Catholic family. Catholicism and Maori descent were not seen as positive ingredients in the marriage mixing bowl in those days.

'I had encountered that already as a student at university. In my contact with young women from time to time there would be negative parental pressure because of my descent. In my case I was more Mediterranean-looking so it wasn't just a visual thing – it had to be a race thing. But in those days most of the families in the city knew who the other families were. They knew that I had Maori in me.

I just weathered it all with Sandra's family. I recognised it as that old Kiwi colonialist racism that usually wears out once people have had some sort of relationship with each other.

'Maori and Pakeha have been vigorously marrying each other for a very long time and I think it's now part of the mix of our society. And you are always going to get prejudice whether it's over race, religion or whatever. There's a fair amount of inherent class prejudice in New Zealand, too. It's sometimes quite difficult to sort out if race is the real cause or if it's an accumulation of things.

'Although Maori and Pakeha have been marrying for a very long time, it is interesting to note the way Maori and Pakeha issues are reported in our media as though they are always two separate entities without any crossover. It's part of the extraordinarily barmy way we have constructed our discourse in recent years and it's also due to the tendency in New Zealand to convert everything to do with Maori into a race classification. Any area of difference is classified on a race basis. We never hear a Pakeha opinion being described as a "Pakeha opinion", but if any Maori dog barks, that will be taken as representative of "Maori opinion". That's all part of the Kiwi milieu.

'When I was studying at the university, I identified as Ngai Tahu and old Frank Winter, the Ngai Tahu Maori Trust Board chairman, was always keeping an eye on me. He was a patron of the University

Maori Club, so anyone of Ngai Tahu descent who failed to attend the club did so at their peril. The Maori Graduates' Association was re-formed a few years later. It was largely concerned with looking after various haukainga back in the rural areas that had been devastated by evacuation to the cities. We organised busloads of students to go back to marae and work in the fields, and at night the old people would come into the meeting house and be with us.

'The first land struggle I took on was on the Whanganui River. I generally took our kids with me on these ventures so they all had considerable exposure to marae life, and when Hana was an infant she would spend her time with the old man Rangi Pokiha when he came to stay with us over the winter.

'I remember my oldest daughter, Rena, knowing exactly what was appropriate in the meeting house. She knew where my bed went in the house and didn't need to be told, and she made all our beds. She would be asked to make a cup of tea when we had manuhiri and she would go off . . . and if they were Pakeha it would be sweet things and biscuits, but if they were Maori there would be a mountain of bread and butter on the table.

'Our children were exposed to a bigger variety of marae experience than most Maori get to in a lifetime and they learnt the rules intuitively. Two who have been involved in the life of Ngai Tahu are our son, Gerard, an archaeologist, and Hana, our youngest. The others have all had associations and contact and links, they know they are Ngai Tahu and know they are shareholders in different blocks of corporations, and some take a bigger interest than others.

'We have one very beautiful daughter who is white-complexioned, blue-eyed and red-haired, and other children who are darker. I can remember, when the red-haired one was very small, going onto a marae at Ruatahuna and one of the old kuia seized on this child as an urukehu. Tuhoe have this tradition of redheads amongst them. Miria was a focus of attention for those old people there. People from outside the circle said she didn't look Maori, so she couldn't be. But I think most race sensitivity and appearance-based stuff is more an urban thing than what happens in rural places.

'Sandra was always supportive, putting her hand into the housekeeping money for me. It was her income that kept the family going. From the early '80s it really started to bite during the period of the Ngai Tahu claim. She subsidised Ngai Tahu for at least 11 years – because she freed me to do what I could do.'

During the '90s, in particular, various comments were made about Sir Tipene being part of the 'Brown Table' and 'a fat cat' coming from a position of privilege. This has been hard for him to stomach at times.

'The only reason I own a freehold home is that my father left me the capacity to clear the mortgage in his will. Some of the criticism was pretty vile at times and there were ugly untruths about my income. The cost of the wages we paid out through the claim period nearly always exceeded our income.

'For the record, we now own this Wellington house freehold and we have a little apartment in Christchurch freehold. We have two cars that are now paid for.

I mortgaged this old house during the claim period. Ngai Tahu paid everyone else's mortgage off after the settlement. Mine was not cleared and that's always been a source of disappointment.

'We had to do it ourselves. Sandra is hurt and annoyed about that, too. Tribes are really pretty graceless institutions – a bit too much like New Zealanders!

'Although the fees we had coming in from my work in fisheries were reasonably substantial, so were our outgoings. At no time I can recall did I receive the highest fees at the Commission and I was the chairman. It doesn't stop people saying things. People want to believe it and they form conclusions. As for the "Brown Table" stuff, most of the Maori leadership in my time have been pohara or could only be described at best as having a low to medium middle income. Amongst a certain level of politicians and the chattering classes of Queenstown, for example, there's been a lot of assumptions about a kleptocratic Maori leadership, and some of that seeps into the lower levels of journalism. But the most destructive thing you can do for yourself is allow yourself to become bitter about it, so I tend to laugh it off. The bit that hurts is when your own people start to believe it – they get their basic intellectual feed from the Kiwi media and you just have to remember that they are, after all, just Kiwis with whakapapa.

'I was called Tiwi by my taua and by my parents. Tiwi was my name, except when I was in trouble – it was then I became Stephen. I was Steve to my mates. The old people speaking to me on the marae would call me Tipene. I was always a combination of those things and I have always been fascinated by the amount of attention my name has had from journalists and commentators. Just recently I heard a well-known person discussing me in this context on national radio. Why he, and the interviewer, picked on an historic artefact like me, I don't know. It's no good worrying, though, you just wear it!

'They criticise me for wearing my taonga over my tie. There is a little one I wore regularly in the 1960s, which used to send some of my colleagues at the teachers' college into paroxysms of anxiety and rage. But I have always worn a taonga over a tie. I wore it because the taonga was there. I remember once looking around the Ngai Tahu Trust Board table and everyone present had a piece around their neck.

'A lot of the behavioural trappings of tribal identity, from taonga to T-shirts, even moko, have become something of a focus for the chattering classes and part of the ordinary Kiwi discourse. It percolates right through politicians' and journalists' discussions and into their pubtalk. "He's Maori but he is more like us." "He could be an Italian or Greek." "He is that sort of colour." "He's of Maori descent but you wouldn't know it." They tear hell out of the person in question because they assert he can't make his mind up whether he is Maori or Pakeha – or split down the middle.

'I learnt very early that coming from two cultural streams doubled your cultural potential, it doubled your sense of identity and it didn't divide it in half. You can look at dual descent as a multiplication sum or you can look at it as a division sum. To suit an argument, New Zealanders will multiply or divide, depending on their intent.

They are absolutely fixated on what Matiu Rata used to call 'biological arithmetic'. Its effect is to make you feel like an object from a stud book.

'It's a persistent hangover from colonialist racism.

'I think intermarriage will continue and it will be interesting to see the form and shape of Maori culture in that situation. On the whole, Maori culture and identity has not been diminished much by the ongoing march of intermarriage, otherwise you couldn't have had the Maori renaissance. I think that the Maori presence in this society will continue to grow and I do not see it being watered down or affected much by intermarriage. Clearly it will be different, though.

'My wife has had her own life, her own profession, her own relationships. I've had mine and we have had those that we share. My world has been imposed on her, much more than hers has been on me. In fact, hers has barely been imposed on me at all. But some circumstances require such a shift or sacrifice or are more one-sided. Sandra knew what the battle was about and she followed it through. She has a high dedication to principles and issues and that has given us a lot of common ground.'

The Mangu/Spencer Duo

JUDGE *Andrew Spencer is a Pakeha appointed to the Maori*

Land Court in 1987. He's the resident judge at Whangarei for the

Taitokerau district. He presided over the controversial Te Roroa

claim for the Waitangi Tribunal (1989–91). Andrew is divorced

from his first wife, who was Pakeha, and has three children from

that marriage. His partner for the last 15 years, Mere Mangu, whom

he calls Maryann, has two children from a previous marriage,

Nga-Atawhainga and Caleb.

PHOTOGRAPH:

Mere Mangu and Andrew Spencer

Andrew Spencer was born in England of English parents, and came to New Zealand at the age of four in 1951. His parents were from what he calls 'well-to-do' families. 'I didn't start school until the age of six because there were no public schools for little boys in New Plymouth for five-year-olds, so I went to a private kindergarten. My older brother went to a private prep school in New Plymouth, because none of the family had ever been to a state school before. That's the way my family started here. It was very much a conservative English, upper middle-class background.

'My father was quite involved with the Maori community in Taranaki. I remember him speaking of a hui in 1952 in New Plymouth – that the kaumatua there were "gentlemen". He thought them courteous and he had a high regard for them. He thought many "Kiwis", so to speak, were pretty rough and "scrubbers" compared to these elderly distinguished Maori gentlemen.'

For a time the Spencers lived in Kaikohe where Andrew's father helped struggling Maori families with budgeting and tried to find them employment opportunities. Andrew says while his father wasn't racist, there was always an underlying 'them' and 'us'. 'He would recognise someone as being Maori as opposed to not noticing the difference, whereas with my upbringing, at Northland College, a mainly Maori school, I never noticed one person as being Maori and another person as being Pakeha. Many of my friends were Maori, Samoan or Cook Island or whatever.

'At university in Dunedin, one of my flatmates was Singhalese or Ceylonese, and I remember a guy saying, "Oh, so-and-so is your flatmate. You know, the dark guy." And I stopped and thought, "Who's this you're talking about?" And then the penny dropped. "Oh, yes. I suppose you are right. You would say he is a bit dark."'

In 1977 Andrew opened his own legal practice in Kaikohe but, despite the high Maori population, he had few Maori clients. 'It was quite unusual, really, because I had a very substantial clientele of Pakeha from the business and farming community. However, I was involved in other things. I was one of the people who set up a work skills trust at that time, called the Mahi Kia Mohio Trust. It was very successful. Unfortunately the government changed its policies after I left and it folded.'

Andrew says Maori people never came to their house, but his Pakeha family did have some contact. 'When I became a judge I was sworn in on a marae. My wife and children all sang my waiata.' Andrew separated from his wife in 1989. 'I took the job as a judge in 1987 so that we could move from Kaikohe to Whangarei and have a fresh start. But it didn't work out.'

Andrew met Maryann when Sir James Henare and Lady Rose came to see him about a matter at the court. Maryann was their driver.

I was having this meeting with Sir James and Lady Rose and next thing the door pushed open and this beautiful woman poked her head around the door.

'Sir James said, "Excuse me, this is my niece, Maryann," and introduced us.

'Later, Sir James said to me, "Judge, you know that woman I introduced you to? She was an army officer, and she's just parted from her husband and she has two young children. She's a remarkable person. She will one day be the leader in Taitokerau."'

Maryann began visiting the court regularly to research a claim for Sir James. 'One day Sir James came in and started to say something to me about Maryann's father's house site. I said straight off, "Sir James, if you think I am going to do you a favour, think again." He was taken aback. He wasn't asking for a favour at all, so I felt a right fool! As a judge, I am particular about not being subject to any pressure from whoever they may be. He was asking that this matter be hurried up because of the living conditions of Mere's father, who lived at Matawaia. His house, where they brought up all the children, had no power or running water. He was getting old and Maryann was going to build a house on the section. He was the sole owner of this block, so in those circumstances there were no favours required. But in most cases, it's multiple land and people will sometimes try to do things without sufficient notice to the other owners.

'I can recall one occasion when I had an Appellate Court sitting in Whangarei and two senior judges came to sit on this case with me. It was almost 10am and we were just about to go down to start the court. Maryann comes rushing in with a bunch of roses for me. I was stunned. She almost bowled my colleagues off their feet! And she said, "Oh, oh, oh, sorry!", but still gave me the flowers. My friends smiled from ear to ear. It was funny. Thereafter, Maryann became a great friend of one of those judges, Chick McHugh. He loved her personality and spontanaeity.'

Once he and Maryann became partners Andrew still lived away from her, in Whangarei. He wanted to maintain a place for his own children to come to. 'Maryann and I decided to live together about eight years ago. For a little time, the fact that my new partner was Maori was awkward for my children, but there's no aspect of that now that they are older.'

Andrew believes Maryann's children found it easier to accept him because their own father was Pakeha. 'But right from the outset my attitude was, "I am not here to replace your father." Nga-Atawhainga and Caleb were taught to address adults as "Mr" and "Mrs" and so on. I was happy for them to call me "Mr Spencer". I wanted there to be a difference between me and their dad. I wanted them to always honour their father. And it was only about three years ago that Nga-Atawhainga stopped calling me "Mr Spencer". So that was quite cute.'

Andrew noticed cultural differences between his wife and his new partner. 'My wife was very Pakeha, very organised, a very good housewife and mother, a very good cook and everything was on time. If we went on holiday, it was always to smart places, never too much roughing it.

'Living with Maryann, different expectations are placed on me. Things are more flexible. I don't have dinner at a fixed time and there's no expectation that the television will be off when I eat dinner, for instance.'

Andrew chuckles as he tries to explain the flow of his life now.

Time doesn't feature at all. And it gets very frustrating when you live for today and forget about tomorrow.

'It tends to be too far the other way. I think there is a happy medium but unfortunately I'm still trying to find my darling's happy medium. There's a lack of accountability for time.'

Andrew passed an important cultural test with his first taste of the Maori delicacy, rotten corn. 'Not long after we first met, my darling boiled up this beautiful big pot of kanga wai and gave me a big bowl of it. I sat down on the back step in the sun to eat the stuff, with lashings of cream and sugar. And I ate the lot and asked for more. She was surprised but I knew what she was trying to do.'

He says he and Maryann have both come across customs they're not used to and decided their own response. For example, Andrew hasn't adopted the Maori view that tea towels should never be washed with body items. 'I tend to think with modern-age detergents there is not the same necessity to carry on with the old style, but, on the other hand, I agree that I shouldn't put my bum on the table. However, you must remember that there are certain things we, as Pakeha, don't do either. Remember, my parents were of a rather traditional background. For example, table manners were really important and how you set the table, in terms of knives and forks, and even who you have to your home for a meal.'

Andrew explains that he is fussy about who he eats with because of his English perspective on relationships. 'If someone has done a foul deed to someone important to you, you don't sit down and share your meal at home with them. If people don't respect you and yours, you wouldn't even invite them into your house.

I remember giving some of Maryann's relatives the bum's rush at the door. People whom I feel do not respect her or myself or what we stand for. An Englishman's home is his castle, as they say.

'We do have our own cultural norms. I am not sure if they conflict or not. I think perhaps Maryann would be polite to anyone who came to the house. I would not! There is nothing racially motivated about my view. There are certain lines you don't cross. That's it. Sometimes Maryann has done people a good turn and they have abused it. So I don't tolerate that. Maryann, on the other hand, isn't like that. Her whanaungatanga is embracing.'

Andrew is usually comfortable in marae settings. 'One thing we do try to do is not be a burden in a material way. I try to observe their rules and customs because I was also brought up that you do in Rome as the Romans do. I wouldn't impose my cultural values upon them but I can't speak Maori. I do it in English. So there is a strong underlying self-esteem . . . or arrogance on my part. I acknowledge that. I respect myself as a person. This has nothing to do with my being a judge. I don't use the judge bit at all. Throughout Taitokerau, during the court hearing, it's "Your honour" and "Judge" etc, but before and after the case it's "Kia ora, Andrew" and "Thanks, Andrew."

'I go to lots of tangi throughout Taitokerau.

If Maryann is in Auckland she might phone me and ask me to go on her behalf and I don't mind at all. I learn a lot and I see it as part of my duty to do that.

'Returning to the tangi and whakapapa is an important part of the whole culture.

'As a Pakeha I don't feel any discomfort about where I belong. I know my English whakapapa. If I wanted to find out where my ancestors were, there would be no problem with that. My sense of place is in the north here somewhere. We have a funny little bach up near Mangonui, we've got land at Rawene, we have places around about. We live at Ngawha Springs village.'

Andrew's patch as a judge of the Maori Land Court jurisdiction runs from Auckland to the top of the North Island and includes Great Barrier Island. 'I feel very privileged when you think I am a Pakeha from head to toe walking in somebody else's world. But when you stop and think about it, what I am actually doing is not in the Maori world. The court is a Pakeha system and I am very aware of it.'

He was branded a radical judge by some politicians when the Waitangi Tribunal reported on the Te Roroa claim. Andrew says the Tribunal merely recommended that the Crown should try to *negotiate* the purchase of general land, which included some waahi tapu sacred to Te Roroa. He was very cross at the time because he felt the Tribunal's report had been deliberately misrepresented.

Andrew was also in the headlines over rating issues in the Far North District. 'I was accused of being partisan to the Maori cause and critical of the well-off Pakeha ratepayer, who was getting rates relief and council services. The reality is that the Maori community, in general, does not receive services and yet they're expected to pay rates.

'There is a major injustice if you look at Maori communities in this area. You will find the council has sold off, and is still selling, Maori-owned "general land" to pay off rates. Some of this Maori-owned land became "general land" 40 years ago, often without the consent or knowledge of owners. This meant these lands were not succeeded to in the way they would have been if they had been Maori land. They fell into arrears of rates and have been sold by the Council.

'Given this history of rating sales, if you look at the services provided to the Maori community as ratepayers they are minimal, and always have been. There is hardly a single marae that has a tar-sealed road.

'If you compare towns like Kerikeri, Opua and Paihia with Kaikohe, the difference is huge. The administrative centre was always in Kaikohe but because of the land values they've shifted everything to Kerikeri and Paihia. The bureaucrats will only come to the north to work if they're stationed in the Bay of Islands. That's where they can buy properties and get increased capital values they won't get at Kaikohe, where most of the residents are Maori. So it's both an economic issue and a racial one. Bluntly, it's white flight to Kerikeri and Paihia and Opua where the affluent Pakeha live, many on lifestyle blocks, leaving the less affluent in Kaikohe.

'I live in the Maori community in Ngawha Springs and wish that more people, instead of being so damn racist, would actually live *in the community*, as opposed to living in what are, in effect, racial enclaves.'

Andrew says he and Maryann never argue about politics, although they discuss them a lot. He believes Maori issues are poorly reported in the media. 'Because every time anything negative is Maori, it is identified as Maori. It's as if Maori people as individuals haven't got any brains. They don't exist as individuals. They exist in a stereotype – a stigmatised type called "Maori". For example, Maryann has just passed her law degree and the likes of the Pakeha community, of Dr Brash and so forth, would immediately have a floating thought, "Oh, she must have had a preferential place in law school and may not have had to get there on merit." Which is nonsense, because she got there entirely on merit. And what's more, she hasn't had any handouts to do it. She has done it with her own resources totally. I am immensely proud of her.

'It seems that Maori are stigmatised to failure. That's the way the wider population looks upon them. But we could reverse that stereotype and say, for instance, that wealthy people must be cheats or they wouldn't have all that money. That's a simple parallel. Neither stereotype is true.

When I first met Maryann, I said she was a 'princess' – and I guess it was by way of my arrogance. I saw we had a lot in common in terms of our upbringing.

'I felt that she had a background and upbringing very like my own. She has a very deep sense of self-respect. Maryann was brought up in a very traditional Maori environment, where Maori language is her first language.

I have a certain diffidence in anything to do with her because I always know that I am second best for her because I haven't got that Maori language.

'It's a joke that I have picked her up on her quaint mispronunciation of words like *cabinette* instead of cabinet. But when I do that, I am very mindful that I couldn't foot it anywhere in her language, or within her community at all, like she fits into mine. So there is a certain humility in my part about that.

'Maryann's traditional upbringing was very special within her own community. And that is really accentuated by the extent to which she lives her tikanga Maori. Despite our differences, I don't think of us as being in a cross-cultural relationship. I don't even think of Maryann as being Maori. It doesn't come into my contemplation.

'Now and again I stop and ask myself, "Is there a cultural explanation for this?" She will tolerate behaviour from her wider whanau and hapu that I find unacceptable. Because of her legal adoption, I think sometimes that she has a stronger feeling of affinity and

whanaungatanga to those people than they perhaps feel towards her.
I don't like the lack of reciprocity. That's why I sometimes react in an
inhospitable way to those who don't offer her respect in return. I am
protective towards her and I make a judgement from my own cultural
perspective. And that is it.'

※

DRIVING *through Moerewa in Northland you can't miss the sign*

on an old wooden building: 'Mere Mangu's Office'. It's where she

ran her general election campaign in 2002 and where she studied

for her law degree just completed at the University of Auckland.

In the election, Mere Mangu polled at second place in the Maori

seat of Te Taitokerau as an independent candidate. She was little

known to the media except for her part in the campaign against

Ngawha Prison, but she is better known in her tribe, Ngati Hine of

Ngapuhi, and other Maori circles. Mere's first language is Maori

and her life is driven by tikanga Maori values. Her original career

was as an officer in the army. She is divorced from the father of her

two children, Caleb Joshua (22) and Nga-Atawhainga (20), mother

to her first granddaughter. She and her partner, Andrew, live at

Ngawha Springs village.

Mere Mangu was born in 1957 in Dargaville at Te Kopuru Hospital. Her birth mother was married to someone who was not Mere's father. 'It was decided by the couple's parents it was not appropriate for the mother and her new husband to start off their marriage with this baby. I was given through whakapapa to another whanau at Matawaia. My maternal grandmother was a niece of my adopted parents, Tauiwi Nori Motene and Tahuri Mangu, so, in a Maori sense, I was still within the bloodline. I refer to my adopted parents as Mum and Dad because I really don't know or have a relationship with anyone else as a parent. I love the life I was given. I was number 13 of their children and they adopted two more mokopuna after me. That doesn't account for all the other children and whanau they nurtured.'

One reason for the comings and goings in the Mangu household was the particular healing lineage of Mere's adopted mother. Mere is still reluctant to talk about it. 'It's not the done thing to refer to tohunga, because people of my mother's generation were brought up when the Tohunga Suppression Act was still prevalent. Sometimes we had whole families with us while she tended to the ill person. Normally it was the mother being cared for.

'We never saw ourselves as poor. We had a full life. Maori was the only language we spoke and the few Pakeha we ever met were at school or church. We worked from dawn till school, and after school till dark. However, in working we had a lot of play. We were taught so many things we took for granted without realising we were being given values. Mum knew no other language but Maori. Dad worked at the freezing works. There was no sexism. Whatever our brothers did, we did. Whatever we did as women, they did. My brothers make the best kai, the best hangi, fried bread etc, . . . as do all the men from Matawaia.

'Although my elder sister was married not long after I was adopted, she and her husband actually cared for me, because they lived at home with Mum in Matawaia. At the age of six we were riding horses and walking into the bush to gather the medicine. We knew all the trees. We knew how to get the plants and bring back the amounts required for Mum to make her healing concoctions.

'We had big vegetable gardens. As children we rode the horses to plough and disc the paddocks. We picked up dung to put in drums for fertiliser and raised chooks. We had a house cow called Rhonee.

'I never went anywhere without my mother. I had a very protected life and I was never allowed to sleep anywhere other than at home. Mum always had dinner ready after school. The routine was to get out of uniform, eat something, get into work clothes for our chores, eat, then work either in the garden or chopping wood. We had no power, running water was from the puna, and we would collect puaka (brushwood from manuka). We arrived home after school in time to listen to *The Archers* on the battery radio. We had no television. We had a cold wash every morning. As the family got smaller, we had an enamel bath around the back of the house and you carried buckets of water to it. On Sunday we would have a hot bath by lighting a fire underneath. It depended where you were in the hierarchy who got the cleanest water.

'I was given a special upbringing. I was 17 or 18 before I was allowed to sweep the floor in the marae dining room. I never served in the kitchen. I was made to stay in the marae with Mum and the elders, and was never allowed outside to play with other children.

'The person on the taumata at Matawaia then was Kako Waiomio. He was a strict but fair man. The elders all treated me well. When we had hui at Matawaia there would be down time between the groups arriving.

Sometimes Kako Waiomio would use the time to instruct me on oratory skills in front of all the other elders.

'Sometimes I'd just stand up and I would be told to sit down without even uttering a word. In all of that you learnt the stance, you learnt the body language, but you never question. You just accept . . . sort of! Fortunately, Mum would explain to me in private what the training was all about.'

Mere says, although women from many other iwi don't speak on the marae, Ngati Hine is different, with its higher Maori language and culture retention, so Matawaia ran in older, more traditional ways.

'I learnt English when I went to school and loved to read. Whenever Pakeha came to the door knocking, I would be the one to answer the door and everyone else would run away and wait for the Pakeha to leave. When Pakeha came onto the marae, I was the host. It was my role to explain to the visitor what was going on and translate for them, as well as answer questions.

'I thought Pakeha were aliens. They just didn't belong. They never came into our homes or to our marae except for a brief visit to pay their respect at a tangi or something, and then they were out of there. My first real contact with Pakeha came when my eldest brother married a Pakeha, followed by another sister and brother. Mum spoke very little English to them.

'At the end of my primary years at Matawaia Maori School, I went to board at Queen Victoria School for Girls. For me it was a wrench from home. However, now when I look back I am pleased I went because it exposed me to Pakeha culture and polished up my English. We had to sit at the table with the other girls and learn to use a knife and fork and serviettes. Miss Berridge was the headmistress then and we had very strict rules. We were never to raise our voices. When you laughed at the table it had to be a subdued laugh.

As a result of being at Queen Vic, I could go into any social situation and know what to do.

'I went to training college to become a secondary school teacher. They accepted me into English and Social Studies but I didn't want to do those subjects.' Mere had confused feelings about the circumstances of her birth and adoption. She knew that her birth mother was teaching English and Social Studies to some of her relatives in a school up north, and Mere wanted to teach Maori and follow her own path.

'It was the first year that mature Maori speakers were being brought in to teach Maori and I wanted to be a part of that. I wasn't allowed to because I was too young, so I rebelled and left.

'When Mum found out she wanted to pack me off to be a police-woman. But I said, "I can't because my brother is in jail. It might come to the day when I have to arrest my brother. What would I do then?" Without telling my parents I joined the army and my brother, the one who'd been in jail, signed the documents for me.

'I went to Burnham to train because it was when they had a women's corp. After that I came back to Auckland and did odd jobs while I was completing my university study and then went into the army fulltime for six years.

'As a child I had never struck racism and, in fact, it wasn't until the army sent me across to Melbourne that I really experienced it. Two Pakeha guys, who had gone with me, protected me from a lot of the racism. The Australians would make references to my colour or shun me altogether as if I didn't matter. At that stage we were young officers and this was in the officers' mess. At first I was dumbfounded. It floored me that they should treat me like that. After the second time I started to think, "I don't have to put up with them." I used to get angry and retaliate at times. I am sharp with my mouth as a form of defence. I tend to wait my time. I may not always deal with it straight away . . . but it will happen.

'The army in general was not racist. I was happy there because I got to see most of New Zealand. I loved bush work and being outside. Queen Victoria School for Girls had helped me understand Pakeha and I got even more used to them in the army.

About this time I discovered that I had been betrothed in the traditional way to a young Maori man who was a friend of mine. Neither of us knew this had been planned by our families.

'I came home from the army for his wedding still not knowing. I had brought him some linen as a present. But as I was leaving for the wedding Mum gave me a bucket to take instead. I arrived late so I wouldn't be seen walking in with my present. I put it under the table and thought nothing more of it. After the wedding Mum told me about the betrothal. The bucket was a way of acknowledging that it was okay that it hadn't worked out. In the bucket were kumara, peruperu and things to start the newly-weds off on a new life.

'I had a Maori boyfriend once who was not allowed to even come to our house. It had something to do with his whakapapa and Mum would not have anything to do with him. At that point, she said to me, "You are not to marry a Maori."

'When I was in the army, there were all those Maori men, but not one of them asked me out. That's probably because at the time I became a fulltime soldier they'd just introduced the new officer cadet training at Waiouru and Maori women officers were a novelty. We did everything the men did. It was harsh training even though I had done the work my brothers did at home. Not everyone can dig their own hole and live in it.

'While I was in the army, friends and relatives my age had all had children. I was feeling left out and I guess I married out of loneliness or need. It wasn't something I had thought through. I went out with this Pakeha guy I met at a party. I got pregnant and married him.

'Our different backgrounds made the marriage difficult for us both. He hadn't had anything to do with Maori until the army, and when I went to meet his family, they hadn't actually had a Maori walk in the door until that day. I guess they were apprehensive, but actually I'd go so far as to say that they did come to love me. In saying that, we were still from different planets. I was used to celebrations where all the family came together.

The only time I ever saw them come together was when one died and then no one actually knew who the other one was!

'For Mum, food was an integral part of people coming together, whereas with them it was very much a cup of tea and finger foods. I have two beautiful children from my husband, Caleb and Nga-Atawhainga.

Mere's children from a previous marriage. Caleb (*left*) and Nga-Atawhainga

They can identify as Irish and Scottish from his ancestry. Although they don't know too much about those particular cultures, they do recognise that they have that whakapapa link, as well as Maori.'

Mere, like Andrew, has a clear memory of their first meeting. 'I went to Maori Affairs with Sir James and Lady Rose, and I was really mad at the difference in service you received, as if you were not "somebody". I went back to meet up with them to say I would be late. I didn't knock but walked straight into the office and there was Andrew sitting there. I was quite shocked because he was young, where my idea of the Maori Land Court judges was old fuddy-duddies. And he was sitting back in the chair with his hands behind his head.

He says he was unconscious of doing this, but he sort of looked me up and down, and I thought, 'who the hell do you think you are?' At the same time I also thought, 'He's really confident, self-assured and debonair.'

'But I didn't acknowledge him. Sir James introduced us and I just spoke to them in Maori and said what I was doing. Sir James told me, in Maori, to pull my head in and not to be so angry.'

Mere's children were still at primary school when she and Andrew met and she was conscious of giving them a good Maori cultural education as well as a Pakeha one. Her father insisted that she stay home with the children, rather than take up a job, and she's glad he did. 'They don't have the depth of knowledge of tikanga that I was given. However, I feel I have exposed them to a range of cultural experiences.'

Mere says Andrew has been really good with her children. Her daughter, who is listening in at this point, agrees. Nga-Atawhainga now calls him 'Anaru'. 'Because we had Anaru in the family, my brother and I adapted more to Pakeha culture than we would have if we had gone straight from Mum to living with Dad. Most of our lives were spent with the Maori community. When we moved in with our Dad later, there were still huge cultural differences. We used to spend hours on the phone talking to Mum. With Mum we always had lots of family around us, but with Dad there was just his partner, so we felt stranded and lonely.

'Another thing that Anaru did was to help us with our school work. English became my favourite subject at school and that was mainly because of Anaru's influence. He was always really helpful with our school work and our education. It was a top priority with him.'

Mere is aware that Andrew doesn't always understand tikanga but she believes neither of them have any insurmountable cultural difficulties. 'He is the rock in our relationship – I can wash up against him and he decides whether to embrace the wave or repel me altogether. He's a fast learner. I can tell him something once and he gets the message . . . most times!'

Andrew's reluctance to welcome everyone who calls has had advantages for Mere. 'Because I have been studying it has been convenient to have that distance. I could never have achieved it with whanau coming all the time. Andrew is open to whanau get-togethers if there's a birthday or something. He doesn't take his stand for no reason. There have been occasions when he believes some members of my family have let me down. I accept that because you have to put value on yourself.

'There are differences in our attitudes where I don't agree with him. For instance, I would come home and my gumboots would be gone. And I would accept they've gone. "Forget it. It's only a material thing and I am not hampered by it." But for him it's a big thing. "Someone has taken that without even asking you!" I say, "If you really want a pair of gumboots go out and buy another pair. Why would you want those gumboots back anyway?"

If it was the last bottle of milk in the fridge, I would give it, whereas he would tend to look after us in the house first.

'I would prefer us to go without, because, to me, we have the wherewithal to buy an alternative. Sometimes people need it there and then, so why not?'

If Andrew has an issue with something about Maori culture, Mere says he'll run it past her and see what she thinks. 'We discuss it until we come to some sort of understanding as to why things are the way they are and why I think the way I do. For Pakeha issues I tend to be arrogant enough to think that I know enough about it not to have to bow down to his view. I am not so accepting of his opinions.

'Sometimes Andrew finds my non-adherence to Pakeha time, or my indulgence into Maori time, a problem. From my perspective I am pleased to know that I can still flow with the priorities of the moment.

'We can disagree on money. We can disagree on a lot of things – but by bedtime it's forgive and forget. I'm really respectful for the fact that he's not abusive, he is not mean, he is very trusting and he loves me.

Time on this earth is very short, and loving feels so much better than being angry.'

Mere has found Andrew very supportive of her interest in politics. It was the Ngawha Prison project which made her think that no one was actually speaking up for the ordinary Maori citizen. 'I decided to stand for Parliament because we, as citizens, are not listened to in our own country. I will stand again for the 2005 election.

I acknowledge that there's a part of Maori society that won't vote for me because of my association with Andrew as 'the Judge'.

'That's okay. People who have been before a judge and didn't get what they wanted are hardly going to back that judge's partner. I suppose you could say I am tainted by association, although I know I am my own person.'

Mere believes Andrew has learnt a lot about the important concepts of Maori culture and it helps her to be comfortable with him as her partner. 'I am absolutely confident in his being able to carry things off on the marae for me. He was really open to learning and so I would like to think that I have influenced him in really good ways on the marae or when Maori things are needed in general.

'He came home one day from Wellington and was absolutely disgusted about the way a respected Maori elder had been welcomed into the Tribunal – over dirty dishes. There was no powhiri for this kaumatua in the proper way. Andrew had taken the Maori values on board as if they were his own, so I thought that was great.

'My response was, "What did you do?" That was the more important thing. And he said that he'd apologised to the kaumatua and got into conversation. And I said, "That's all that is expected of you. As long as you know and you acknowledge it, you can move on – as it is not necessarily your role to put things right."'

Mere feels no disappointment that Andrew does not speak Maori.

'That's okay, because sometimes you hear these Pakeha who come on to the marae and attempt to speak Maori and are absolutely atrocious at it. I would prefer that they didn't. I mean, we know who they are. They don't have to pretend to be something that they are not. So I prefer Andrew to be who he is, rather than have him stand up and make a mockery of the language. I think what's in his heart is more important to me than what comes out of his mouth.'

Mere says Andrew was not aware of the extent of racism from Pakeha towards Maori in the north.

She says he didn't understand what she meant when she spoke of racism in the business community.

'Many Pakeha business people were his clients when he practised law there. So one day she showed him what she meant.

'At one shop he had introduced me to the owners and they were falling over themselves to say hello when I was with him. So I waited a few days and went back in. I told Andrew to stay outside. I waited and waited to be served. Then finally I said, "Now you go in." And he was hardly at the door and they were there to serve him. I just wanted him to be aware, to have an understanding of what goes on for some Maori. One may be treated as a second-class citizen. There's a need to educate and make others aware and change that attitude.

'My mum told me I had to marry a Pakeha, and Whina Cooper was always an advocate for mixed marriages, but I don't think it is a good mix if you don't know yourself. It is just another layer of difficulty in a marriage. Andrew has had to adapt to more than just Maori culture. He's not used to social difference in a family situation so it is new for him to include people like gang members, homosexuals or ex-prison inmates in his family circle.

'We are both adults, educated in some things but dumb in others. That's okay with me. It works.'

BERNADETTE *Maniapoto (née Honywood) is a Pakeha grandmother who was born on a farm near Dipton, in Southland, and moved to Invercargill when she was 13. She knew nothing at all about Maori until she met her husband, Nepia. Bernie, as he calls her, is the mother of six children including the singer-songwriter, Moana Maniapoto.*

Bernie was 24 and working as a receptionist in an Invercargill hotel when a girlfriend asked her to a party. 'My friend said these five Maori

PHOTOGRAPH:

Bernadette and Nepia Maniapoto

boys would be there. So I went along and met Nepia. I thought he was quite nice and handsome. We got chatting and he asked me if he could phone me up and take me to the pictures and I said, "Yep," and I was excited about going.'

Nepia was 32 and had been working at the Ocean Beach Freezing Works in Bluff for four years. 'After we had been out a few times, I said to Nepia, "You had better come home and meet my mother." She met him and didn't seem to have any reaction to the fact that he was Maori. My parents were separated. My father was good as gold about Nepia. And when I told my only brother, "I'm getting married and he's a Maori," he said, "Doesn't worry me if he is Chinese or what the hell he is."'

Bernie soon learnt something about racism when one of her aunts made it very clear that she did not approve of her marrying Nepia.

She told my mother, 'Oh, she'll be living up there in a pa with sticks around it and grass skirts.' She had no idea.

'She was always very nice to him face to face, but the funniest thing happened later. I sent this aunt photos when we were away visiting my brother in Australia, and after she died one of my nieces sent them back to me. My aunt had cut Nepia off every photo! I had never realised the true extent of her dislike for my marriage.

'The Maoris down in Invercargill are very fair, and I didn't even know they were Maori until after I met Nepia. We used to mix with his small crowd mainly, but when we were invited to things on our own, that used to be a laugh. We would go in and you could almost hear the conversation stop in the room. They weren't used to Maori. After a while he would start playing the guitar and singing and they thought he was the loveliest guy out.

'One time, we wanted to get this flat, and I went down and had a look and it was nice, and I said, "Can I bring my husband?" They said,

"Yes", so I took him down and showed him through. That night the landlord rang up and said, "I'm sorry, but I've made a mistake. I've already let it to somebody." Nepia said, "I know why he said that." He said to my mother, "You ring up and see if the flat's still available." So she phoned and it was. It was horrible! I couldn't believe it. It was tricky finding flats. I didn't believe it went on until it happened to us.

'I was hoping the babies would be darkish, but mostly they turned out in-between. They were beautiful babies.

people used to be quite interested in us, because we would be walking along with our pram and they'd take a good look.

'It was quite a thing because there weren't many Maori down in the south. As the years went on, heaps more Maori came.'

The couple travelled up to visit Nepia's parents at a farm north of Turangi at Te Rangiita in their holidays, but Bernie says it was a long journey by train, boat and bus – and costly because they were relatively poor. When they made the journey with one of their babies for Nepia's sister's wedding, Bernie learnt a lot about whanaungatanga. Nepia's parents and other whanau members gave them enough money to fly home to Invercargill and stay in a hotel in Christchurch on the way. 'Different ones from the whanau came along with a little koha in an envelope for us. It was lovely but I wasn't used to it. It was quite different to how Pakehas are.

'Nepia's parents came down to Invercargill and his mum was just lovely. We were really struggling and I said, "I've only got one pair of shoes." Off we go the next day. I came home with that many pairs of new shoes! They weren't well off themselves but they shared what they had. And when the children went to stay with them they were properly spoiled.

'My first tangi was when Nepia's mother died suddenly at 65 of diabetes. At the tangi there were all these people. I was overwhelmed by the wailing and the whole thing because I had no idea what was involved and I didn't know what to do.

It was the biggest number of Maoris I'd ever seen in my life. I told Nepia, as a joke, that there were too many Maoris.

'Nepia didn't criticise me if I made cultural mistakes. I was interested to find out about things. He would talk to me in a nice way and say, "We don't do it like that." Some of the food they ate was hard-case. Fish heads! I could not believe anybody would eat those things! And rotten corn. It was an interesting life and there was always something new to learn.

(*l to r*) Niki, Bernie, Keri-Lee, Moana, Nepia, Maru

'I was very keen for the kids to know their Maori culture. We have only one son, and I hoped he would speak Maori and go to a Maori school. I thought it was really important. When we decided to shift up to the North Island, I asked Nepia if we could send Moana, our eldest, to St Joseph's Maori Girls' College – and we did. We sent three kids to boarding school and three missed out. We couldn't afford to send them all.

'In our early married days, we would sit up in bed and Nepia would teach me these Maori words and it seemed to get so complicated with all the different meanings, but I did have a little try. He was a good speaker.

'Moana was 10 and my youngest, Lisa, was just a baby when we shifted up to Rotorua in 1970. They were exposed to more Maori language and culture then. Nepia's father spoke Maori all the time. In the holidays they learnt how to make piupius and all those sorts of things. Maru went to the Maori boarding school, Hato Petera, and he got right into his Maoritanga.

'We made the move to Rotorua because my mother was our only family in Invercargill. My brother was in Australia. So we asked my mother to move up with us. A bit after we arrived we bought two units in Rotorua – one for her and one for us. My mother was very happy about becoming part of a Maori family. She just fitted in. She would make little goodies for the children when they came home from school.

'I felt very lucky to have married into Nepia's family myself. We lived with his dad and his older brother for a while before we bought the units. Nepia's father was a lovely man. Maori was his first language and he would be trying to tell me something in English then he would revert to Maori. He was a real gentleman, a big man. Everyone always made me welcome. It's like now. We have some great times when we get together down at the bach. They get on their Maori band wagon, and I say to Dave (my Pakeha son-in-law), "Come on, Dave, let's give them our views." And then we try to give them the Pakeha side.

Often I go to things where I am the only Pakeha, but I don't feel any different.

'Sometimes Nepia might say, "Maoris shouldn't have done that," and I will say, "Why not?" He doesn't run Pakehas down, but I find myself sticking up for Maori more than him sometimes, because he gets a bit hoha with some of the Maori things that happen.

'I went to the foreshore and seabed hikoi when it came through Rotorua. Afterwards I was going for my daily walk and I met this quite flash Pakeha. She didn't know I had anything to do with Maori. And she said to me that she lived in a flash area but the area next door was mainly Maori. She said, "I wish sometimes I could just put a bomb in there. It's just like that hikoi. I was so disgusted with it. They would be all on the benefit those ones." I said, "I doubt it very much." So we had a few words!

'There are some terribly racist ones out there. I don't know if it's getting any better. Sometimes I think it's getting worse.

when I hear snide remarks, it sometimes gets a bit too much and I will say, 'Actually I am married to a Maori,' and they will say, 'I don't mean every Maori. There are always good ones.'

Bernie admits to being a bit conservative, at first, when Maori activism became prominent in the media in the 1970s. She thought they went 'a bit overboard' sometimes. But she says she wasn't 'uptight' about it. 'I remember the rugby match in Hamilton during the Springbok tour. We were watching it on TV, and then Moana phoned. "Hi Mum. Just ringing to tell you I'm all right." She was right in the middle of the grounds when the game was stopped! Moana was a bit of a protester. She painted the placard to take to the game, and wanted her father to drop her off where all the protesters were meeting, and he said, "Well, you can leave that placard behind." I thought it was good that they could have their say.'

Moana would discuss such issues with her mother, and Bernie says her daughter knew what she was talking about. 'I have learnt a lot from Mo. Sometimes we would have good talks and she explains things so well. I will ask her things, and we will talk for hours.

'When I read the papers, I sometimes think they beam in on Maori unfairly. It's always a big issue when something comes up about Maori, but if Pakeha do the same thing it is swept aside.

'On the odd time I'd get upset as a mum. People say Moana is an "activist". I don't know what she's supposed to have done. Just because she has an opinion on things, she's been given that label. I think it was great that she took the opportunity to say what she wanted and explained things. Only a minority do that.'

Moana is the eldest of the Maniapoto girls. Then there's Trina, Keri-lee, Lisa and Niki. Their brother, Maru, teaches maths and computing at Rotorua Boys' High School. Trina works in administration for Mana Maori Media. Keri-lee and Lisa both teach Maori language and Niki is in administration at a kura kaupapa.

'I am proud of my six children. They've all done so well. I think we've been so lucky with them. In the end I'm not worried about other people's perceptions of them. I think, "Just let them be."'

✖

TRINA *Maniapoto is the second child of Bernie and Nepia Maniapoto.*

She married a Maori but is now divorced. She has a 14-year-old

daughter, Katarina, and an 18-year-old son, Nepia, named after

his grandfather. Trina is a backing vocalist in her sister's music

group, Moana and the Tribe. She believes she knows why Bernie and

Nepia's marriage has been a success.

'Both Mum and Dad were really hard workers and great parents. Dad worked long hours every day to keep food on the table, and Mum would be at home taking care of us six kids. She would sew, knit, cook, you name it.

'I can remember Mum adapting really well to everything Maori. She learnt how to bake rewena bread and fried bread beautifully, and how to cook boil-ups. However, she would cringe if Dad tried to cook a pig's head in her nice clean oven. He would have to cook it when she was out for the day and clean up before she got home.

'She fitted into the whanau and the Maori lifestyle easily. She got on well with all Dad's family and I remember many whanau gatherings with mountains of good food and lots of singing. All Dad's family could sing and play various musical instruments.

'Once we arrived in Rotorua, Dad and his family often took us to hui at marae – land hui or marae committee meetings. We were also lucky to go to Maori arts and crafts courses at the institute in Rotorua to learn how to do taniko, make kete and piupiu.

'Today, Mum (even though she probably doesn't even realise it) has a place and knows her role in the marae. She knows what to do before manuhiri come. She will go about setting up the wharenui with all the bedding and do the cleaning and cooking. She is a bit of a gun now at catering for crowds. She knows how to do budgets for big hui. She knows what kai to cook, how to run the kitchen, where everything is kept and is usually one of the last ones to leave the marae after doing the final clean-up. She works really hard there. I know she feels really at home at Waitetoko, our marae, and very comfortable alongside other whanau.

'She has a go at using Maori words to her mokopuna, some of whom are good Maori speakers. If she gets a word wrong, the mokos think it's a huge joke and will crack up laughing – and she'll just laugh with them.

'One thing my Pakeha mum is amazing with is whakapapa. She can link that cousin to this one, and go back a couple of generations and she knows exactly who married who, and whose grandfather that is and where they are from. All of us kids find ourselves asking Mum after an occasion at the marae, "Mum, who was that lady?" And then off she goes. She can make all the tribal and whanau connections. She's amazing like that.'

NEPIA *Maniapoto was a long way from home when he first met his Pakeha wife, Bernie, at a party in Invercargill. He was born in the timber-milling settlement of Mokai, which lies inland on the western shores of Lake Taupo. He was the second of five sons to his father Hema Maniapoto (Ngati Tuwharetoa, Ngati Raukawa) and his mother Mamaeroa (née Hamiora of Te Arawa). He also had an adopted sister. Nepia went to Te Aute College and later trained to be a farm manager, but when that didn't work out he joined the army and served in Korea. He loved life in Southland, but Nepia's greatest joy is being with his immediate and wider whanau.*

When Nepia was born in 1929, Mokai was a busy settlement in comparison with today because of the timber industry. 'My father was a post splitter, which involved felling huge totara trees with a cross-cut saw on his own, and then breaking the timber down to tidy totara posts. How he managed on his own is unbelievable. He took the posts to the road by horse and sledge. For all his work he received four pounds per hundred posts. Later he became a farmer.

'At home we spoke some Maori but we were banned from speaking it at school. The focus was on being educated. The key thing during that era was discipline. We knew our father had a pair of size 11 hobnail boots. We never got that punishment but we knew it was there. He was very strict.

'We had two homes, one in the village and one in the forests, and our main mode of transport was on horseback, loaded up with all the domestic essentials. Up in the forest there was no power, so lighting was by candles and kerosene lamps, but heating was no problem as there was plenty of firewood. Our main concern when we were young was whether Santa Claus would find us or not – but he managed to.

'My older brother and I walked to school and we were allowed to leave early to walk home. At night the banks along the road were lit up with glow-worms.

'From Mokai we moved to Te Rangiita, on the south-eastern shores of Lake Taupo, when most of the Ngati Tuwharetoa land was being developed for farming in the 1930s. The main families in the area were about a half a dozen Maniapoto whanau and three Pakeha families, the Flights, one of which was made up of 12 children. We were all very close and it was very special. Everyone learnt Maori songs and action songs and had beautiful singing voices. Even now, although age is creeping up on most of us, that whanaungatanga is still very strong and is a very special treasure.

One thing that always strikes me about the mid-'40s was that Maoris weren't allowed to purchase beer to take away. So my father and his brother gave their money to a Pakeha to buy their grog.

'I have no idea how that came about or when the law was changed – but it certainly appeared racist to me.

'We had a very Maori way of life. We ate trout, wild pork and venison. All the families had their own crops on the farm and everybody worked together growing vegetables.

'My brother and I both signed up for the Korean war in 1953. There were big farewells at marae on both our father's and mother's side when we left, which was nice. We were in the artillery, back from the front line.

'At 28 I moved to the far south to work at the Ocean Beach Freezing Works at Bluff. I met many chaps there from all parts of the North Island, some good rugby players, good musicians and good singers. From our talent we formed a rock 'n' roll band called the MRB (the Maori Rhythm Boys). It was very popular, especially with blonde Pakeha girls, which proved that there was no racism there.

'Back home my brother Huri and I had been members of the Maori concert party set up by our famous aunty, Guide Rangi. So we decided to form a Maori concert party made up of our mates and some Maori lasses from Bluff. We performed at the Civic Theatre in Invercargill. The venue was chockerblock on all three levels, and everyone was blown away. It was the same at Bluff.

'I mention these two events because we made a huge contribution towards racial harmony in the south. But we've always classed South-landers as very special people. They welcomed us to their homes. That was how I met Bernadette. The locals always enjoyed our company and especially our singing.

I began chatting with one of the Pakeha lasses at a party, Bernadette, and we've been chatting together ever since.

'Most of our mates married Pakeha spouses and it was the best thing that ever happened, as our families have come through with flying colours. In our home we live a nice simple lifestyle, no hard or fast rules, just respect and care for the home. We don't have any arguments on a cultural basis, but at times we express our own views and look at both sides.

'We look at what's being said in the newspapers and sometimes I think Maori issues are covered poorly. What really gets to me is, when a Maori beats the system of thousands of dollars, the person's race comes to the fore. But when the other side beats the system of millions of dollars, he is just Joe Bloggs, and Rodney Hide (the Act MP) doesn't make any noise.

'We left it up to our kids to decide their choice of identity – Maori or Pakeha. It is entirely up to them and must come from the heart. My family and grandchildren are well on track with the Maori language and are very fortunate. In our early days we were punished for speaking the language at school and it looked as though the language was going to be lost, however it's on a roll now.

'Bernie had two aunties in the South Island. One thought I was the cat's pyjamas but I wasn't very sure where I stood with the other one, until she passed away and I saw what she did to a photo of Bernie and me with her brother, Michael, and his family. This aunt had cut me out of it with a pair of scissors. So that proved just how much I meant to her. I couldn't help but have a big laugh. She didn't make me feel uncomfortable – it was inside her, not me.

'When we moved back to Rotorua in 1970, we brought Bernie's Mum with us so that we could take care of her. Years later when my mother-in-law passed away, Bernie said, "There won't be many at the funeral because they didn't know Mum." But friends and some of my aunties and cousins turned up at the funeral service conducted by a Maori Catholic priest. It was a lovely service, especially with the singing of my whanau. Afterwards my brothers put down a hangi and the singing continued. When Bernie's cousin and husband were due to head back to Christchurch, they said, "It was the best funeral that we have ever enjoyed."

'I think there probably were odd occasions where the children struck racial prejudice, just as Bernie and I did when we were looking for flats in Invercargill, but our kids could handle it. I think they taught themselves how to speak up. They were all switched on.

'We are very proud of our kids. Every one of them.

It seems common that children of cross-cultural marriages will take up the Maori side.

'The grandchildren are coming through the same – with all the reo. Our cross-cultural marriage has certainly worked. It's our family that makes our lives. And Bernie is part of my family now. When she dies I would expect her to be buried at our own cemetery at Waitetoko.'

MOANA *Maniapoto, Bernie and Nepia's eldest child, is the lead singer and songwriter for the music group, Moana and the Tribe. Her music and performances by the group have won critical acclaim throughout New Zealand, the Pacific, Asia, Europe and the United States. She writes about what touches her as a Maori woman and mother, and about social and political issues affecting Maori. It's not surprising that she's made music her career because she says the passion of the Maniapoto whanau is rugby, song and marae. Moana married Willie Jackson and had a child, but she now has another Maori partner. Although she identifies as Maori and speaks out for Maori, her mixed heritage gives her a broader perspective on New Zealand race relations.*

(l to r) Katarina Maniapoto, Moana Maniapoto, Amiria Reriti – aka Moana and the Tribe,
performing in Germany

Moana Maniapoto had a very Pakeha start to the first 10 years of her
life. 'My Pakeha grandmother lived close to us but I had little to do
with my Maori relatives, except when my other grandmother and
grandfather came to Invercargill to visit.

'At that time I didn't identify myself as Maori. There was another
Maori family in the street but as a child I didn't notice the difference
between them and any other family. In the '60s in Invercargill we lived
in a very close suburb. Everyone knew everyone else's family and their
business. When Mum went to hospital to have another child, we would
stay with the woman down the road who had 10 kids. And people ate
at each other's places. It was a lovely place to grow up. I went to ballet,
gymnastics and theatre like all the Pakeha girls.

'We went to the odd kapahaka practice and people called my dad
"Mr M" because they couldn't pronounce "Maniapoto". But me and my
sisters and brother couldn't pronounce it then either. We just listened

to what everyone else said. Dad would use a few phrases in the house like "Haere mai ki te kai, haere ki te moe (or hoi hoi)" – the ones you use for kids. But there was nothing that suggested to me anything particularly distinguishing. I didn't notice my mum was fair and Dad was dark.

'It wasn't until I moved up north that I realised what it meant to be Maori. We went to my grandfather's house in Rotorua after my grandmother died and all the hundreds of people there were nearly all relations, and I thought, "Oh, my God!" It was enormously different. There was no marae in Invercargill then and Mum never took us to a funeral so we didn't know about death. Once in Rotorua, we went to a tangi every couple of weeks and became really comfortable around dead bodies.

'I didn't appreciate the value of this until I saw some of my adult friends freak out because they'd never seen a dead body. I think it's healthy to understand death so I took my son to funerals from when he was three or four. Death is natural, it's a cathartic experience and it's important that children don't get frightened at seeing their grandparent dead. They get used to it and it's easier to handle.

'I guess moving to Rotorua was a bit of a culture shock for all of us, except Dad. Mum told me about her astonishment at the tangi for my father's mother, who was quite a well-known, respected woman in Te Arawa. Mum's recollection was being in the kitchen all the time. She said, "All these people just came to the house. They came and came. They kept coming and ate and ate. There were dishes everywhere. And they slept everywhere. On the floor or wherever they could find a place."

'Initially we moved in with my Maori grandfather and Dad's eldest brother in Rotorua. Five of us kids slept in bunks in one bedroom and Mum and Dad and the smallest kid were in another room. It was absolutely fantastic.

Koro (my grandfather) was in his eighties, and the older he got the less English he would speak.

'He was really old school. I spent a lot of time listening to him telling stories. I loved that.

'I won a Ngarimu essay in Maori once, but if Koro asked me to pass the salt in Maori, I would just about die of fright. I was good at academic Maori but he would freak me out when he spoke. I also did dumb things (in a cultural sense) like feeding the cat with a saucer from the cupboard. He would come and grab my ears and twist them and say, "You don't do that! Don't put human things with animals." So I learnt lots from him.

'My Pakeha grandmother was also engaging with us every day because she lived in the other side of the two flats we bought in Rotorua. So we would have our Maori grandfather, with his big cups of Nestlé's condensed milk coffee and gingernuts to dunk in it, and my lovely Pakeha grandmother who would leave a plate of beautiful cinnamon toasts on a plate at the door. She'd have the full serviette thing with silver rings. She was very genteel, very slender and gracious and always a mass of dash. Her hair was always done even though our family was the only social life she had in Rotorua.

'Koro was also dignified and well mannered. He always wore his hat and carried a walking stick. They were both from a different era – special gentle people. My grandfather was always driving to the Land Court, hui, tangi etc. and giving us the heebie-jeebies because he was a terrible driver.

'When my Pakeha grandmother died, Mum was sad, thinking it would be a lonely funeral cos my grandmother didn't know many people. We were her life. Dad said, "I don't know what you're worried about." Mum had no experience of the process of running a funeral. But in the end it was all taken care of. There were karanga. It was like a tangi but in a church and all Dad's aunties from Whakarewarewa were there. There was lots of singing, then a big hakari at home afterwards with all the family. It must have been lovely for my mother. I felt very moved by that.'

Moana was amused by the aunt from Southland who cut her father out of the family photos.

'When I was touring with my "radical" bilingual bands in my university days, I would go and visit that aunt and she was always so happy to see me. She was quite plummy and used to play bowls. And she would say, "I never quite understand why you're always so into this Maori thing. You do have another side, you know." And she made little comments like, "You're at university. Well, that would be your mother's side coming out!"

'Dad didn't exist for her. Even as a teenager I could sense she had an issue with how strongly I identified as being Maori. At that time I wasn't able to analyse it. Now I think she was probably a product of her time and environment, not being familiar with anything Maori.

'It's interesting that on my father's side his mother was more upset that one of my uncles was going to marry a Ngapuhi woman, rather than having any concerns about my dad marrying a Pakeha. My Aunt Rose (the one from Ngapuhi) told her to get over it and that she wasn't part of the raids on Te Arawa in the nineteenth century! They ended up having a good relationship.

Our whanau is a really close one and Mum slotted into the whanau life. She almost assimilated into it and became part of the marae.

'It was probably easier for her because she was uprooted from her own life in Invercargill.'

Moana remembers her mother being critical of the 1975 land march and the sight of the protesters marching over the Auckland Harbour

Bridge and later the Bastion Point occupation. 'But it wasn't bitter. At that time my parents believed everything written in newspapers, which was common then. It wasn't until I met my friend Jane Kelsey at Law School that I realised you can't believe everything you read. My father and his whanau are very quiet and humble. And our marae and our area was very strong. Our land holdings, our turangawaewae, weren't threatened. I know they had lots of engagement with the Land Court when I was a kid, but Dad never said anything about Bastion Point or the land march. Recently, I was pleased to find that they went out of their way to go to the foreshore and seabed hikoi when it came through Rotorua. My mother writes to me about my sisters and their work in the kura and how proud she is of them.

'For years I was regarded as the radical in the family and I probably was. Because I was a lot more identifiably political than them. I worked on a project with a Pakeha nun researching colonisation and Dad took notice of what she said about our racist history. He said, "I hate hearing that stuff because it makes me so angry and frustrated." We all have ways of coping with that kind of information. But I think that my father and his brothers and the family have been living a very strong Maori life – very marae-centred, very whanau-orientated – and that's always been a little haven for all of us. It's very safe. There was no violence in our family. Cripes, we never said bloody or bugger in earshot of our parents until we hit our thirties.

'The difference for me was that I was in Auckland and at the university. It was a different world during the Springbok tour and so on. When I went to university, I got a bit more "conscienced" about the Treaty, and I married into the Jackson whanau, all of whom were active in various Auckland networks. Nearly every conversation was about politics. That was a surprise to my family. The Jacksons were a wonderful family but, when the two whanau first met, Mum and Dad said, "Gee, they talk a lot of politics!" In our house the conversation then was more about rugby and everyone's jobs. My parents are working-class people who did as much as they could to open up opportunities for us. So I was the first to go to university from my whole extended whanau.

'I knew Mum and Dad had experienced racism as an interracial couple in finding accommodation in Invercargill. And I'd hear talk in the family about why Maori weren't picked for certain sports teams. My uncles weren't picked for instance. They'd never say directly, "It's because he was a Maori." But they would have the discussions and it would pop up.

'I didn't experience racist comments personally until I was an adult. When I got admitted to the bar in Rotorua the judge made a little speech and said something like I was "a credit to my race". I thought that was shocking. Another thing that really gobsmacked me once was someone saying, "I hope you have a good life and lots of lovely little piccaninnies." I couldn't think of anything to say! I could feel this heat coming into my face – like when you have really bad news and are about to faint – then I just thought, "She's a nutter."

'Other things have been more subtle – patronising or condescending. It's the paternalistic attitude. It's the institutionalised racism that you come across. That's why me and my friends started up a Smoke-free Coalition and a Maori Music Coalition. We were fed up with other people thinking they knew how to take care of us.

'Organisations ask us to be involved in a decision, then they ignore it and carry on as before. They say, "Oh, we just thought . . . " And we say, "It's not your job to think what *we* want to have done." These people don't understand it's not their role to make decisions off their own bat for *our own good*. We can do that for ourselves.'

Although Moana can see that her parents have made a success of their cross-cultural marriage she has never been an advocate of interracial relationships herself.

when we were first at university the so-called radical element was saying, 'You have to marry each other.'

'"And if you don't find decent Maori men, then you are better to hook up with a decent Maori woman." It was very staunch.

'In those days the first requirement for a partner was that he had to be Maori and we would have a wish-list that he would have a knowledge of the Treaty of Waitangi, take part in kapahaka, be handsome of course, and speak Maori, have a few clues and would not bash you. We laugh about our criteria now – we're a bit more relaxed. I see a lot of Maori women with Pakeha men who treat them really well.

'Nowadays, I suppose I'd be a little bit more realistic and not so gung-ho about Maori marrying Maori. Although I do see it has lots of compromises when you marry Pakeha – just watching other friends' lives. There's a lot more explaining about why you need to do things. Relationships are about compromise anyway, and marrying someone from another race seems to add this other layer.

I see Maori women with quite right-wing Pakeha husbands and I don't know how they work it out.

'I have noticed that when the drink comes out then all the slagging stuff surfaces. Some people obviously wear masks until then. I don't know how people cope when they are in a relationship like that.

'Mum and Dad are very private people and undemonstrative. I think their relationship has worked in the way that they created this whanau they are proud of and with everyone very staunch and successful in their fields, almost all bilingual of their own choosing. It's a warm, close family. They have never sworn at each other. They are very respectful. They are mates, friends, companions. They've built a strong, loving whanau. They're proud that none of us has gone off the rails. And none of our lot are shy about speaking out either. All the grandchildren are lovely. We're really lucky.

when my ex-husband, Willie, and I decided that we were going to talk to our son, Kimiora, in Maori, Mum was worried about it initially. She said, 'That's great. How am I going to talk to him?'

'I said, "You just carry on speaking English." The whole family thought it was a bit radical in the early '90s. But then when the child could jabber away in Maori at four, they all got excited and my sisters started learning Maori. Lisa and Maru are better than me now. Some of my nieces and nephews are fluent as well. Now Mum is very happy with that and has a fantastic relationship with them all.

'Mum's heritage is part of my identity and I am very interested in finding out more about her family tree. She and Dad went to England once and Mum comes from quite a flash family! It's in the *Burke's Peerage* book and every year they write and ask if she wants to update their whakapapa. There are lords and all that in her family. The Honywood family tracked her down in New Zealand and so she started connecting with relations from England. When Mum and Dad went there they decided to go and see Lord and Lady Honywood somewhere. My sisters joked to Dad, saying, "You hop in the front and look like the chauffeur!" We all cracked up. But they had a great time. The English rellies thought Dad was a bit exotic. That's the flip side of it all – people thinking you are exotic.

'In a physical sense I am very aware that Mum is not Maori. However, she is extremely comfortable in her role and place in the family. I think that's wonderful. I think of myself as Maori because I think it's crap to talk about fractions like one-quarter this or three-eighths that.

The obsession of people to quantify how much Maori a person has really demonstrates where they're coming from.

'When you get politicians saying there are no full-blooded Maori around, there is another agenda operating behind that. It's an attempt to have us all die out so they don't have to deal with "living Maori". Being Maori isn't quantifiable in a physical sense. It is a cultural, spiritual, family, personal, emotional kind of response that you have to it. I am also proud of my English, Irish and Scottish blood.

'My appearance is confusing for some people. Funnily enough when I was at school with lots of other Maori, because I have a honky nose, I looked a bit too Pakeha. Then in Pakeha circles, I looked more Maori. I think as I have got older I look more Maori. Because I identify so strongly as Maori it used to annoy me sometimes that some people would think I didn't look as Maori as I was supposed to. I am very aware to never make assumptions about people, because you see blonde, blue-eyed people at wananga, and they write down their hapu! I understand how hurtful it is for them to have people constantly commenting just because, through no fault of their own, they don't look the part.

'It is worth noting that we mispronounced my brother Maru's name for most of our life, until our mates corrected us. (We didn't roll the "r" and used a long "a".) The reason was that Dad, and other Maori at that time, would anglicise the sounds *so they would not annoy anyone.* I spent the first 20 years of my life hating my name and feeling that I was annoying everyone by having this long-winded hard-to-pronounce name. Then I spent the next 20 years deliberately annoying people and insisting it be pronounced properly!'

Moana sees it as part of her role to try to break down barriers between Maori and Pakeha. It doesn't always work because some Pakeha believe she should stick to being an entertainer and keep out of politics. 'My friends and I try to bring people on board, to understand what the issues are about. It's not a Maori and Pakeha situation. It's a justice thing. Through music, speaking and workshops we want to bring Maori and Pakeha women together and create an environment where Pakeha can ask questions and get answers in a non-threatening way. Women go back into their families and talk about these things.

'It was a shock how quickly white New Zealand reacted to Don Brash's Orewa speech in 2004. I was disappointed because over the last 20 years we thought we had made some progress, but how quickly everybody turned on each other! Pakeha were feeling deprived, Maori feeling scapegoated, Maori in defensive mode and Pakeha thinking they'd been given an open licence to whinge and moan, even without the facts. Some Pakeha said to me, "It's really good this is out in the open." But is it?

'I asked them what was in the Treaty that they wanted to get rid of and they couldn't really say what was bothering them. They didn't have basic information. When people react emotionally to a bunch of headlines without thinking, that's worrying. If you're not educated enough about issues, then you won't really understand why one side is passionate about something.

'It's a mistake to brand all Maori as being the same or all Pakeha as the same. I am trying to avoid those generalisations.

I try to look at race relations in New Zealand as not being a battle between Maori and Pakeha. It is between the informed and uninformed and it's about justice. It's not about race.

'People try to make it into a race thing but it just so happens that, because injustices haven't been addressed, Maori are the most deprived.

'If I look at possible models for our nation, maybe Mum and Dad have come up with a formula in their own very understated way.'

BETSAN *Martin is a Pakeha researcher, philosopher and Treaty*

of Waitangi educator who's been in a relationship with a Ngati

Tuwharetoa kaumatua for six years. In her previous marriage she

had three girls and two boys. In 2004, Betsan made a symbolic

seven-day fast as a 'lament' for the proposed Crown ownership of the

foreshore and seabed and advocated the need for the government to

support Maori common law rights. She and her companion, Rakato

PHOTOGRAPH:

Dr Betsan Martin and Rakato Te Rangiita

Te Rangiita, spend considerable time apart because he lives on

Lake Taupo and much of her work is in Wellington.

Betsan Martin was born to New Zealand parents of Scottish origin towards the end of the war. Both families had migrated here in the nineteenth century. As a child in Wellington, she knew little about Maori, and nothing about the Treaty of Waitangi. 'I went to a private school, Queen Margaret, from the age of four until I was 17.' And, as an adult, her limited contact with Maori continued. 'I married a Pakeha professional man and we had five children, living a white middle-class sort of life. The marriage ended in 1985.'

During the latter part of her marriage, Betsan became very interested in social justice and theology and she completed a degree at university. 'I later became an Anglican priest, although I have not practised in the church for many years. In the early 1980s there was a huge endeavour in the Anglican church to inform us about the Treaty and move to bicultural partnership in the church structures. I was captivated by the Treaty of Waitangi and the history of our country. I thought, "I've lived here all my life and haven't known about this!"

when my youngest son was very little, I read about kohanga reo, and thought, 'Imagine if my son could attend kohanga reo.'

'After a lot of thought, I went to Kokiri Marae in Seaview in the Hutt Valley and asked if my son could go there. So, from a very early age, David became immersed in Maori language and the culture of the marae.

'I began work in the Anglican Family Centre in Lower Hutt, which had Maori and Pacific Island staff in leadership. The Family Centre was a crucible for relationships with Maori and Pacific people, and my

Treaty education work began there. The centre had a close relationship with Kokiri Marae where David was at kohanga reo.'

After David (Rawiri) had been at the kohanga for a month, one of the staff took Betsan aside to say they were very happy to have Rawiri but wondering whether she would undertake to keep him in Maori-medium education throughout his schooling. Betsan made the undertaking. She had some concern that her husband might have other views about it, but it was early in their separation and she felt unable to discuss it with him.

'When the time came a few years later for Rawiri to leave kohanga and move on to a kura kaupapa Maori, I was issued with court proceedings by his father and my ex-husband and taken through a legal process to stop him going to the kura. The children and I had to go to psychologists. A counsel was appointed for the children and for me. Psychologists came to Kokiri to investigate . . . which was very embarrassing. I thought it was hopeless. However, the court ended up saying something like Rawiri was very well adjusted, so my daughter, who was a little older, should go to the kura too! Susanna went into total immersion Maori education very soon after the decision.'

Betsan had reservations about the court putting seven-year-old Susanna into a kura because she felt her daughter had not been prepared for such a big change to a total immersion Maori education environment. 'I would not have done that myself. I believe it was quite hard for her. Susanna, who was called "Huhana" at the kura, stayed in total immersion until she was 12 and was never entirely happy at school once she left Maori education.'

Susanna lives in Paris now and has become a fluent French speaker – no doubt helped by her bilingual education.

'David once said, "Mum, you don't realise what a hard time we sometimes had being the only Pakeha. And we had a lot of changes to cope with." Total immersion education was a new system, and when we moved to Auckland that also meant a lot of changes.

From my perspective, Rawiri and Susanna's Maori education
was a great gift. Every child in New Zealand could be speaking
Maori and English.

'However, it was pretty demanding on my kids, because they were put, not only in another cultural and language environment, but in another social environment. Certainly Kokiri extended the concept of whanau to include us, as Pakeha.

'Interestingly, my oldest daughter, Kirsten, has a Maori partner, Toko, and my grandchildren have gone to the same kohanga. In their household they have these three fluent-speaking children and their uncle David. So we have ended up being a family closely involved in Maori education, although John and Kelly, my other two, have not been directly involved.

'My passion for the Treaty sometimes surprises Maori. But as a Pakeha, I believe that respecting tangata whenua and what was agreed in the Treaty is the key to a stable and sustainable future for our country. All I can say is that I read the Treaty and felt the page was alight. It has taken me out of my conventional life.

'I met Rakato because someone who knew of my interest in the Treaty told me I'd be interested in his work. I attended a seminar Rakato held and it became clear that our thinking was so aligned that we were drawn together. Actually we climbed Tauhara mountain at night and a big moon was up . . . Gradually I began to meet his whanau and go to the marae with him.'

Betsan loves going to marae and enjoys powhiri – even when she can't understand all of it. She hasn't found the language easy to learn, perhaps because she started late. 'I take a course and then I'll korero with Rakato, who is a beautiful fluent speaker. I speak Maori to him and he responds, but then we fall out of it quite quickly.'

It was the Treaty that inspired Betsan's PhD, along with postmodern philosophy on the ethics of difference. She explored ways for Western philosophy and liberal traditions to move beyond war, the suppression of women and violence against indigenous peoples.

While the Treaty inspired her study, much of the philosophy was based on a new ethic in relationships in which the 'difference' of the other is upheld and respected – an ethic that applies to sexual difference as well as cultural difference.

'Rakato took me to Hirangi marae in Turangi and I was amazed by the carvings and the story he told me about them. It was revelatory because much of what I had written about in my PhD appeared to be expressed in carving. A male and female were represented there together, with creativity and social regeneration arising from their interaction. It was two different cultural approaches to the sexual relationship.

'My thesis drew on the idea that where male and female qualities are both strong, then society evolves creatively; where they are out of balance and the feminine is suppressed, society becomes patriarchal and monosexual. As I interpreted it, the carver, in a uniquely Maori way, had represented the full mana of women and of men as the two pillars of the house, expressing symbolically the full strength of the tribe.

'Pakeha also need to uphold feminine spirit and values along with masculine qualities. And, when it comes to culture, instead of respecting difference we've tried to assimilate Maori.

For me difference is more interesting than equality because we don't all want to be the same.

With all that intellectual theory going on in Betsan's mind, it's no surprise that her relationship with Rakato presents her with a range of complexities. 'I appreciate Rakato not just as an individual but as a tribal person. He fulfils a role in his tribe, which is different to my background and culture. Rakato is a kaitiaki and I have total respect for that. He has brought me an entirely new understanding of the land.

'When we walk over the fields, he says, "That's Pihanga the mountain, and now we are walking on the palm of her hand. And that's her extended arm over there." I came to see the landscape through totally different eyes. It's magical.

'Almost every day, Rakato is on the land. His passion is to protect the environment and encourage people to become involved in self-sustaining projects on the land. I've observed that Rakato's knowledge is respected in Tuwharetoa. He's called on for his depth of cultural wisdom and he's a great mediator. To my mind he has a marvellous analysis of tribal affairs.

'Some of my work and my family are away from Turangi. At first I thought this suited both our situations. Now I think there are other expectations of our relationship. The love that arose from our shared visions has held us together. One can't explain the out-of-the-ordinary circumstances that bring people like us together, nor the enchantment that makes us persevere with difficulties.

'Through Rakato I have become very involved in his local hapu development. Nga Runuku are building a marae on ancestral land and projects associated with it as kaitiaki of the land and people – kai mara, or organic vegetables, ecotourism, restoring the wetland, looking after the waterways. It is a big environmental project, using solar and wind energy and the ecology of the land and waterways. I've been able to contribute with fundraising and with seminars and administration. Working with members of the hapu is a priority.

'I can't tie our relationship up in a neat package. Although six years together seems a reasonable time to me, in some ways it's only a first moment – especially in a tangata whenua understanding of time. Friends have said, "If you go to Turangi, can't you get him to come to Wellington some of the time?" I know that's not viable because, effectively, kaitiaki means you don't leave.

'I am open-hearted about living in Turangi with Rakato, his family, whom I love dearly, and the community there. Finding a way to combine this with my family and work has been hard in our relationship.

I'm aware that some kuia consider that Rakato should be with a Maori woman to correspond more with his tribal commitments, especially at this later time in life.

'The kuia have always been quite marvellous to me, but it is not entirely possible to read the silences.

'I am following his late wife, Margaret, and his other partner, Fiona, who both had children with him, children who are Maori, who have whakapapa. I recognise that being together when you're younger and having children as Maori and Pakeha together weaves you more into the community. Coming together later brings the complexities of diverse family commitments, as well as of friends from other worlds.

'We are at a time in our lives when we want to make the most of our experience and both of us are very serious in our commitments. Sometimes our cultural differences make these very similar paths seem divergent. And I want to maintain close relationships with my children and grandchildren, and this means being where they are – as well as being with Rakato. My work on the Treaty and on a charter for human responsibility can take me around New Zealand and overseas as well.

'I love and appreciate being part of the Nga Runuku project. Rakato speaks about a two-hulled waka, a vessel for a long journey. He describes it as joined by a platform that represents qualities that bring people together, such as "generosity, unconditional love, shared purpose" and so on. He speaks of women at the front giving birth to the future and men behind, "safeguarding the wisdom and whakapapa of the past". It is a metaphor of great significance to both of us. My telling of it is oversimplified, and it is really his story to tell, but it may be enough to indicate our hopes and the challenges of keeping two differently crafted hulls together to hold a shared course.'

RAKATO *Te Rangiita bears the name of his tribe Te Rangiita, whose rohe is on Lake Taupo, north of Turangi. He was born in 1937 and lived with his elderly maternal grandparents in an 'isolated fashion' at a small farm which had traditional gardens and orchards. He had what he calls a 'tohunga' upbringing by wise kaumatua. He chose to marry a Pakeha woman, Margaret, who died in 1994. He has two sons Te Riini and Pia to Margaret, and twins Ana-marie and Potiki to a later Pakeha partner, Fiona, whom he describes as 'a fine mother to the twins'. For the past six years Rakato has had a new Pakeha companion, Betsan Martin, an intellectual with a big family of her own.*

Rakato Te Rangiita had no childhood relationship with his natural parents, leaving him with a sense of regret even now, but he was raised 'in kindness' by his grandparents. They were illiterate people who lived strictly by tribal tikanga and went to all the tangihanga and the hui of the hapu around Lake Taupo.

'I was nurtured by child-bearing women of the various marae we stayed at. My sense of who I was, and who my family was, is that all the people of the tribe brought me up. I became their common child. I was trained to love, feel, think and live tribe.'

'My grandparents made sure I wasn't Christianised. I was brought up in traditional Maori spirituality and dedicated to special training from a very young boy.

'My first wife, Margaret, was Pakeha and when the whanau found out that I planned to marry they went to see her. They needed to know that she could live in the tribe without falling victim to it. Margaret was prepared to take that on. It says something about my family's acceptance of her that the hapu of Ngati Te Rangiita paid for our tribal wedding – much to the surprise of her relatives.'

Margaret was a staff nurse in an operating theatre when Rakato met her and this professional background proved to be an advantage for his people. She started a health scheme for Tuwharetoa, the first of its kind in the country, and worked hard in the tribal community. Rakato says he, in turn, supported her and regarded her as a leader. When Margaret died 10 years ago she received a tribal burial – lying in state on two marae.

Rakato's own career was in the prison service and he was able to bring Maoritanga into his work. One thing that grated on him and the Maori prisoners was the mispronunciation of Maori by staff and their objection to its use. 'It took time, but eventually we were able to use our own language there without too much gritting of teeth by the staff.

'When I left the prison service, I put together a seminar on personal leadership. This is how I met Betsan. Most of the participants were Maori, but this wahine Pakeha turned up and at the time she was a Treaty trainer. I found her very interesting with much to share, so we gravitated together.

'In our relationship we have mostly lived apart because, due to her work, Betsan lived first in Auckland and later in Wellington. This situation is not really satisfactory. There are needs in the relationship and we would both benefit if she spent more time here or I spent more time with her elsewhere. But my work is here.

'The hill behind where I live, Te Hemo, is the home of our atua kaitiaki [tribal guardian], brought to Aotearoa by our tupuna, Ngatoro-i-rangi. I was born and raised within sight of this puke maunga. It is the centre of my universe. I am attached to it by a short lead – which becomes shorter as I grow older. The differences between Betsan and me are not helped by my own silence about tapu matters and the particular (and maybe peculiar!) values of a regional tribe and its hapu.

'Communicating with atua Maori as a tohunga is, of necessity, isolated work. Nor is it the domain of people who are not dedicated to it, whether Maori or Pakeha. Living apart is appropriate for me in this work but separation from my partner is also at the cost of aching hearts.'

Rakato does move about a little within his own tribal district. He visits the waahi tapu, or spiritual places, of the various hapu. 'Waahi tapu are recognised by iwi as places of knowledge, history, spirituality, identity and heritage. I was trained as an oral keeper of waahi tapu. This apprenticeship began when I was 18 with the revered, feisty and now long-deceased kaumatua Rawiri Hemopo, from the headwaters of the Whanganui River. My training ended with the passing of Hoeta Wall of Waitahanui. Over 45 years I passed through the hands of a long list of kaumatua and kuia of the many hapu of the iwi, including my natural father from Ngati Turangi. I came to love them all and I have visited almost 700 of their long list of waahi tapu. They walk with me daily as conscious reflections of the spirit tribe that guides us.

'In our relationship Betsan is separate from this tapu work of my culture. However, the work she is doing is valuable to Maori and certainly is important to my hapu. Pakeha women have a certain level of freedom not always open to Maori women. In addition, Betsan has keen intelligence, empathy and a get-up-and-go spirit.'

Rakato finds a common understanding with Betsan about the need to uphold feminine principles alongside male ones. 'Wahine Maori are suppressed by the influences of other people's religion and culture, by Maori and Pakeha men – and by Pakeha women. Tuwharetoa once had an order of female tohunga but they became redundant quickly with the advent of colonisation and Christianity. The altar, or tuahu, of the mana wahine was lost and their many atua were cast aside.

'So much potential is still waiting to be set free by the work of female tohunga. So much harmony and growth could result, to the benefit of all cultures. It may be outside the thinking of the current establishment but it is a confirmation of our tikanga Maori. Wahine of Betsan's intelligence, leadership qualities and training could possibly fill this gap to some degree . . . supporting the momentum. It requires courage, sensitivity, persistence and skill. However, it might be politically sensitive in my world and must not be derailed by any conflict.'

Rakato talks briefly about the meeting house, Tuwharetoa I te Au Pouri, which had such a profound effect on Betsan when she first saw it. He explains that the spiritual harmony of the union between the male and female figures on the house was hugely significant to the tribe's ancient spiritual teachings. 'The marae is often referred to as the "neutral marae" because the female pole of paepae whakanoa (power of extension and expansion) and the male pole of paepae tapu (power of restriction and depletion) were in balance – with the central pole, their child, holding up the peak of the building in-between.

'I have been drawn to Betsan regardless of having long since decided that I have had enough with flighty matters of the heart. I find her beautiful. Her work with development of my new hapu marae is a difficult leadership task that she's given as a commitment of heart which has stamped its mark on our hearts also. She's managed this along with all her other commitments.

'I've hoped that she would settle with me in time – not as a worker for the hapu but as a companion of the heart. I am not sure if this will happen. An issue in the background for me, and Betsan, is a viewpoint among the hapus that I should be involved now with Maori women rather than a Pakeha. There are no children involved in our relationship. So it leaves her under a bit of pressure if she is to sit comfortably in the tribe. She has a hard row to hoe, but she's got the intelligence and what it takes to actually get there.

'Those are all the issues that are sitting there behind our personal relationship and influencing us. It's a cross-cultural relationship at kaumatua level!'

❦

TOKORANGI *Kapea is a commercial lawyer who works for a bank. He has also worked on Waitangi Tribunal claims and as a Treaty claimant researcher. He's married to Betsan's oldest child, Kirsten Gendall, and they have three children, Tarikura (12), Rawiri (9) and Matariki (3). 'Toko', as most people call him, chairs the management committee at his youngest son's kohanga. He was brought up in Ngati Ruanui country, in South Taranaki. Both his parents are Maori. His mother's links are to Te Ati Haunui-a-Paparangi, Te Ati Awa and Ngapuhi. His father is Ngati Apa.*

(*l to r*) Rawiri (9 yrs), Tokorangi Kapea, Matariki (3 yrs), Kirsten Gendall, Tarikura (12 yrs)

Tokorangi Kapea says his father can speak some Maori and his mother speaks a little, but they didn't speak it much at home. He heard it mainly through the wider family of uncles and aunties and grandparents. 'I was brought up around the marae. We had big Maori families on both sides with a sprinkling of Pakeha. In my parents' generation most have married Maori but among my cousins there are many Pakeha partners as well.

'I suppose it was just a reality of New Zealand society for people like me, over 30, that many of us would marry Pakeha. There were no immersion classes so most have grown up in classic state schools. Unless you lived in the wops where there were mostly Maori, you always grew up and hung around with Pakehas and at some stage you hook up with them.'

Toko remembers a few issues about being different. There were not many Pakeha who could pronounce his name correctly. 'It's just one of the issues that Maori face. I understood very quickly that Pakeha people didn't get your name right or pronounce Maori properly. They just didn't know how.'

Toko says in the 1970s and '80s a Maori who chose to could sneak through the whole education system and not learn about Maori matters. At the most they might learn a few Maori songs. 'It was like that for lots of my Maori friends and cousins. On my mother's side, there are about 13 first cousins but no one could speak Maori – and yet we were a pretty pro-Maori family. I had a really great Maori teacher at school and I participated in the school Maori cultural club. I have wonderful memories of that – with all of my friends. Unfortunately, though, I didn't come out of school being able to speak Maori; I picked some up at university.

For all intents and purposes I'm just like a Pakeha Kiwi, it's just that I'm brown and I happen to have chosen to go to kapahaka and hung out at the marae a lot.

'It's a bit different now because there are schools where you could go through all your education and just be around other Maori. I think, too, that maybe people identify more strongly as Maori than they did say 10 to 15 years ago because of the language revival and all that.'

Toko and Kirsten met when they were studying at Massey University and lived in the same hostel. They were friends at first and then their relationship deepened. Toko says it's interesting how people have intermarried quite freely in New Zealand compared with many other countries. 'The racial divide can be quite superficial at some levels.

Racial tension may be really bad politically in this country, yet socially Maori and Pakeha can get on with each other.

'You could take a position on, say, the Treaty of Waitangi or the recent foreshore and seabed issue, and have couples who totally disagree with each other, yet go out and drink with each other and start having kids and they can agree to disagree in passing. That's quite amazing.

'My marriage to Kirsten isn't like that, though. I've been quite fortunate because my wife's quite informed. We both studied sociology and that's helped us to be well informed on those sorts of issues.'

The couple made a decision to send their children to kohanga reo and kura. Toko says it means that their kids live in two parallel worlds. They meet Pakeha mates at activities like scouts or soccer. They can visit their friends and enjoy PlayStation or go to the movies and generally hang out in the wider world, but the next day his daughter will be speaking Maori all day as part of a completely different world. 'And that's what a lot of Pakeha people can't grapple with.

'A lot of Maori people can't grapple with it either. Many of my Maori friends aren't sending their kids to kohanga. They have this misconception that Maori is not particularly relevant or useful and they want their kids to know English and supposedly succeed in the Pakeha world, so they send their kids to the state schools without Maori. It's the same reason our parents weren't good speakers and why my generation missed out, too.

'Kirsten and I have taken the position that we want our children to be able to move between the two cultures.

we're taking the view that, in the long term, having Maori as well as English is beautiful for a number of reasons.

'I hope one day they'll pick up other languages more easily and become global people.'

While it's clear that Toko and Kirsten have shared goals and a warm relationship, Toko says they recognise that Maori and Pakeha really do communicate differently. 'It's very hard to explain because it's so subtle. With Maori there's quite a lot of chucking off at each other. But it's very light-hearted. It can also be, "Don't rise above your station."

When I am with Maori I do switch over into other little mannerisms and different little sayings that I may not normally say when amongst Pakeha friends. You almost don't know you're doing it.

'As a couple, we have noticed differences because of those little quirky cultural things between Maori and Pakeha. It goes right down to micro levels – different communication styles, right up to how families interrelate and get on with each other. The whole of my first cousins are like my brothers and sisters. First cousins just walk in the door and you feed them and park them up somewhere and that's the way it is. They might stay for one day, they might stay for ten.

'My dad, for example, stayed with us for a long time. I've had cousins roll in and out at different times. Overall this kind of thing has worked really well but I think, at her end, Kirsten's trying to figure out how things work.

'In terms of my relationship with Kirsten's family, it's been really good with both her parents. Betsan, her mother, is very politicised so that makes it interesting sometimes. Kirsten's dad is in the legal profession – which I understand as a lawyer myself.

'Betsan stays here from time to time, so we catch up on different issues. Over the last 20 years she's got more involved with social justice issues. She's travelling all over the world doing bits and pieces. Fascinating dinner table discussions come up.

'Just the same, I challenge her views a lot. I'm just being picky mostly. She's very "green", very pro-Maori. I'm very pro-development, business development for Maori, and she takes the approach, "Keep everything as it is." And I say, "Nah, nah. That's too old. Gotta move on. Get out of grievance mode," hence my commercial lawyer background. Fundamentally we agree. We're talking around the edges. It's just "how", I suppose. We want the same things.'

The continuing trend for Maori to choose mixed marriages is taking place internationally as well as in New Zealand. Many of Toko's whanau are part of a substantial Maori migration to Australia, where the identity of children of Maori descent may raise interesting questions in the future. About eight or nine of his father's brothers and sisters are now settled in Australia. His mother, brother and sister are there, too. His father spent 15 years there. Most moved to Australia in the 1980s during the Rogernomics era when jobs were scarce in New Zealand.

'We've got lots of little brown kids who are Maori but they're Aussies. Their kids will play for Australia one day – maybe in the Wallabies or the Kangaroos. Which country is going to do the haka?'

Overall, Toko believes that race relations in New Zealand might benefit from mixing of the cultures in families. 'A cross-cultural marriage doesn't mean that you are necessarily going to have people who are any more informed about each other's culture. However, mixed marriages, potentially, could make conflict in our society more difficult.

It would be difficult for a full-on revolution to occur because there's been so much intermarriage here.

That doesn't mean he advocates mixed marriages for everyone. 'When it comes to marriage, you just go where the love is and love should deal with the rest of it. And if my kids want to marry a Maori or a Pakeha I would say that it's irrelevant if that's the person for them. But people should not expect partners to change just because they're sleeping together and having kids.'

KIRSTEN *Gendall is a Pakeha, the eldest of Betsan Martin's five children, sister to David and Susanna and raised in the seaside suburb of Eastbourne. She works as a researcher and evaluation*

adviser in a government department and has a BA in Sociology and

a Masters in Social Science Research. She lives in Wellington with

her husband, Tokorangi, and their three children, where she's on the

board of her children's school.

Maori were so much off the radar in Kirsten's early life in a predominantly Pakeha middle-class community that she can be very specific about the few contacts she had. 'One of my friends was the bus driver's daughter and I visited her house. And I remember thinking, "Oh, this is a little house." I didn't see our house as flash but it would have been compared to hers. Looking back now I can see the social differences that were there but I certainly wasn't aware of them then. She was the only Maori person I knew until I went to Queen Margaret College where there were even fewer Maori and only one in my year.

'In the sixth form I learnt some New Zealand history. It was fairly bland stuff around the wars. I don't remember hearing anything about the political/social context around it. It was "this is what happened" and that was that.'

When Kirsten was 16, her parents separated and her awareness of Maori and their language and culture began to open up. First came the news that her baby brother, David, was to be placed in a kohanga reo.

'I was very close to David and protective of him. I didn't know what the kohanga was really about. I didn't like the way he screamed his head off and was unhappy when he first went there. Now I have seen my own children screaming their heads off before they settle in somewhere. Just the same, I believe there was an element of difficulty for David, at first, to be put into an environment where he didn't understand any of the language. I was thinking, "What's it really like for him?"

'David, and my youngest sister, Susanna, had a very different life from my own. They both had a total Maori immersion education and a working mother. My upbringing was monocultural and I had a stay-at-home mother. But, about this time, I went away to Massey University and didn't really get involved with those changes.'

Reflecting on it now, Kirsten believes the lives of her sister and brother were enriched by their Maori education, although they faced challenges, too. 'They have turned out as well balanced as any of us. But, for myself, I would not have liked an education like that. I would have been constantly anxious about not fitting in.'

At university in Palmerston North, Kirsten's world was widening out further. Massey had a strong emphasis on Maori learning and she met Toko in the hostel where she was living. They became friends and through him she met many more Maori.

I was aware that Toko was Maori, and that I was Pakeha, but it was not an issue for me.

'I was attracted to his relaxed manner and sense of humour and we got on well. He's extremely personable and can get on with anybody. He liked me because I had a car. It was a beat-up Mini but a very practical asset.

'We were rather casual friends at first. He went to Australia to be with his family over the four-month summer breaks. When I finished Massey and said I was going back to live in Wellington, Toko said, "I'm coming with you." And then I realised that . . . oh, we had what you might call "a committed relationship". About four years later we had our first child.'

Armed with the experience of total immersion Maori education within her own Pakeha family, Kirsten is very comfortable with the idea that her own children are at a kohanga reo and kura. 'They are there primarily because they are Maori and I want them to learn their own language. I also believe that the emotional security and experience of kids is important in their educational success – and they are getting that in the environment they're in. They began kohanga at the time their language was developing, and we had tried to use basic Maori words and phrases at home, so it was not completely foreign to them. It was a natural progression for them to go on to a kura.

'Our kids are very competent verbally in English, and Rawiri, our nine-year-old, has already taught himself to read in English without any lessons. I suppose every child's experience will be different, but my view is that our children will be all the better for their Maori education. If I have any issue at all, it's that we don't make the effort to speak more Maori at home.'

In her marriage to Toko, Kirsten has noted some cultural differences.

Toko's father came to stay for a while and there was never a definite time frame around it. He was here for three years.

'I suppose he wouldn't have known how long he was going to stay either. Mostly it was good because our children could spend time with him. He'd been in Australia all their lives until then. Of course, there were times when we had little things to sort out and usually Toko was the one who communicated with his dad over the sensitive subjects. When I was about to have our third baby we both felt we needed more space so his dad moved into another house we owned just down the road.

One of the things I noticed most about having his father in the house was the funny things in the fridge – like tirotiro, which is sheep intestines.

'There was often food in the fridge that I would think, "Surely no one's going to eat this. It's been here for weeks or months." And I'd do a big clean-out and throw it all out and he'd come home that night and say, "Where's those mussels?" And I'd say laughingly, "Oh, Toko threw them out." And he'd know it was me. And he'd say, "Oh, it's all right, dear." And he probably had his own views about the vegetarian dishes I cooked. After some meals he'd say, "Oh, this is nice. What's this, dear?" Maybe he would have preferred more meat and potatoes.

'When I'm with Toko's family I'm quieter than I might be in my own family where, as the oldest, I can be quite bossy. It may be just because that's usual with in-laws. But perhaps at first I was hesitant, at a subtle level, to be sure that I didn't make a cultural blunder. I often used to (and sometimes still do) look to Toko to give me the cues about what is appropriate for me to say or do.'

The stereotype that Maori have a more relaxed approach to life than Pakeha is played out in Toko and Kirsten's relationship. She says it's probably a combination of gender and personality, as well as culture. 'Toko and I are very different personalities. I'm more organised than he is, but that may be a gender thing. Overall I am probably more serious than he is and he's generally much more laid-back.

One challenge to my cultural thinking in this marriage has been about financial matters.

'Toko is generous with money and I'm comfortable and supportive of that in general. His generosity also works in my favour as he shares so generously with my family and friends, as well as with his. But I don't really like it if I feel that he's taken for granted and not appreciated. I'm sure some of my Pakeha middle-class friends would find this sort of giving quite foreign. It's not actually a problem for me, but I know it's different to how many of my Pakeha friends would operate financially.

'It is probably true to say that Pakeha need to adapt more than Maori do in a Maori/Pakeha cultural relationship. Toko, of course, has had to live all his life in another majority culture. I'm very willing to make many of the adjustments necessary. When it comes to tangi, for instance, I'm often the one who says, "We have to go, Toko," if someone in his whanau dies. I suppose there are also many Pakeha women who would not agree to putting their children in total immersion Maori education.

'I've done these things so subconsciously that I don't even think about it. I wanted to do them. To some extent Toko has had to adjust to me, too. It's a bit of a cultural leap eating my vegetarian organic food!'

❀

___

DAVID *Gendall is a 21-year-old Pakeha student at Otago University who was educated in total immersion Maori schooling until he was 12. At times he complained about this to his mother, Betsan. David, often known as Rawiri, says his father was uncomfortable about his Maori education. However, increasingly David is able to analyse the Maori influence on his life and bring new understanding to it.*

While it was often a challenge to be a Pakeha kid in a Maori education environment, David Gendall is changing his mind about it now he's an adult. 'I was brought up differently to the rest of my friends and obviously being the only white kid in class wasn't easy. It was like being in another country and sort of isolated because, for eight or nine hours of the day, I was a Maori and then I'd get home and I was a Pakeha again. I used to ask Mum, "Why can't I be normal?" But I see now that it has its good sides.

'I've got two perspectives on the world. I feel sometimes it sort of isolates me because a lot of my friends aren't necessarily in tune with that kind of thing. For example, the foreshore and seabed issue – my Pakeha friends have the classic uninformed perspective of it. I think I have an informed one because I know Maori values and customs.

'Looking back, I can say now that my experience was generally

Back (*l to r*) Oliver Petitjean, Susanna Gendall, Betsan Martin, John Gendall, David Gendall, Tarikura Kapea (granddaughter)
Front (*l to r*) Rawiri Kapea, Kirsten Gendall, Matariki Kapea, Jocelyn Martin, Kelly Gendall

positive. I can't really compare it to anything else because obviously I've only had one life. When I was young I could speak Maori and I did kapahaka. I could hold my own in those things and I was just accepted as being like that. But as I got a bit older I used to get a bit of flak for being the only white kid in a fairly staunch Maori marae. You get the odd guy saying, "Why don't you give us our land back?" and that kind of thing. Of course, I had no idea of what they were talking about at the time.

'It was funny because, at one stage, for a year at primary school, I led the kapahaka group. The whole time I guess people were asking, "Why's the white guy leading the Maori dance?" It must have looked ridiculous.

'Sometimes I get derogatory names. Pakeha friends have given me the nickname "Raw" because Rawiri is the Maori word for David. I find "Raw" offensive but I can't really say to my friends, "Hey guys, can you not call me that?" It wouldn't occur to them that it would be culturally insulting but it's something that I feel. I know it's all in jest but after a while it grates.

I suppose if I was brown I could call it racism. But how can you call it that when it's two white people talking to each other?

'There are no words to describe why it's offensive. I don't know how to say it other than to state the obvious and let people draw their own conclusions.

'My Pakeha father is in the legal profession. He's had a fairly straight and narrow life, working hard and all the rest of it. Initially I don't think he was that thrilled about me going to kohanga. It would have been the last thing he'd have expected Mum to do. He never said anything, but I remember him dropping me off at kohanga once or twice, if I was staying at his place, and he was never really that interested. Later, I won awards for getting good grades in Maori at high school because it was so easy for me. But my father never said much. He did congratulate me but was not that enthusiastic.

'I've been thinking about my education a fair bit recently.

I've been overseas and it's a funny thing, that I don't have a defined identity as such. When you're raised Maori but you've got white skin it's strange. I find it hard to relate to either Maori or Pakeha.

'I suppose if Maori was night and English was day then I'd be the twilight or something. I don't feel completely one or the other, so I can't really be ignorant to the other perspective. It's quite hard to explain.

'I went to a mainstream high school and carried on with Maori in the third and fourth forms at bursary level. In academic terms it was good. I could do university-level things when I was about 13, because I could speak and spell written Maori. I guess the main benefit would be, as my mum would say, "an unconscious alternative perspective" or something.

'I read that people who are bilingual are less likely to face senility in old age. They have more agile minds and are better at solving problems. I was in Ireland for six months and I met a lot of other foreign people there who said I could pronounce their names as well as they would pronounce them. That's because I have the experience of a different language and I suppose my mind isn't just limited to a single thought process. When you approach another language and perspectives, you have to forget what you already know and be open.

'With respect to cross-cultural marriages in our family I suppose my influence there, of going to kohanga and stuff, may have got the ball rolling. My sister, Kirsten, and her husband, Toko, have put all their kids into kohanga. I speak Maori to them every now and then, but not predominantly because it's just easier to talk in English and it doesn't exclude anyone.

'However, for the most part, the only place I speak Maori is at Kirsten and Toko's house.

None of my friends, not one, would have the same level of language that I would, so I can't have a discussion in Maori.

'People know "kia ora" and "ka kite" if you're lucky, but not much more.

'I sometimes think French would be more useful than Maori. Even when I'm with those who speak it, English would always be the main language, although if I'm talking to an elder or somebody I know from way back, then I'll talk Maori to them. And it's cool because we have something in common.

'I've grown out of being insecure about my Maori education, but I still feel people don't understand some of the things that for me are just clear as day. I have been brought up with Maori values, so I have respect for elders and regard for the land and so on. The unwritten rules of Maori customs are ingrained in me. Unlike my Pakeha friends, I'm totally comfortable on a marae.

'I don't like how society generally has a subtle negative attitude towards Maori. Everybody knows that the crime rate and that sort of thing is predominantly Maori and all those kind of negative stereotypes.

People hang on to those stereotypes and, because I have this Maori part of me, I feel sometimes that I don't connect with a lot of my Pakeha friends.

'In the same way that Maori is not a written language, it's such a spoken language, it's something you feel and experience rather than being able to *say* how it feels. There are few words to describe someone in my situation because it's fairly rare.

'I am studying geography and management at Otago and it's my last year. I think it will definitely be an advantage to put on my CV "fluent speaker of Maori". People *are* interested. All my friends know that I had a different upbringing and some of them think it's kinda cool. But they don't know what it was actually like to be there for all those years. It was my life and my upbringing and I can't change it and it makes me who I am today. I guess I'm thankful for it, because a lot of my friends I just look at and think that they're stupid. I do appreciate my friends but there is so much they don't understand.

'I remember once trying to explain to them the Treaty stuff and trying to explain it as if to a three- or four-year-old, "*You* signed. There were *two* treaties. One was technically different from the other and yadda yadda . . ." They would refuse to accept it. And we just don't talk about it. It gets swept under the carpet. It's a strange predicament but I guess I'm used to it now, so it's kind of become normal.

'One thing that I dislike about New Zealand is how Pakeha culture is based on things like rugby, and where we actually do have genuine culture – Maori culture – it's exploited to hell. Like the haka and the koru. I feel I'm a part of a society that's treading on what I value. I don't wake up every day and think, "This is hell!" but it's something in the back of my mind.'